Through the Keyhole

Through the Keyhole

Sex, Scandal and the Secret Life of the Country House

SUSAN C. LAW

Cover image: © istock
Back cover: © The British Library Board

First published 2015

The History Press
The Mill, Brimscombe Port
Stroud, Gloucestershire, GL5 2QG
www.thehistorypress.co.uk

British Library Cataloguing in Publication Data.
A catalogue record for this book is available from the British Library.

ISBN 978 0 7509 5669 7

Typesetting and origination by The History Press
Printed in Great Britain

CONTENTS

	Acknowledgements	7
	Introduction	9
Part One	**The Foundations of Aristocracy**	**17**
	1. Marriage for 'Love or Gold?'	18
	2. Land and Power	34
	3. Duties and Pleasures	42
	4. Lord Bully *v.* Lady Di	50
Part Two	**Vice and Virtue in Print (1760s–1770s)**	**57**
	5. 'The Fashionable Vice'	58
	6. The Black Duke	63
	7. Noble Reputations	78
	8. 'The Good Old Peer'	88
	9. Wicked Lord Lyttelton	95
Part Three	**Staging Adultery (1770s–1780s)**	**105**
	10. Courtroom Dramas	106
	11. Adultery Trials for Sale	114
	12. Secret Assignations	123
	13. The Purity of Noble Blood	129
	14. 'A Prodigious Swarm of Trashy Writers'	135
Part Four	**Moral Reform and Scandals (1790s–1810)**	**143**
	15. Moral Reform	144
	16. Scandalous Entertainment	157
	17. Courtesans, Lords and Ladies	164
	18. 'A Sin of the Deepest Dye'	173
	19. The Earl of Morley and 'A Certain Liaison'	181

Part Five   Changing Roles (1810–1830s)   **191**

   20. Public Roles and Private Lives   192
   21. Facts or Fictions?   199
   22. 'The Spell is Broken'   205
   23. Pages 'Dried With Diamond Dust'   212
   24. Elephant Ellenborough, 'A Dandy Among Politicians' 220

     List of Illustrations   232
     Notes   233
     Bibliography   246
     Index   254

Acknowledgements

Researching this book has involved an extensive cast of characters, both living and dead. First, I should like to acknowledge the countless members of the Georgian aristocracy who have shared their lives with me during the past eight years. Second, I am indebted to the present Lord Cobham for access to papers held in the Hagley Hall private collection and permission to reproduce material from them; to the Earl of Denbigh for kind permission to quote from archive documents; and to Lord Ellenborough for his friendly interest in my research and the loan of family records. I would like to thank the following for permission to quote from their collections: The National Archives, Chatsworth House, Plymouth & West Devon Record Office, Bury St Edmunds' branch of Suffolk Record Office, and Warwickshire County Record Office. I am also grateful to the staff at each of these archives and the Bodleian Library in Oxford, for their assistance with my research inquiries.

It has been a truly long and winding road which led to the production of this book, and along the way I have been lucky enough to draw on the support of numerous people who helped to make it happen. My thanks to academic staff and postgraduates of the history department at Warwick University, who shared a wealth of knowledge. And to my special brew Earl Grey for proving that a cup of tea can solve everything. I am grateful to all my friends and family who have each played their own unique part, especially my parents James and Penny for a lifetime of love and encouragement, and my husband, Clive Radford, whose steadfast support and home-baked bread have made it all possible.

INTRODUCTION

It was just after breakfast at nine o'clock on a bleak winter morning when the housemaid Elizabeth Hopping hesitated by the parlour door, torn between apprehension and curiosity. A muffled thudding sound was coming from the adjacent room, echoing through the stillness of the old manor house. She crept towards the oak-panelled door, heart pounding beneath her stays, and swiftly crouched down to peer through the keyhole. There was no mistaking what was going on next door.

With a horrified gasp Elizabeth instinctively drew back. Her hands were shaking, and she pressed both palms flat against the smooth polished wood to steady herself as she bent her head for another look. On the far side of the parlour by the gilded oval mirror, Lady Abergavenny was leaning back against the hall door, her petticoats bunched up as high as the garters on her stockinged legs. Pressed up against her in a passionate embrace was her husband's friend Mr Lyddel, his coat unbuttoned, doing something that a man ought not to do. Dazed and shaken, Elizabeth scurried away down the back stairs, scarcely daring to think about what she had seen. She whispered her secret only to a laundrymaid, afraid that no one else would believe the shocking discovery.

Richard Lyddel, 'a very civil, modest, well-bred gentleman', living only seven miles from Lord Abergavenny's country estate in West Sussex, was a regular visitor to the house, often riding over to stay for a week at a time as a welcome guest of the family. But as the months passed, suspicion grew among the servants about the unseemly intimacy between him and Lady Abergavenny. The house porter William Smith noticed that every time Mr Lyddel called, he was told by the mistress that she would not be at home to anyone else during his visit. Laundrymaid Mary Hodson saw the couple kissing at the window of an upstairs dressing room, then hurriedly closing the shutters, and on several occasions one of the housemaids was ordered to leave the room with the bed still unmade when Mr Lyddel came to her Lady's chamber.

By the autumn of 1729, Matthews, who as his lord's gentleman was entrusted with family business matters, was becoming increasingly worried that the couple were involved in a criminal correspondence. During the week of 13 October he was dealing with the engrossing of tenants' leases, working in an apartment beneath the White Room where Mr Lyddel was staying. Seated at his usual writing table, he was absorbed in the task when a sudden noise from above made him stop abruptly halfway down a page, quill poised over the inkwell. He could plainly hear a man's voice and the sound of the bed creaking in the White Room, and rushing out onto the main staircase he saw Mr Lyddel appear and call for his man. Running as hard as he could, Matthews found one of the house servants and told them to send up the valet, then ran up the back stairs through the long gallery just in time to see Lady Abergavenny emerging from the White Room looking very red and disordered. The next morning he again heard noises in the room above and, determined now to find out the truth, dashed up the back stairs, along to the end of the gallery, and removing his wig lay down out of sight to wait. Shortly he heard the bolt drawn in the White Room and Mr Lyddel appeared, looking around furtively, then the mistress came out carefully spreading her petticoats to prevent the silks rustling.

On Thursday of that week he heard similar suspicious noises in the bedchamber and decided to report the matter to Mr Osman, the house steward, as he could not bear to see his lord betrayed in this fashion. On Friday and Saturday morning the two men waited together for the lovers to meet, and both heard the White Room bed creak, the door unbolted and saw her ladyship come out holding up her petticoats as before. With such clear evidence now of a clandestine liaison, they knew Lord Abergavenny had to be told the truth; they initially asked his mother if she would break the terrible news, but she was too upset to confront him. Eventually on 6 November Mr Day, a neighbour and relation who managed the family estates in several counties, agreed to take on the difficult task and asked his lordship to take a walk in the fields with him as he had something to discuss. Clearly alarmed by his grave manner, Lord Abergavenny pressed him to speak out at once, and when he heard what had been going on between his wife and Mr Lyddel was at first too shocked to believe that his close friend could have done such a thing. But faced with the facts of his wife's blatant infidelity, he agreed that the pair had to be surprised in the very act of adultery as final, incontrovertible proof.

At six in the morning on 8 November, Matthews, Mr Osman and Mr Day all squashed into a closet adjoining the White Room where Mr Lyddel slept and settled down to wait. Suddenly at nine o'clock they heard a noise, and peering through the keyhole Mr Osman saw her ladyship enter the room, slip over to the bed and say in a low voice, 'I cannot stay with you now.' Uncertain if she had left the bedchamber, they waited impatiently for a few more minutes to see what would happen next. Then, hearing sounds within, Matthews cautiously opened the door, and the three men tiptoed softly to the bedside and flung back the curtains.

Startled by the sudden intrusion, Mr Lyddel, wearing only a shirt, froze and cried out, 'Oh God!' Lady Abergavenny lay there beside him on her back in a very indecent posture, with her naked legs exposed. Even more shocking, she was heavily pregnant. 'Dear Matthews, do not ruin me. Do not ruin me,' she begged, hastily trying to cover herself. Matthews told her they had been sent at her husband's direction, and to Mr Lyddel said in disgust, 'Sir, I thought you would not have been guilty of so foul an act.' Mr Osman said, 'For you Sir, to come so frequently, in such a shew of friendship, and to wrong his Lordship after such a manner as you have done, is a crime for which you can make him no satisfaction.' Mr Lyddel replied, 'It is very true, I can make no satisfaction,' and offered to take his horse and ride away, and never return to the house again. But they locked him in the room alone, and when Lady Abergavenny sent a servant to check on him later that morning he was full of remorse and greatly agitated, exclaiming, 'I am a vile wretch; for God's sake do not speak to me.' Matthews set off immediately for London to instruct the family lawyer Mr Staples, and he swore an affidavit so that legal proceedings could be started against Mr Lyddel for criminal conversation.

At three o'clock that afternoon Lady Abergavenny was sent away in disgrace to her father General Tatton's house in London. Less than a month later she was dead.

~~~

The shocking tale of Lady Abergavenny had all the right ingredients of a juicy scandal – illicit sex among the upper classes, betrayal, remorse and punishment of the guilty couple. It revealed a tantalising glimpse into the secret existence of the aristocracy, which was usually safely hidden from public gaze behind the forbidding stone walls of their country houses. The compelling story went on to be printed and reprinted for more than a century in newspapers, periodicals, books and pamphlets, to the delight of generations of readers who could enjoy the vicarious thrill of peeping through the keyhole at the personal lives of the rich and powerful. Even better, they could relish all the titillating details of a sexual intrigue presented in the guise of a morality tale.

It was Lady Abergavenny's sudden death on 4 December 1729, shortly after childbirth, which gave the story extra dramatic resonance because it seemed like divine retribution for her sins. Already widowed after a brief marriage to his cousin Edward (the 13th baron) who died of small-pox, the 24-year-old Catherine had been married to William Nevill, 14th Lord Abergavenny, for four years at the time of her adultery. The couple already had two children, a boy of two who was a godchild of the king and a one-year-old girl, but the new baby died with his mother soon after birth.

Despite his wife's death, Lord Abergavenny went ahead and sued her seducer in a civil action for criminal conversation (popularly known as 'crim. con.').[1] At the hearing on 16 February 1730 at the Court of Common Pleas, he was awarded the enormous sum of £10,000 (the equivalent of £600,000 today) in damages against Lyddel, which reflected the heavy penalty inflicted in such cases where there had been a dishonourable betrayal of male friendship.[2] Speaking in mitigation, Lyddel's defence counsel told the court he could not afford to pay large damages as his estate was heavily mortgaged. In fact, he had more than ten years earlier been disinherited by his father, Dennis Lyddel, a former MP for Harwich, who took the unusual step of passing his estate, including the family home Wakehurst Place in West Sussex, to his wife rather than his eldest son, Richard, who was known as 'a profligate rake'.[3]

Whether Lord Abergavenny was aware of his friend's bad reputation is uncertain, but there was plenty of gossip that he knew about and had actually encouraged his wife's extramarital affair with the intent of suing for financial gain. He was clearly a man quick to avenge any perceived slight to his honour, as the previous year he had actually sued his own aunt, Anne, the Dowager Lady Abergavenny (mother of his deceased cousin Edward), 'for scandalous words spoken'. The action for Scandalum Magnatum, an ancient offence of slandering the nobility, was heard by Lord Chief Justice Eyre at the Court of Common Pleas in May 1729. He claimed £10,000 damages but was awarded the still considerable sum of £2,000 by the jury. The 'remarkable trial' was widely reported in the London press including the *Daily Post, Fog's Weekly Journal, London Evening Post* and *London Gazette*. Whether the defamatory words concerned his wife's infidelity or the legitimacy of their children we cannot be certain, though it would seem highly likely because only charges of this seriousness would be deemed to warrant legal damages of such a punitive nature.

Two years after the adultery trial Lord Abergavenny remarried and had an imposing mansion built for the family at Kidbrooke Park near East Grinstead. Catherine may have been genuinely in love with her seducer, or was she merely the careless debauched young wife of popular imagination? As for Lyddel, he did not end his days in the debtors' prison where many thought he deserved to stay, but went on to lead a respectable public life as MP for Bossiney in Cornwall. How he managed to pay off his debt is unknown.

Whatever the actual facts of the case and motives of those involved, the sensational story took on a life of its own in the commercial press as publishers seized the chance to make a quick profit from the scandal. The first brief articles appeared in the *Monthly Chronicle* and *Daily Post* reporting Lady Abergavenny's death at a lodging house in Soho. They were followed soon after by a deluge of print about the adultery trial, including lengthy coverage of all the smutty details in the *Monthly Chronicle*, the *Grub Street Journal*, the *Whitehall Evening Post*; pamphlets such as *An Account of the Tryal of Richard Lyddel Esq*, and *The Whole Tryal of Richard Lyddel*; and several verses including *A Poem, Sacred to the Memory of the Honourable Lady Aber---y*.

The case also inspired Henry Fielding's play *The Modern Husband*, which opened at Drury Lane Theatre in February 1732 and criticised the law enabling husbands to claim damages for adultery. The story was then reprinted at intervals over the next century in various different forms, proving especially popular in books of collected adultery trials such as the seven-volume *Trials for Adultery: or, The History of Divorces* (1779–80), and later in the succinctly named *Crim. Con. Gazette* (1838–39).

Both at the time of the scandal and long afterwards, public opinion was divided about whether Lord or Lady Abergavenny deserved the most sympathy. Writing to a relative on 5 December 1729, the day after her sudden death, one observer remarked disapprovingly that everyone was talking about 'the strange behaviour of Lady A … the woman is pitied – "poor thing!" her "stars" are blamed; she was *unlucky*, indiscreet not to manage more cunningly, and by the generality of the world she is more condemned for not hiding her fault than for committing it.'[4] As ever, it was not so much the actual sexual indiscretion of a public figure but being found out that created the scandal and provided a lucrative target for publishers.

The potent allure of sex, money and power has always created a keen public interest in gossip and speculation about the hidden private lives of the English aristocracy. A complex mixture of envy, derision and curiosity seems to be at the heart of an enduring fascination with a glamorous world far removed from our own. Today it is the private lives of show business celebrities, politicians and wealthy public figures that fill our modern media of print, television, film and digital sources. But the origin of this public appetite for sensational tales of high-profile scandal lies at the birth of the commercial mass market for print in Georgian England.

In the late eighteenth century there was serious national concern that an epidemic of adultery threatened to destroy the whole structure of English society. Four separate anti-adultery bills were introduced in Parliament to try and tackle the problem as the number of divorces increased and a series of aristocratic lawsuits for crim. con. caused public outrage. Publishers cleverly exploited stories of adultery for commercial and political motives, but these attacks on the aristocracy's moral fitness to rule ultimately undermined the traditional basis of hereditary power and marked the first steps in its decline.

Printed literature appeared in many different guises in Georgian England and proliferated so quickly that it seeped into the fabric of daily life. This rapid development of large-scale commercial publishing and the press meant that it soon became a powerful agent of social change, playing an active part in manipulating public opinion on important topics of the day. The fuel which fed this growing entity was of course cash, and publishers were constantly searching for new topics which would increase their readership. Stories of sex and power revealing the secret private lives of the aristocracy were guaranteed to be popular and saleable, so it was not surprising that their potential as a profitable commodity was quickly realised.

Although only a small proportion of peers were involved in trials for crim. con., adultery within the upper echelons of society developed into a prominent public issue as publishers effectively exploited the market demand for nobility by presenting salacious details of their personal lives as entertaining morality tales, often deliberately distorting reality by magnifying those aspects which would appeal to their readers. The publication of adultery cases as titillating entertainment magnified what was actually a minority activity into a perceived epidemic of immorality, and the scandalous private lives of a small number of peers came to be seen as emblematic of a morally corrupt class as a whole. This flood of print gradually helped to change perceptions of the aristocracy and acted as a catalyst for widespread public debate on their previously unquestioned status as leaders of society.

The public seems to prefer its aristocrats as entertaining stereotypes, presented as easily recognisable figures such as the scandalous duchess, the lecherous lord, the Regency rake and the eccentric earl. But what lies behind the lurid newspaper headlines and the bare facts of published exposés? I wanted to explore the stereotypes of aristocratic vice popularised by the commercial print culture of periodicals, pamphlets, newspapers and novels, and compare them with personal accounts written by those actually experiencing adultery themselves.

During the five years researching and writing this book, I spent many hours immersed in boxes of material at archives all over the country, sorting through bundles of musty old letters tied up with ribbon. I pored over the inkblots and scrawly handwriting of manuscript letters and read the yellowing pages of diaries in worn leather covers, trying to piece together the personal stories of some of those involved in complicated and deeply human dramas of infidelity – passionate, moving and often tragic.

One of the greatest pleasures of this historical detective work has also proved to be the greatest challenge, namely the enormously rich and sometimes daunting archival legacy of the aristocracy. The existence of this wealth of material has of course provided a mass of original documents to draw on, but the sheer volume of sources and their often fragmentary nature meant that the task of selecting and unearthing individual stories has been particularly difficult. Even the archive catalogue records of a single titled family and its estates over generations frequently run to many hundreds of pages. These family papers have now mostly been deposited in the safety of county record offices, although many collections still remain in private ownership.

Precisely which documents survive from the stacks of dusty boxes amassed by each family is to some extent an accident of fate, depending on both the actions of descendants and the historical priorities of earlier county archivists who were working to specific agendas. For peers, especially those with prominent political careers, extensive and assiduously catalogued collections of their papers, correspondence and journals exist, but extracting any evidence at all about their personal lives from this mass of public documentation can be almost impossible. For noblewomen the opposite problem exists, as few personal papers have been deemed interesting enough to be kept for posterity, and those that do still exist can be hard to locate within voluminous dynastic records, where they are frequently hidden in unclassified boxes of random 'family' or 'miscellaneous' papers.

When investigating the sensitive topic of infidelity, it is not surprising that some of the potentially most revealing material was destroyed by close relatives at the time or by morally censorious later generations, trying to ensure that such delicate family matters remained strictly private. Sexual misdemeanours are best kept as guilty secrets, locked safely in the comforting embrace of the country house. Because, as unlucky aristocrats who found themselves victims of the press discovered, public scandals can have dreadful and far-reaching consequences.

Part One

The Foundations
of Aristocracy

'Nobility at this period, is but a
degenerated race of men, whom
education hath only informed of new
vices … [they] debauch themselves
and their inferiors – ruin their own
honour, and the kingdom's.'

Rambler's Magazine, 1822

1

Marriage for 'Love or Gold?'

The shocking number of extra-marital affairs among the aristocracy had become the subject of heated public debate by the late eighteenth century. Outraged critics protested that 'this horrid vice' of adultery 'is at present become epidemical. It rages like pestilence – almost every newspaper furnishes us with repeated instances of this crime. Surely the air is become infectious and infection daily increases.'[1] In another sermon, sold as a printed pamphlet, an irate Scottish clergyman thundered:

> Adultery makes us brutes, or rather proves that we are so ... [it] is a crime so odious and complicated, that it violates at once, the laws of God, and the laws of man, the harmony of nature, and the harmony of virtue, which is nature's law. Adultery indicates the absence of every divine and social feeling ... this vice is as common as it is base, as fashionable as it is odious.[2]

But such strong views were not confined to religious moralisers who might be expected to enlist such an apocalyptic vision in an attempt to chasten their congregations. Many others felt equally alarmed about the prevalence of infidelity. A series of sensational legal trials for criminal conversation and a rising number of aristocratic divorce cases were given extensive publicity in an expanding commercial print market which thrived on the popular appetite for scandal. Measures to curb the problem were debated during anti-adultery bills raised in Parliament during the 1770s and again in the early 1800s, highlighting the issue and deepening fears that the immoral behaviour of the ruling class would spread down the social hierarchy, corrupting the whole of English society and fatally undermining national stability.

Speaking during the Parliamentary debate on the 1800 Adultery Prevention Bill, the barrister and future Lord Chancellor Thomas Erskine said he believed 'the crime of adultery ... to be one of the highest public offences'. An earl's son who had witnessed at first hand its far-reaching effects during his professional career over several decades acting as counsel in crim. con. actions, he argued:

> All other injuries, when put into the scale with it, were as nothing. What, then, was wanting to compleat the definition of a criminal offence in a civilized nation? What but its public consequences? and was there any other private wrong which produced so many? The sanctity of marriage, a contract which was the very foundation of the social world, was violated.[3]

The devoutly Evangelical William Wilberforce became better known for his anti-slavery campaigning, but he also believed adultery to be the single most important issue facing the country at the time, and 'of much more importance than any question about peace or war, or any constitutional question; for ... if the crime is suffered to go on unchecked, nothing could have a greater tendency to destroy the whole fabric of society.'

Aristocratic adultery was seen as such a serious threat to national stability because it undermined not only the institution of marriage, which was the cornerstone of society, but also the authority of the aristocracy as its natural leaders, whose inherited power depended on a legitimate bloodline and exemplary personal behaviour. The importance of marriage as the foundation of hereditary landownership and power meant that adultery within elite ranks had immense implications, not only for married couples and their family dynasties but for wider society also.

No one was really interested in the sex lives of ordinary folk or adultery cases within the lower ranks of society, by shopkeepers, lawyers or farm labourers. They may have caused a fleeting local scandal, and the few cuckolded husbands able to afford legal action may have found the trials reported in the local press, but they did not threaten the existence of the State or affect the entire structure of society. Adultery had many different meanings (personal, legal, religious, social and, ultimately, political) but was technically defined as voluntary sexual intercourse by a married person with someone other than their spouse. In his definitive *Commentaries on the Laws of England*, William Blackstone used the phrase 'the crime of adultery', but explained that adultery as a public crime was left to the jurisdiction of the spiritual courts, while temporal courts recognised it only as a civil injury as an action of trespass by the adulterer against the husband.[4] In the eyes of the Church, adultery was a sin which contravened the seventh commandment and was one of the grounds for marital separation, along with extreme cruelty, granted by the ecclesiastical courts. Adultery cases could also be brought under common law, following the introduction in 1670 of the legal action for crim. con. which awarded monetary damages to cuck-olded husbands.[5]

Marriage was regarded as the basic unit of society and was therefore vital as a stabilising force: 'Marriage … though it be in itself one of the smallest societies, is the original fountain from whence the greatest and most extensive government have derived their beings … the good of the whole is maintained by a harmony and correspondence of its several parts.'[6] The philosopher John Locke argued in his *Two Treatises of Government* that man and wife formed the first society given by God, who decreed that this 'conjugal society' should be a lasting union in order to nurture the resulting offspring.[7] Maintaining the happiness of both partners was essential for a long marriage, and anything that disrupted marital harmony was ultimately a threat to the wider social order.

A widespread belief that all was not well with English marriage existed throughout the late eighteenth and early nineteenth centuries, as reflected in the repeated and often vehemently expressed opinions published in periodicals, essays, books and pamphlets. In 1772 an essay contributor to the *London Magazine* observed, 'At the amazing rate adultery has prospered of late, men will be afraid to venture upon matrimony … At the best, it is but a losing game … our women have advanced a degree farther in the science of adultery than ever women did before.'[8] Although written with more than a tinge of irony to raise a smile in the reader, it effectively highlighted the potential consequences of popular trends in behaviour. By 1799, a serious pamphlet penned by the anonymous 'Friend to Social Order' regretted 'the present lamentable state of the malady, in this civil war of lust'.[9]

This public debate referred to the prevalence of infidelity in all ranks of society, not only within the aristocracy, and such perceptions of rampant adultery continued into the next century. In 1821 a contributor to the letters column of the *Ladies' Monthly Museum* summed it up in graphic rhetoric, writing:

In an age like the present, when the scorpion of infidelity … boldly raises its head in our streets and high places … the heart of every true Briton, patriot, and Christian, must view with abhorrence the dissemination of principles, which, if not timely checked will eventually destroy every social tie, and plunge the country in all the horrors of anarchy and confusion.[10]

As in the earlier sermon which had envisaged adultery as an epidemic, this writer also imagined adultery as an alarming aspect of predatory, untameable nature, here in the vivid metaphor of a dangerous scorpion.

So what exactly had gone wrong with English matrimony, and why did more couples appear to be unhappy with their relationships? One of the main problems was a subtly changing attitude to the actual meaning of marriage, and the thorny issue of whether love or money mattered most in the choice of a spouse. Marriage itself was basically an economic institution, but during the eighteenth century a growing awareness of the concept of romantic love brought higher expectations that partnerships should also provide emotional fulfilment and companionship. Finding the ideal spouse could therefore be especially difficult in aristocratic families where, prior to the early 1700s, parents had arranged matches mainly for dynastic and financial advantage. Despite changing attitudes, however, romantic love matches did not completely replace arranged marriages.[11] The unpredictability of human nature and the complexity of mixed motives meant there was always far more to the choice of spouse than a simple love versus money calculation.

During the eighteenth century there was a decline in peers' sons marrying heiresses from 40 per cent to 10 per cent, although this was not due to any major shift from economic to personal reasons dictating choice. On the contrary, marrying girls from titled families as a way of enlarging estates became less popular because promises of future inheritance did not always materialise, and the certainty of a large marriage portion paid upfront was more attractive. A marriage could not be described simply as being either arranged or romantic, because it may have felt like a very different experience for bride and groom, with one choosing for romantic reasons and the other for family duty. The reality seems to have been that there was no radical change in the motives for marriage during the Georgian period, and most alliances probably continued to mix financial and personal motives, finding a balance that could be anywhere on the scale between coldly utilitarian and deeply romantic. Regardless of more rose-tinted notions of love which some thought were being fostered by literature, the actual experience of marriage was not exempt from the pragmatic financial considerations governing many other aspects of life. This was especially true in people of rank and fortune whose main priority was the continuity of landed estates, but also for those of the lower orders who aspired to rise socially and coveted the prestige of marrying a title, which was a valuable asset in the competitive marriage market.

It is clear from personal letters, and the printed advice literature, pamphlets, essays, periodicals, novels, poems and plays of the era, that hard-headed mercenary motives for marriage were widespread, continuing throughout the eighteenth century and on into the 1830s. Contemporaries repeatedly voiced deep anxiety about the prevalence of the wrong motives for marriage based on 'ambition', which they blamed for the rising number of separations, adultery and divorce cases plaguing society.

Some of the major concerns were deftly summed up by the humorous *Dictionary of Love*, which was reprinted through four editions between 1776 and 1795. Words listed under M included 'money' and 'matrimony', with money defined as a 'term of infinite power in the present modern System of Love. The possession of it alone confers the title of lover, as it does a Lord. A bank-bill genteelly conveyed, beats all the fine things a Catullus or Tibullus could say.'[12] This clever satirical contrast between the old classical ideals and the hard facts of life continued for the term matrimony, where 'Sordid interest is now the great master of ceremonies to Hymen, of which it pollutes the sanctuary.' The anonymous author launched a scathing attack on parents who sacrificed their children to money, claiming they were worse than an ancient tribe who burnt their offspring to honour the Canaanite idol Moloch, because 'the pain of those sold for interest is a lingering one, and often as sure as death'. The dictionary explained that, 'At present, the fashion is to *commit* matrimony; since … it is rather a crime than a virtue; many enter into it with no better design than a highwayman on Hounslow-heath, *to take a purse.*' It described love as a business transaction under the definition of Rival, as an 'out-bidder' for the hand of a lady by a man of fortune wanting to 'beat down her price'. The enticements needed to win a woman were in proportion to her personal worth, so that a duchess 'may fall to a diamond necklace, and a chambermaid to a taudry ribbon'.

Whatever the motives, marriage remained a perennial challenge, and in an age fascinated by gaming many people accepted that marriage was the biggest gamble of all. In a letter dismissing the congratulations of a friend on his recent wedding Thomas, 2nd Baron Lyttelton, explained, with characteristic frankness, 'Marriage is the grand lottery of life; and it is as great a folly to exult upon entering into it, as on the purchase of a ticket in the State wheel of fortune. It is when the ticket is drawn a prize that we can answer to congratulations.'[13] And another correspondent, referring to the notorious Lady Abergavenny scandal, remarked, 'My Lady A's behaviour, and some more wives of the same stamp, has so disgraced matrimony, that I am not surprized that men are afraid of it.'[14]

In *The Forced Marriage,* a play written in 1770 by a well-known and widely published London doctor, the reluctant bride's servant pointed out that as marriage was 'a lottery at the best', it had 'little chance to prosper' if love was sacrificed to a father's avarice.[15] The play picked up on the popular debate about marriage motives by charting the tragic consequences of a match between a lord's daughter and a rich elderly nobleman, who the father thought was 'above her proudest hopes – a prize scarce to be dreamt of'. It dramatised the conflicting viewpoints of the father (who claimed his motive was paternal love, with age and life experience giving a more reasoned basis for choice than youthful passion) and the girl, who dutifully refused to elope with her real love, went mad and died at the prospect of this forced match. The loyal maid, a character embodying the voice of reason, protested that, 'it looks so like base prostitution, that the more I think on't, the more it shocks me'. And in the preface, the author declared that he wrote the play 'to expose a most cruel and absurd tyranny too common in life'.

It is significant that neither this play, nor other writings, used the term 'arranged marriage' as it was understood that all matches involving legal settlement of land or money required arrangement by relatives and lawyers, but this had no relevance to any personal emotions involved. Couples distinguished by their notable lack of feeling could be described as marrying for 'interest', 'ambition' or 'fortune-hunting', while marriages of substantial mutual affection were 'love-matches', although this particular phrase was mainly found in novels and periodicals.

Men and women were equally likely to harbour mercenary motives, as were people of all social classes who saw marriage as the best means of securing status and wealth. The American philosopher Benjamin Franklin condemned 'muckworms' with a 'thirst for riches' in the opening section of his *Reflections on Courtship and Marriage* entitled 'Many unhappy matches are occasioned by mercenary views'.[16] He harshly criticised the 'abominable prostitutions' seen daily in so many marriages and asked, 'How many play the harlot for a good settlement, under the legal title of a wife! and how many … to repair a broken fortune, or to gain one!' First published in 1746, the hard-hitting essay was reprinted three times in England where it obviously struck a chord with a largely middle-class readership, by arguing that marriage should be founded on mutual friendship and esteem, not based on 'mere motives of interest' which were 'repugnant to reason and nature'.

English authors who themselves frequently came from the moral middle classes could also argue self-righteously that 'love alone shall regulate thy choice', although they too were not immune from the financial priorities of a commercial and aspirational society.[17] The barrister Richard Fenton was an affluent young gentleman who could afford to be scathing of social climbers in his poetry but in real life actually married a baron's daughter, whose money conveniently helped to fund his antiquarian and scholarly ambitions. One of his poems decried those heartless people who marry upwards:

> Base, let them suffer to be bought and sold,
> And barter all their happiness for gold;
> Or, lur'd by grandeur, for a title wed,
> And risque their peace to share a noble bed.

It was obviously easier to ascribe base motives in other people's marriages than to admit that your own motives might not be entirely pure or disinterested.

Ambition was present in all social classes but the mercenary motive was believed to rise in proportion to rank, so it was noticeable in the landed gentry and especially prevalent among the nobility, who had the most at stake in terms of land and fortune, as well as the bonus of a title. Far greater economic and parental pressure was therefore imposed on aristocratic children, particularly eldest sons who would inherit and daughters who depended on a generous marriage portion for future security. The different meaning and practice of marriage for the aristocracy meant that they were thought to be most likely to marry for the wrong reasons and therefore to have unhappy marriages.

These imperatives of inheritance and lineage were reflected in the correspondence between Basil, 6th Earl of Denbigh, and various family friends. Among many letters of congratulation on the birth of his grandson in 1796 was one which commented, 'I hope … that the House of Denbigh will never want plenty of lineal successors.'[18] The acceptance that financial matters were a natural component of aristocratic marriage was illustrated in another letter to Denbigh from Charlotte, Marchioness of Bute, who had herself been a wealthy heiress as a bride. Summing up the recent union of her husband's brother William Stuart, Bishop of St David's, she tellingly linked happiness and cash in the same short sentence, 'The Bishop and his wife seem very happy, she had twenty thousand pounds.'[19]

Marrying well was viewed as an important family and social duty for young aristocratic men and women. Parents went to great lengths to achieve a match that would be mutually satisfactory to both families in terms of status and fortune, and therefore lengthy legal and financial transactions were required when large amounts of inherited land and money were involved. The vast ten-page marriage settlement document signed and witnessed at the Old Bailey in 1747 for the marriage of Lady Mary Bertie, daughter of the 2nd Duke of Ancaster, and Samuel Greatheed, the wealthy son of a St Kitts sugar plantation owner, showed how the interests of both parties were carefully protected. Lady Mary's £15,000 marriage portion (roughly £900,000 today) was specified as providing £5,000 to Greatheed 'to and for his own use and benefit', plus a further £10,000 to be kept in trust for the bride and her future children.[20] In addition, a parcel of land on the St Kitts plantation was granted to Lady Mary's trustees to assure her future income in the event of Samuel's death. This family alliance of new money and ancient pedigree clearly brought benefits to both parties, with the consolidation of rank and two fortunes. While Lady Mary secured a wealthy husband who had lucrative West Indies investments and prospects in public life as a newly elected MP, Greatheed gained the social prestige of marrying into a duke's family and a cash settlement he could invest in his estate. During the eighteenth century a portion of around £25,000 in cash (around £1.5 million now) rather than land was the norm from girls marrying a peer, though adjustments were made to take account of inequalities in rank. Untitled brides or those outside the landed gentry were required to bring a larger sum when marrying up the social scale, while the widow's jointure would be more generous for noblewomen marrying down. At the pinnacle of society, the marriage portion of HRH the Princess Royal was a staggering £80,000 (£4.8 million today) in 1797.[21]

Many parents were naturally hoping for a judicious blend of the practical and emotional when arranging their children's marriages, such as the politician and author George Lyttelton, 1st Baron. He had spent considerable effort in 1763 negotiating a suitable match for his only son, Thomas, with Anne, daughter of Lieutenant-General Warburton, who would inherit £50,000 on her father's death.[22] But eighteen months later the marriage settlement had still not been finalised; Thomas, travelling in Europe on the Grand Tour, expressed his frustration to his uncle, writing, 'I am betrothed to a woman whom I would give the world to enjoy, and whom I cannot marry until ... the General has sold his estate ... I prefer Miss Warburton's love to that of any other woman.'[23] He was delighted that Anne seemed to be equally smitten, 'my sweet girl ... professes herself, in the language of desiring love, to be *mine, and only mine.*'[24] However, after reports of his gambling and youthful misconduct in Italy, the match was called off, and his father took a largely pragmatic view: 'Upon the whole, I flatter myself he may do better elsewhere, as Miss Warburton's present Fortune was rather too scanty to make him easy; and no-one can tell how long her Parents may live', adding that the union might have been 'less happy than I could wish'.[25]

Despite the apparent mutual affection of the couple expressed in their letters, in later life Thomas had a very different view of the match, rationalising that youthful obedience to paternal authority had made him consent to a marriage in which he and Anne were mere pawns in a family negotiation: 'A rich and amiable young lady was chosen to the happy and honourable task ... to shape me into that perfection of character which was to verify the dreams of my visionary relations.'[26] It is difficult to be sure whether this cynical viewpoint had some truth or if the power of hindsight had distorted his memories of genuine youthful feelings. But the case shows how there could be several different interpretations of an apparently 'arranged' marriage.

Older couples free of parental interference had greater personal freedom to choose, but they too needed to be aware of the delicate balance between emotional and practical considerations. The second marriage of Basil, 6th Earl of Denbigh, showed the complex and shifting motivations of both partners. Although proudly proclaiming noble descent from the princely line of Hapsburg, the family had a long history of financial problems, which had led to the loss of an estate in Rutland after Denbigh's accession to the title.[27] A major motivating factor throughout his life was therefore the need to secure extra income, which he managed via a series of generous court sinecures including lord of the bedchamber and by marrying twice, both times to an heiress. The first was a traditional arranged marriage to Mary Cotton, a baronet's daughter with a substantial marriage portion.[28] From their remaining letters, the couple appeared to have been ill-matched in terms of temperament, his being a lively nature enjoying bawdy jokes and drinking, and hers governed by devout religious belief. In one letter to a relative, Denbigh joked about 'the diversions of London' and its opportunities for adultery, adding, 'Ho! ho! – lay in a good Hock of Wine, for we intend to pass many a merry day with you this Winter.'[29] In contrast, one of Mary's earnest letters, which was left to be opened after her death, urged her husband to consider his immortal soul and reminded him of 'my repeated attempts during Life to awaken you to a Sense of the imminent Danger you run'.[30]

Only nine months after her death in 1783, the earl was remarried at the age of 64 to Sarah, Lady Halford, the rich widow of a neighbouring Leicestershire baronet, whom he already knew from social events in the elite county circle. The match was a considered two-way financial deal to which the bride brought substantial estates but retained all rents and profits 'in her full and entire possession', while the earl settled on her both land and his London house.[31] Denbigh's initial comments expressed his practical rather than emotional requirements of marriage, when he wrote to a friend, 'If good sense, chearfulness, and an amiable Disposition in a Wife can conduce to Happiness, I think I have every prospect before me of being so.'[32] But there was also great affection between the couple, and he wrote later, 'Lady D ... has been my only comfort for nigh this two year'.[33] On superficial appearances, the marriage could be described by observers either as a pragmatic marriage made for financial considerations to a baronet's widow of independent fortune, or as a love-match by two older people of independent means who had known each other for some time. Neither of these interpretations would be entirely accurate, as it was a far more complex picture in which affection, rank and money all played a part in the decision for both partners. Mercenary motives could co-exist with real attraction or develop later into a genuine marriage of affection.

Although a couple's personal considerations could be less clear-cut than the public façade of a marriage might indicate, commentators reflected a society where mercenary motives did now seem to predominate and many people believed that 'a woman in this country has very little probability of marrying for love'.[34] The situation was especially difficult for girls because 'men *chuse*, and women only *accept*' and sometimes the best they could hope for was that esteem might later develop into limited affection.[35] Parents overcome by ruthless ambition were thought to be the main cause of unhappy marriage, and writers repeatedly used the term 'prostitution' for this heartless trade in daughters, which they warned could lead to adultery.

One author argued that as 'marriages are generally made by the … authority of parents; and their children are only actors who have parts given them, sometimes very difficult … to perform', it was as unjust to blame them for the consequences, as to blame a player who recited a bad part for the faults of the dramatist.[36] The writer viewed crimes of adultery as the 'probable and necessary *consequences*' of matches created by avaricious relatives, and urged legislators to punish parents 'for the profligacy of children they had … inhumanly prostituted'. In similar vein, the aptly pseudonymed Augustus Lovemore warned that a girl 'hurried by her parents into a wealthy marriage, drawn by variety and dissipation … into innumerable temptations, may … fall into the most fatal error'.[37] A writer in the *London Magazine* of April 1770 remarked that both men and women were real fortune-hunters, but young ladies were 'too often the dupes of their own, or their parents' ambition'.[38] A pretty girl with a portion of £500 would turn down a mere tradesman in the expectation of a carriage, while more than £1,500 meant that she 'sets her cap at a coronet'.[39]

Mercenary marriage was seen as a growing problem right through into the mid-nineteenth century, with regular warnings about the perils of fortune hunters appearing in print. Writing in 1829, the political reformer William Cobbett described those who love 'according to the rules of arithmetic' as 'despicable' and propagating 'a species of legal prostitution'.[40] Women's magazines took a particular interest in the debate, publishing essays such as 'Which should a young lady prefer in matrimony – love or gold?' in 1815 and 'The calamities of heiresses' in 1828, both of which argued strongly against bartering personal happiness for wealth.[41] The extent to which these ideals were actually reflected in real marriages is of course difficult to gauge, but a combination of personal and strategic familial interest, depending on individual couples and their social rank, is the most realistic assessment. For the aristocracy, family duty usually remained more important than individual preferences.

Because the choice of partner and the experience of matrimony had a major impact on most people's lives, the topic had strong market appeal that was exploited by the commercial press in popular formats including pamphlets, books and essays giving both serious and satirical views of marriage, alongside novels, plays and poetry. Outside the confines of stern religious tracts, writers took an entirely realistic view of marriage, offering practical advice on how to cope with difficulties and citing the power of reason as the guide to conjugal harmony. This pragmatic approach was exemplified by *A Father's Legacy to his Daughters,* a popular work by the eminent physician Dr John Gregory which went through fifteen editions between 1774 and 1796. It outlined the considerations in choosing a husband, warned against the false expectations raised by romantic novels and wisely summed up the secret of a lasting marriage in which the 'tumult of passion will necessarily subside; but it will be succeeded by an endearment that affects the heart in a more equal, more sensible, and tender manner'.[42]

The habit of novel reading was repeatedly criticised for corrupting morals and setting up distorted, overly dramatic expectations of real-life romance. One popular publication warned girls to 'shun as you would do the most fatal poison, all that species of reading … which warms the imagination … and raises the taste above the level of common life' or it will 'embitter all your married days'. In the cautionary memoir and conduct manual describing the causes of her own scandalous marital separation, Lady Sarah Pennington recommended plays as being morally instructive, but said that novels and romances should be avoided for their 'pernicious consequences' in real life. Not only were their moral parts 'like small diamonds amongst mountains of dirt and trash', but they 'give a romantic turn to the mind, which is often productive of great errors in judgment, and of fatal mistakes in conduct – of this I have seen frequent instances'.[43]

Sensible guidelines for husbands based on 'reason, virtue, and honour' were also laid out in *A Letter from a Father to a Son on his Marriage*, which advised men not to discard all the little attentions of courtship: 'Be … as you were before marriage; polite and complaisant … tender and attentive'.[44] It gave guidance on behaviour in married life including care in personal cleanliness, avoiding food disliked by the wife and how to cope with 'diversities of temper'.

An amusingly cynical but widely held idea of marriage was encapsulated in *Cupid and Hymen; a Voyage to the Isles of Love and Matrimony*, an ingenious tale which described marriage as a beautiful island of illusion tempting unwary travellers, who found instead when they arrived a threatening landscape of briars, precipices, morasses and serpents.[45] The island had two ports named Love and Interest, the latter a trading port 'full of immense Riches, where Fathers and Mothers … put off their Daughters, who are set out for Sale in their Warehouses'. It was divided into provinces inhabited by the Discreet, the Ill-matched, the Ill-at-Ease and the Jealous, while the capital of the head province Cuckoldshire, named Hornborough, was a city 'as large as London, to which it bears a very great Resemblance', peopled mainly by the wealthy elite.

The book also included several ironic portrayals of marriage, including a bachelor's financial estimate of the expenses of married life, and a married man's reply which jokingly quoted the justification of wedded love as being the 'perpetual fountain of Domestic Sweets' from *Paradise Lost*, Book Four. Very few serious references were made to Milton's famous passage 'Hail, wedded Love' in literature discussing matrimony in this period. Instead, it often cropped up as an ironic commentary on the contrast between the pure sexual married love in the Garden of Eden, and the wanton behaviour of modern lovers. These included the use of Milton's opening lines in a pamphlet about the adultery of the Duke of Cumberland, and in a satirical guide to seducing young ladies.[46] Most readers would have been familiar with the passage and picked up on the implied reference to its well-known fourth line, 'By thee adulterous lust was driven from men'. Milton may have shaped more traditional aspirations for marriage, but for most people this proved to be an unattainable Protestant ideal of perfection which was sadly confined to sermons and religious essays.

Contemporaries strongly believed that the high incidence of marriage for the wrong motives posed a serious problem in society generally, but particularly in the upper echelons where far more was at stake. In her novel *The Sylph*, published in 1779, Georgiana, Duchess of Devonshire, expressed the fashionable cynical opinion of the reasons for marriage in a letter from the libertine Sir William Stanley to Lord Biddulph asking, 'don't every body marry? those who have estates, to have heirs of their own; and those who have *nothing*, to get *something*'.[47] Later in the novel, the bitter words of the heroine, Julia, reflected the author's own experiences in an emotionally stunted marriage to the 5th Duke of Devonshire: 'Marriage now is a necessary kind of barter, and an alliance of families; – the heart is not consulted; – or if that should sometimes bring a pair together … love seldom lasts long.'

Marrying for 'interest' did not necessarily rule out love or sexual attraction, and fortunate couples managed to combine a measure of both, but many young people continued to put family duty before their own personal wishes and this could have serious consequences later on. This was true for Lady Elizabeth Hamilton, who was reluctantly persuaded by her ambitious mother to marry the wealthy Edward Smith Stanley, 12th Earl of Derby, instead of her real love, John Sackville, the 3rd Duke of Dorset. The couple married in 1774 after a brief courtship, but within four years Elizabeth was involved in an adulterous affair with Dorset, left her husband and found herself exiled to the country in disgrace for the rest of her life.

A similar case of thwarted youthful passion leading to infidelity was that of Lady Elizabeth Belasyse, who in 1789 reluctantly married Bernard Howard, the 12th Duke of Norfolk, to please her parents despite being in love with the Hon. Richard Bingham, with whom she later had a passionate affair. Speaking as the defence counsel during their trial for adultery in 1794, Thomas Erskine criticised the 'legal prostitution of parental choice in the teeth of affection' and described in dramatic rhetoric how the unwilling bride was 'stretched upon this bed as a rack – a legal victim to the shrine of heraldry, torn from the arms of a beloved youth to secure the honours of a higher rank'.[48] The court heard how Elizabeth had often slept alone on a couch in tears and told her maid that she would rather go to Newgate prison than to sleep in her husband's bed. Erskine used the case to frame a general attack on noble conduct, warning, 'Let the aristocracy of England, which trembles so much for itself, take heed to its own security … Instead of continuing their names and honors in cold and alienated embraces … let them … marry as Affection and Prudence lead the way'. His compelling speech explicitly linked loveless marriages to the pursuit of alternative comforts by taking part in 'rounds of shallow dissipations', and he told the court that Elizabeth was able to hold open assignations with her lover at popular public venues such as Kensington Gardens, the opera, Ranelagh Gardens and fashionable watering places.

Marital harmony was difficult to achieve at all levels of society but aristocratic couples had to deal with specific pressures created by their rank and fortune, both in the making of marriage and in the everyday experience of married life. The main points of class difference highlighted in contemporary writings were the prevalence of the parental arranged match, the freedom to travel widely and mix socially, the temptations offered by public amusements in town and the conduct of husbands in neglecting wives either for duty or for other women. All these issues were believed by critics to make adultery more likely within an elite corrupted by wealth and leisure, who rejected 'tender sentiments, which … refine the moral character' and instead wasted their lives in entertainments and 'unmeaning criminal commerce'.[49] The meaningless flirtations conducted at public amusements were satirised in *Cupid and Hymen*, where the island inhabitants known as the Contented Cuckolds enjoyed unconstrained lives of pleasure, dancing and feasting, at operas, balls and masquerades, in pursuit of novelty for its own sake because as everyone knows, 'Lovers are … like fish, the freshest are always the best'.[50]

Impressionable and naïve young wives were especially prone to become addicted to the 'fashionable follies of the great world' by indulging their vanity in the 'gaiety and dissipation' of town life.[51] This popular view of aristocratic marriage was described in the epistolary novel *The Mercenary Marriage,* a morality tale about the vain and socially ambitious Laura, who vowed to herself, 'I *must* raise myself ... to that rank in life which I was, undoubtedly, born to enjoy'. She then rejected the younger son of a peer with a fortune 'too small to be mentioned' to marry wealthy Lord Glandour.[52] In contrast to *The Sylph*, the peers in the novel were all portrayed as virtuous men with strong moral values who became the innocent victims of Laura's single-minded ambition. Her addiction to dissipated London life soon led her into trouble, culminating in secret assignations in Kensington Gardens with her former lover, which were discovered by her husband. He sent her away to the seclusion of his remote Scottish estate as punishment, explaining that because he had no proofs of adultery he could not procure a divorce: 'If I cannot get rid of her entirely, I will keep her by way of punishment ... as she loves nothing so much as perpetual appearance in all public places, in order to be admired'. Laura was eventually allowed to return to London but only plunged deeper into a fashionable life of dissipation, until her husband eventually discovered her alone with a lover in her dressing room. Unable to face the shame of divorce she died, dramatically begging her husband to 'forgive a wretch, undone by vanity and ambition'. The novel graphically illustrated the temptations of town life for young women, and how adultery could develop from harmless flirtation in public venues to the ultimate violation of the marital home.

The unique problems of aristocratic marriage were also highlighted in *Letters from a Peeress of England to her Eldest Son*, which said wedlock was 'less calculated to make people happy than any other institution, human or divine'. The same book suggested that elite marriages were less contented than those of tradesmen, saying 'Cupid often flies the gilded room and damask couch, and is found in humble spaces ... magnificence and content are wide asunder'.[53] Marital discord was attributed to a surfeit of leisure, to familiarity fading into indifference and to the neglect of boring husbands who became engrossed in the all-male activities of field sports, politics and gentlemen's clubs. The passage of time alone could create disenchantment, when 'the gay and well-dressed Strephon of twenty years old, turns at forty into a slovenly and bald-headed foxhunter, or grave politician'. But whatever the causes of unhappy marriages, the anonymous and presumably fictitious peeress was strongly against divorces, which were 'desperate and shameful remedies to evil'. Instead she advised that, 'through all the changes of mind and person, man and wife may still be friends', and should continue to maintain outward appearances by enacting 'a picture of amity and concord'.

Nobility carried with it certain expectations of correct behaviour, so members of the landowning class had specific pressures on their marriages, which were made largely as dynastic alliances to protect the hereditary bloodline. Arranged marriages and mercenary motives continued well into the nineteenth century but these pragmatic considerations existed alongside varying measures of love, individual hopes or romantic dreams. Clearly loveless arranged marriages were not the only cause of adultery, but many people believed they were greatly to blame.

2

LAND AND POWER

The English country house estate has for centuries been a visible symbol of privilege and status, a living theatre of public power and display where dramatic stories of everyday life are staged. But at the same time it is an intensely private place, hidden in acres of secluded parkland and protected from prying eyes behind the forbidding stonework, rows of tightly shuttered sash windows and firmly closed doors.

As the solid foundation of leadership and authority, the great country estate operated as a public private place. It served both as a domestic space for the extended family, servants and close acquaintances but also as a public backdrop for social, political, agricultural and other essential business activities. And, crucially, for each successive generation living within the house, the building itself was the impressive physical evidence of family continuity and a confident statement of its enduring rank and power.

A noble family dynasty was created by a mix of the bloodline, the name and the landed estate, but while the family name was important, the country estate itself was most significant in securing continuity by inheritance. As a result, the ancestral home seemed to possess an intrinsic mystique, evoking strong emotional responses from each successive life tenant who became the new link in the chain joining past ancestors and future descendants. It formed part of an inviolable social contract between generations which the statesman Edmund Burke had summed up so well as 'a partnership not only between those who are living, but ... those who are dead, and those who are to be born'.

The roots of aristocratic power are buried centuries deep beneath England's history, and by the late eighteenth century the landowning elite had reached the height of its influence as the most exclusive, most powerful and most land-based aristocracy in Europe. This 'self-reproducing oligarchy' of the English aristocracy had become a tighter closed circle than at any other period, which undoubtedly underpinned its all-encompassing power and social cachet.[54] The foundations of such undisputed leadership which lay in the possession of land and property were based on traditional beliefs that ancient hereditary rule safeguarded the continuity of the state.

The first titles were handed out by grateful monarchs in recognition of support in battle, and being raised to the peerage had always been a possibility for a few fortunate families who became distinguished for their military, political or legal service. But the process typically took at least two generations via the steady incremental steps of 'trade, a fortune, the acquisition of an estate, a baronetcy, membership of Parliament'.[55] The number of nobles gradually increased over the centuries, but it still remained very much a small and exclusive group. Only 1,003 people held an English hereditary peerage during the whole of the eighteenth century, with a total of 189 peers existing in 1780, rising to 267 peers in 1800.[56] Gaining membership of the aristocracy became far more difficult, and landownership became more concentrated in fewer hands. Many elite landowners managed to amass huge fortunes in the new market-driven economy and consolidated their position by pouring this wealth into developing their country estates.

The word 'aristocracy' was first used by the Ancient Greeks to signify rule of the best, but in early modern England it had become synonymous with social rank based on inherited honour or high esteem. Aristotle believed that 'those who are sprung from better ancestors are likely to be better men, for nobility is excellence of race'. The word aristocracy specifically denotes a form of government, and the term came into common usage in eighteenth-century English society as referring to 'government by the best in birth and fortune'.[57] By the late 1700s this traditional definition began to be overtaken by a new meaning of aristocracy as a social group.

Fundamental to this aristocratic ideology was the basic belief that social order reflected a natural moral order, and that those at the summit of the status hierarchy possessed honour as an inherited virtue. Bernard Mandeville, the influential Enlightenment writer on social theory, defined honour simply as being 'the good opinion of others' and, significantly, he identified the importance of a public show of honour, which he argued 'is counted more or less substantial the more or less noise or bustle there is made about the demonstration of it'.[58] The concept of honour as a dual-facetted quality, encompassing both an inner personal virtue and an outward display of superior birth underlies the traditional rationale for elite rule. When this equation of rank with virtue became the subject of increasing critical debate in the late 1700s, it inevitably called into question the whole basis of an intrinsic social order and highlighted the link between the public duties of a ruling elite and their behaviour in private life.

The traditional view was upheld by the writer and literary authority Dr Samuel Johnson, who was best known for his dictionary. He believed strongly that in all civilised nations the principle of hereditary rank contributed 'greatly to human happiness'. He observed:

> I would no more deprive a nobleman of his respect, than of his money. I consider myself as acting a part in the great system of society ... there would be a perpetual struggle for precedence, were there no fixed invariable rules for the distinction of rank, which creates no jealousy as it is allowed to be accidental.[59]

Aristocratic leadership of a stratified society originated in assumptions about the stability of land itself as a dependable long-term investment, and a deeply rooted belief system that landownership conferred an entitlement to rule on the major stakeholders possessing a share of English soil. This in turn underpinned notions of a stable, disinterested ruling class of landowners who were financially secure enough to be able to govern for the public good.

Various different and often interchangeable terms were used during the Georgian period when referring to members of the aristocracy, the most common ones being 'the nobility', 'the peerage', 'people of rank and fortune', 'the great' and 'the higher ranks'. The five ranks of the peerage with membership of the House of Lords were, in descending order of importance, duke, marquis, earl, viscount and baron. Baronets were technically commoners as they did not sit in the Upper House. Because of the complexity of inheritance laws there were inevitably plenty of grey areas, as for example in the case of a peer's eldest son who was technically a commoner until he succeeded to his title, or younger sons who remained commoners unless they later went on to inherit.

By the end of the eighteenth century there were just 400 families with substantial estates providing annual incomes of more than £5,000 (roughly £300,000 now), including those of peers plus some of the wealthier baronets and upper gentry. Together they made up less than 1 per cent of the whole population, but they represented the upper echelons of a landowning class in 'its greatest days of political, social and economic supremacy'.[60]

By the early nineteenth century aristocratic families needed a minimum yearly income of £10,000 (£600,000 today) or a large estate of at least 10,000 acres in order to finance the running of their country house and the requisite attendance in the capital during the London season. For a landed aristocracy with a rural economic power base, maintaining a hold on power into the industrialised nineteenth century depended on adapting ideas of what leadership meant in a changing society. This included investment in emerging economic development projects and performing duties in local and national affairs in line with an innate belief in the value of public service. This adaptability in embracing new roles, together with an unshakeable personal confidence in their position as natural leaders, enabled English aristocrats to survive sporadic attacks on their hereditary privileges.

Although aristocratic influence continued to increase throughout the eighteenth century, the peerage admitted only a handful of newcomers from outside its traditional ranks. During the century 229 new titles were created but only twenty-three of these had no previous family links with the nobility, eleven of those being successful lawyers, such as Lord Ellenborough's father who was created a baron in 1802 on becoming Lord Chief Justice. However, these newcomers were already wealthy enough to possess substantial property or a useful circle of influential friends and relatives. The father of the 1st Earl of Morley was plain John Parker, an MP from a wealthy landed Devon family owning a large country mansion at Saltram near Plymouth, who was raised to the first rung of the peerage as a baron in 1784.

Beneath the upper echelons of the peerage and baronetage, only a limited number of newcomers moved up into the broader elite comprising the county gentry, who lived in smaller country houses of perhaps 5,000sq ft. These newcomers were not business- or tradesmen but came mainly from the professions, and they were viewed by some contemporary observers as part of a positive 'biologically rejuvenating process' of the upper classes which promoted better social stability.[61] The potential profits to be made from a stream of philanthropic and economic or agricultural improvement initiatives created many new opportunities for successful men, who could now qualify by means of their personal income instead of landed estates to join this broader ruling class. By the end of the eighteenth century old conflicts between landed and new moneyed interests had begun to fade. There was growing acceptance by the traditional landowners of professionals, old merchant and banking families, although both groups united in their scorn for rich but vulgar industrialists. Although they were often perceived as an exclusive tribe, the aristocracy was constantly recreating itself through inter-marriages which linked peers, their downwardly mobile younger sons, landed gentry and new trade money. While some wealthy newcomers moved up the social scale through the purchase of an estate or via marriage, peers' younger sons did not have titles and in effect became gentry, while titled eldest sons often married heiresses from among the gentry, professional and merchant classes to bring welcome financial aid to debt-ridden family estates.

Alongside this gradual shift in the composition of the ruling elite came an era of consolidation between the 1780s and 1820s in which the previously separate elites of England, Ireland, Scotland and Wales merged to create a broader British aristocracy and strengthened the basis of landed power, which began a gradual decline only after the 1832 Great Reform Act.[62] A key factor in this consolidation was the change in patterns of land ownership, caused by demographic changes in the first half of the eighteenth century which produced a shortage of male heirs and a glut of aristocratic heiresses. This in turn led to the amalgamation of many landed estates through marriage alliances and the sale of other estates when the natural male line died out. Land reached such a premium that demand from prospective purchasers exceeded availability, and land prices were hugely inflated by the popularity of 'terramania'.

Everyone acknowledged that land was both the foundation and the symbol of power, and naturally the longer a family had owned its land, the more powerful it was likely to be. It could take a family several generations to reach the upper echelons of the peerage through the gradual accumulation of wealth, land and status. Robert Bertie, the 1st Duke of Ancaster and Kesteven, for example, was also 4th Earl of Lindsey and 17th Baron Willoughby de Eresby, showing the steady ascendance of rank by this ancient Lincolnshire family whose original barony had been a Norman title.[63] *Burke's Peerage*, which was first published in 1826, emphasised that the traditional origins of noble status lay in landownership, explaining to readers that 'the tenure of land was, in the olden time, the test of rank and position, and even now ... it remains the same'.[64]

The English aristocracy owned a larger percentage of the nation's land than any of the other European elites. No precise figures are available covering the period prior to the only official survey of landownership known as the New Domesday Survey, which took place in 1873. However, the survey's finding that 25 per cent of England was owned by 363 landowners, who were mostly titled and holding estates of more than 10,000 acres, is very likely to reflect broad ownership patterns in the preceding century.[65] A further 30 per cent of land was held by 3,000 landowners (mostly untitled gentry with estates of 1,000 to 10,000 acres) and just 3 per cent was owned by the Church, Crown or government.

The English landed elite therefore owned a total of 55 per cent of national territory, a sizeable proportion compared to French nobles with estates over 1,000 acres who held roughly 25 per cent of the country before the Revolution and 20 per cent afterwards. In Prussia owners of equivalent estates covered 40 per cent of the country, and in Russia (where nobility was not linked to land ownership) only a mere 14 per cent. For the English aristocracy, then, owning land, safeguarding the family estates and passing them on intact for future generations was an integral part of what it meant to be a peer. And this fundamental connection with land went much further than the material facts of acreage, stone and mortar, to a deeply ingrained belief in the possession of land as a dynastic trust held for posterity by a series of life tenants.

This guarantee for future generations was provided by the legal devices of strict family settlement and entail, where primogeniture ensured that only the eldest son inherited both the land and title, while financial provision was made for other family members in the form of pin money for wives, jointures for widows, marriage portions for unmarried daughters or sisters and capital or annuities for younger sons who became commoners, unlike their European counterparts who retained titles, legal privileges and easier access to government or army posts. In contrast, Continental noble estates were repeatedly divided on the death of each consecutive owner, leading to the fragmentation of land ownership and a massive proliferation of titles which decreased their worth. In Prussia, for instance, there were 20,000 titled families in 1800 and in Austria-Hungary, more than 200,000 nobles. The French system of primogeniture ended with the Revolution, although nobles had before that generally left smaller proportions of land in entail than English peers, and gave larger fortunes to their younger children.

Primogeniture and entail therefore played a major role in making the English elite the smallest, most exclusive, richest, most powerful and most land-based of all European aristocracies. The impact of these legal safeguards was not only financial but powerfully emotional too, binding as it did the families to their estates, position of authority and social status in perpetuity, and consequently shaping their attitudes, lifestyle and personal behaviour. Inheritance and the continuing preservation of the family estate was inevitably a central preoccupation for peers. And it naturally had implications for marriage strategies by creating an insistence on the absolute certainty of wifely fidelity in order to protect the dynasty from the threat of an illegitimate impostor inheriting.

The very essence of aristocratic identity was rooted in the family estate, to the extent that the identity of each individual heir in turn became subsumed into the longer-lasting and more important symbol of the family power base. This deliberate conflation of heir and estate was expressed in the letters of Anne, first wife of the Duke of Grafton, who when writing to her estranged husband used the abbreviation 'Euston' to refer to both the family home Euston Hall in Suffolk and her eldest son, Lord Euston, though she used the Christian names of all her younger children.[66]

The close identification between the owner, the ancestral home and past generations helped to confirm the family's privileged position in the eyes of outsiders. The country house estate was a permanent reminder of aristocratic wealth and status, even at times when the family was not in residence. It also became the focus of a vast network of business and social activities that reinforced lasting bonds of interdependence within the local community. Peers had varying degrees of involvement with the management of their estates, depending on personal aptitude and the size, location or diversity of estate interests. Some landowners, like the Duke of Devonshire, left everything to a professional land agent or estate steward, while others took a close interest in day-to-day matters, such as the 2nd Marquess of Bute who personally managed all his six estates.

Estates were developed gradually over successive generations as a confirmation and reflection of the family's increasing wealth and rank. Between the 1780s and 1820s a flurry of country house building consolidated elite power, both at a practical level by providing local employment opportunities, and as a symbolic material display to impress local society and visitors. Many new houses were constructed, and older properties were extended in keeping with the latest architectural fashions or completely demolished to make way for larger buildings erected in their place. Magnificent sweeping parklands were designed to complement the classical grandeur of these new mansions, while indoors the family's superior rank and taste was shown off by the latest fashionable décor and furnishings, portraits and sculptures, antiques, vast art collections and opulent libraries.[67] Visiting country houses to marvel at their design and fabulous interiors became a popular pastime for the aspirational middle classes on holiday, who could enjoy a personal tour of the rooms conducted by the housekeeper for a small gratuity. Most grand houses held dinners several times a year for their tenants and local tradesmen, providing a hospitality which helped to cement its relationship within the community.

The incremental improvement of a landed estate to match the family's rising status was undertaken by the Feildings who had owned Newnham Paddox on the Leicestershire border since 1433 and first rebuilt the house in the early seventeenth century to coincide with their elevation to the peerage as Earls of Denbigh.[68] Family fortunes continued to rise, and in 1754 the house was largely demolished by the 6th earl, who was unfairly mocked by Horace Walpole as 'the lowliest and most officious of the Court tools'. The old-fashioned house was rebuilt in showy Palladian style designed by Launcelot 'Capability' Brown and featured a nine-bay frontage with corner towers. The work took over fourteen years to complete and cost £6,220. A similar development took place at Combe Abbey, a magnificent building on the site of an ancient monastery which was already the third largest mansion in Warwickshire when the wealthy 6th Lord Craven added an extra storey in the 1770s. He also commissioned Brown for a six-year project redesigning the parkland to include an enormous lake. Country houses like this were very expensive places to run and lucrative sinecures from government posts were a major source of income for many Georgian peers, including George Lyttelton who in the 1750s earned enough from his junior post at court as Cofferer to the Household to rebuild his family home Hagley Hall as an impressive Palladian-style edifice.[69]

With such vast investments in estates which they saw as a fundamental part of their aristocratic identity, it is not surprising that the English aristocracy spent more time in their country homes than most other European nobles. English aristocrats were completely adaptable 'amphibious' creatures who felt equally at home living in the two very different environments of the city and the country. But although they spent most of their time in the country, political and social necessity demanded that for several months each year they lived in London, where life was a hectic round of duties and pleasures.[70]

3

DUTIES AND PLEASURES

Social and sexual relationships are inevitably entwined with public life, and this was especially true for the aristocracy during previous centuries. They inhabited an exclusive world created from a complex network of blood ties which centred on the House of Lords, where family politics and private interests merged seamlessly into public life devoted to national issues.[71]

Managing the strenuous demands of their local, national and domestic commitments meant that most aristocratic families led a busy life, constantly on the move and travelling hundreds of miles all over England to take up residence in various town and country houses. Each year would take on a familiar routine as they moved on to the next place with the changing seasons. Four to six months were spent living in London so that peers could attend Parliamentary sittings, which ran from December to July, and the whole family could enjoy the capital's social Season from April to July. One month was usually spent in Bath or at another popular spa resort and one month, visiting friends or relatives, and for the remaining three to six months they returned to the main country estate during the summer. By the end of the eighteenth century, taking part in the fashionable London Season had become essential to keep up the family's social status, by allowing them the time to nurture useful contacts and introduce eligible offspring to prospective marriage partners.

Aristocracy was firmly rooted in the country estate, but it required active participation in a parallel city life of politics and sociability. Everyday aristocratic life was therefore lived permanently in a state of transit between various places, with the small inner circle of family performing their public roles in front of a series of different backdrops and audiences. This regular commuting between locations for work or pleasure had the advantage of opening up a much wider world of activity that previous generations had not been able to enjoy.

Vast improvements in the condition of roads and more comfortable sprung carriages made journeys much quicker and less arduous, so travelling soon became increasingly popular. During a six-month period in 1766 Viscount Bolingbroke, who neglected his pregnant wife to indulge in a riotous bachelor lifestyle of drinking, whoring and gambling, spent several weeks at a friend's Norfolk country house, returned home to his main residence in London's Grosvenor Square for the summer and took trips to the races at York for one week and at Newmarket for three months. He then moved to a new temporary house leased in Hyde Park Corner for six weeks before taking up permanent residence at a grand house in May Fair.[72]

More responsible peers who were committed to a working schedule also managed to intersperse leisure with their routine duties. This resulted in a busy timetable of meetings, social events and informal networking with friends, relatives and others who belonged to the exclusive overlapping circles of influence at the peak of Georgian society. This natural interplay between informal personal life and formal public arenas of power was recorded in the journals of Edward Law, Earl of Ellenborough, who joined the Wellington government as Lord Privy Seal in 1828 and went on to hold a series of high-profile political positions. In his diary entry for 20 April 1831 he noted reading a report of a Parliamentary debate when he got up in the morning; visiting the home of his political colleague Sir Henry Hardinge, who came down to meet him in a dressing gown; later on, meeting two other Members of Parliament as he rode up Charing Cross; discussing politics while visiting a furniture shop; returning to the House at 5pm; walking in the park with Hardinge; and attending a private dinner at Lord Beresford's with Sir Robert Peel, various peers and foreign visitors.[73] There were no clear-cut boundaries between working and personal life in the daily round.

Another picture showing the complex interplay of public duty and private domestic life over a broader period emerges from the meticulously kept diaries of Elizabeth, second wife of Augustus Henry FitzRoy, the Duke of Grafton. They gave a detailed description of the hectic annual routine that incorporated family activities, local duties, pleasure trips and the political demands of her husband's career. During a typical year, the couple divided their time between the main family residence of Euston Hall in Suffolk, a country house in Northamptonshire, a London townhouse and a smaller house in Newmarket. The number of miles covered on these frequent journeys was incredible. Over the course of one month in the spring, they travelled in the post chaise from London to Northamptonshire, then on to Newmarket for one week before returning to Euston Hall, spending another week in Newmarket, then returning to London. Such long carriage rides could be gruelling especially on cold and dark winter days, so it is not surprising that after a particularly arduous trip from Suffolk to London in February, with one disturbed night spent in lodgings, the duchess recorded stoically, 'We were neither of us very well after our journey and did not go out.'[74]

Grafton was often apart from his wife for several days at a time attending to political and business tasks, although after resigning from the Cabinet in 1783 his lighter workload meant that he was able to spend more time at home on his hobbies of hunting and racing. In 1789 the couple spent twenty-two weeks on their Suffolk country estate, mainly from October to February. They lived at the London townhouse for just over three months from February to April and mid-May to the end of June. Five separate weeks were spent at Newmarket races throughout the year. The duchess spent nine weeks at Wakefield Lodge, and the duke three months, often travelling there alone on estate business while his wife and children remained at one of the other homes.[75]

Because country landownership was the whole basis of aristocratic power, peers played a substantial role in their local communities in addition to their wider national Parliamentary, military, court or diplomatic duties. As wealthy owners of vast tracts of land often in several counties, they had enormous influence on the entire local economy, which was dependant on the country house estate for employment, housing and charitable aid. As centres of production, employing a hundred permanent staff and perhaps 200 to 300 people during major building work, the large country house estates were far bigger in scale than most industrial enterprises of the time. It was through everyday life in this local context that hereditary rule made an impact on the majority of the population. Not only did landowners control employment and housing but they also influenced all aspects of community existence through both formal channels of local government and informal social leadership.

Sensible peers were well aware that the foundations of influence lay firmly within their country estates and took their local duties and reputation very seriously. Writing from his country seat in Gloucestershire, Lord Ellenborough noted in his diary for August 1831, 'Recd. by the coach a letter from Hardinge. He thinks the Gov. nearly at an end … recommends my return to town this week, but I have told him I have engagements on Wednesday, Thursday, Friday and Saturday and that my breaking them would offend my neighbours & create speculation.'[76] The awkward conflict between fulfilling a local role in the community and pressing national duties was sometimes hard to reconcile. But despite his high-level political post and the critical state of Earl Grey's government, Ellenborough was reluctant to risk upsetting local opinion by cancelling his commitments at such short notice.

As the link between Parliament and parish, the counties played a vital intermediary role in government through the regulation of all aspects of everyday life. Each county was headed by a lord-lieutenant (a fairly substantial post usually filled by a peer), supported by a sheriff (a demanding, unpopular job taken on by the gentry) and justices of the peace, who were established landowners with the minimum property qualification of land valued at £100 a year. The JPs effectively ran the county through their responsibility for legal cases and administrative matters at Quarter Sessions. From the early nineteenth century they met at monthly or fortnightly Petty Sessions, dealing with a wide range of issues including licensing alehouses, road repairs, the county militia, the Poor Laws and relief, prisons, asylums and policing.

Social leadership of county society was also an important, expensive and time-consuming occupation, which included hosting dinners and balls for tenants, neighbouring gentry and visitors, and involving the community in family events such as coming-of-age celebrations, marriage, christening or funerals. Sporting events, including fox hunting, shooting, cricket and horse racing, acted as useful occasions for social mixing between different ranks.

The actual length of time spent in the country varied greatly, depending on personal choice and the extent of responsibilities elsewhere, particularly for families who owned several estates in different counties. While Lord Hertford visited his Warwickshire seat Ragley Hall for just nineteen days in August 1770, the Duke and Duchess of Devonshire spent around three months annually at Chatsworth in Derbyshire and the rest of the year at either their London townhouse, in Bath or in Chiswick. This extensive travelling, followed by the annual ritual of returning home and bringing examples of the latest fashionable clothing, furniture, carriages and interior décor, gave the family an added mystique and enhanced its status among local inhabitants who themselves rarely travelled as far as the nearest market town. The relationship between landowner and community combined the close ties of deference and dependence accrued over generations with the detached perspective of spectators watching a grand performance. This strangely paradoxical bond shaped attitudes to an elite leadership which was both public and deeply personal.

Naturally the degree of commitment to local activities differed between individuals, between different generations of the same family and according to rank or wealth. While some peers had relatively little involvement, others took their public duties very seriously and became closely involved in all aspects of community life. Notably dutiful peers included the 8th Earl of Winchilsea, an active magistrate who also worked for charities including friendly societies, parish workhouse schools and an allotment scheme; and also the 2nd Earl of Radnor, who regularly attended Quarter Sessions in both Wiltshire and Berkshire as a magistrate and chairman of the bench. Although the extent of involvement in public roles had always been largely a matter of personal choice, by the 1790s, when debates about aristocratic morality and privilege peaked, it was not only performing public duties that mattered but actually being seen to do so by society. What has been called 'a rhetoric of public service' came into being, so that increasing numbers of peers became figureheads for charitable causes such as parish schools and hospitals.[77]

Alongside this more superficial display of public spirit existed a range of traditional roles in county governance for the aristocracy that had always prided itself on being a 'service elite' which gave its time freely to ensure the efficient administration of the country.[78] As permanent residence was a prerequisite for fulfilling local duties, it can be difficult to assess the extent to which peers took an active part. There was increasing criticism of absentee landlords who abandoned their traditional duties, especially after 1760 when landowners were enticed away from their estates for longer periods by fashionable urban pursuits, spa and seaside towns, and European travel. As they neglected local communities for the Parliamentary and social demands of city life, their rural duties were passed down the social scale to clergy and professional men. Nostalgic portraits of paternalist landlords became popular, both in fictional stereotypes and in memoirs of actual exemplary models of benevolence. A poem titled *The Country Justice*, published in 1775, lamented the lost 'golden days of Hospitality/ When liberal fortunes vied with liberal strife/ To fill the noblest offices of life', and attacked the evils of fashionable pursuits that had persuaded the wealthy to desert the countryside. However, by the end of the century the growing impact of a religious revival and the ideals of Romanticism, with its emphasis on individualism, began to reawaken social conscience and a more pressing sense of moral duty among the elite.

Everyday life for aristocratic men combined both the exercise of power and the ritual display of power. In London they dealt with political, business and charitable matters, attended Parliament, and joined their families for social and leisure activities. In residence at their country estates, the daily routine could include estate management, work on industrial or agricultural improvement schemes, local government or charitable duties, public appearances at local events, hobbies like hunting or riding, and socialising at public occasions and private family gatherings. Aristocratic women also took part in many different activities, depending on whether they were resident in town or country, or away visiting friends.

Increasingly, both sexes took advantage of more extensive opportunities for social mixing in the exciting new public spaces emerging as part of a modern commercial culture. This centred on the increased buying-power of the middling classes, which was being boosted by England's rapid economic development and a growth in overseas trade. The newly affluent and families of old money were all keen to sample the novel cultural delights, designed to stimulate what was summed up by the writer Joseph Addison as, 'the pleasures of the imagination.' This holistic concept of culture, that included theatre, music, painting and literature, can be traced back to the previous century when a reassessment of knowledge was sparked by new philosophical debates and scientific discoveries. In *Essays on the Nature and Principles of Taste*, published in 1790, the fine arts were described as 'the arts which are addressed to the imagination' and whose 'object is to produce the emotions of taste'.[79]

This modern way of thinking, together with changing ideas of taste, transformed the arts from an elite pastime to something enjoyed by all social classes who enthusiastically embraced the commercial culture. The new egalitarianism did not deter the aristocracy and prosperous landed gentry from making the most of an expanding choice of leisure activities and visiting coffee houses and pleasure gardens, assemblies, theatre, opera, concerts, art exhibitions, circulating libraries and shops filled with books, periodicals and prints. By joining the eager throng aristocrats, who had previously led largely private lives within the confines of their own domains, now became more visible to a wider public at these commercial leisure venues, and popular interest in their lives led to growing publicity.

The burgeoning commercial culture had a particular impact on the lives of elite women, who could now enjoy for the first time wider social opportunities mixing in these public spaces and attending cultural events in London, larger towns, spa and seaside resorts. And, surprisingly, it was accepted practice that aristocratic women often went out to public events and private evening parties without their husbands, as part of a mixed group of fashionable acquaintances.

Elizabeth, Duchess of Grafton's diary recorded her busy social life with twice-weekly trips to the opera, attendance at private parties, dinners and assemblies with friends, while her husband was either at home, away on business or socialising separately. On 1 March 1789 she wrote, 'I went to Ly Stafford's, small Party. Duke and Henry at home'; on 3 March, 'I went to the Opera, in the Box. Left the Duke at a Whist Party at home'; and on 5 March, 'Duke went to the House of Lords, no business. I went to a Party at Mrs French's and to an assembly at Ly Sutherland's.' On 21 March the duke was away at his country estate, and the duchess remained in London, dining out before attending the opera.[80] The couple seem to have created workable overlapping but parallel lives, which gave both of them the freedom to pursue their own different interests.

This practice of separate socialising in fashionable society meant that married women had plenty of opportunity to develop friendships, flirtations and even more intimate relationships with other men. But it could also leave more innocent wives prey to the unwanted advances of unscrupulous admirers, as Georgiana, Duchess of Devonshire, had found in her early married life. Her *roman-à-clef* novel *The Sylph* was based on her own bruising real-life experiences of high society as an amoral group addicted to gaming, seduction and illicit sex. Her husband had, right from the start, made no secret of his many infidelities and later installed Georgiana's friend Bess at Chatsworth in a bizarre *ménage-à-trois* which lasted many years. Georgiana's own love affair with Charles Grey, the future prime minister, ended in heartbreak in the early 1790s when she was forced by her husband to end the relationship and give up their illegitimate child. In *The Sylph*, the naïve young bride Julia married the debauched Sir William Stanley and was shocked to discover that married couples were not expected to appear together in society:

Sir William never goes with me to any of these fashionable movements. It is true, we often meet, but very seldom join, as we are in general in separate parties … it is the business of everyone to endeavour to put a man and wife asunder, – fashion not making it decent to appear together.[81]

The fashionable social freedom to go out alone and mix in a wider circle brought with it the advantages of new personal introductions which were useful for political networking, finding career openings for younger sons and eligible marriage partners. But as well as making it easier to pursue such highly respectable connections, it was inevitable that these public arenas also created ideal meeting places for those tempted by more dangerous liaisons.

4

LORD BULLY *v.* LADY DI

It was the dirty marks on the parlour couch that gave the lovers away. Great clots of dirt and boot blacking were smeared over the fabric at one end, which looked as if they came from a man's shoes, and a fine sprinkling of white hair powder dusted the arms and pillows. The whole couch was all tumbled, and the cushions scattered on the floor or shoved back anyhow. It was left in this untidy state many times for the servants to find and, even more suspicious, the window shutters were closed with the curtains down at eleven or twelve in the morning.

These seemingly trivial domestic details described by the household servants were part of the damning evidence of adultery used in court when Frederick St John, 2nd Viscount Bolingbroke, sued his wife's lover for crim. con. in 1768 and became only the fifth English peer ever to divorce. The ill-fated union had begun promisingly enough when the handsome and highly eligible 24-year-old married Diana Spencer, the lively eldest daughter of the Duke of Marlborough, in September 1757. It seems to have been a conventional match made for practical reasons on both sides, not least to secure the bride's £10,000 dowry (roughly £600,000 now) as extra funds to finance Bolingbroke's extravagant taste for racehorses, porcelain and silver. The couple soon produced three children but their relationship grew strained as Bolingbroke, later nicknamed Bully the Battersea Baron by the press, spent most of the time enjoying his old pastimes of hard drinking and gaming at his club White's, and racing at Newmarket. He was a compulsive womaniser, pursuing a long-standing affair with his married mistress, the society beauty Lady Coventry, until her early death from poisoning by white lead make-up. At the same time he was conducting liaisons with a series of other women and, more dangerously, was also a regular customer at Covent Garden's seedy brothels. He had repeatedly infected his wife with venereal disease.[82] Increasingly miserable with the situation, in September 1765 Lady Di finally decided she had had enough and left home while her husband was away visiting his friend Lord Orford at Houghton Hall in Norfolk.

She first took lodgings in Clarges Street, London, and then in April 1766 moved to a house in Berkeley Square, where she at last had the freedom to pursue a deepening friendship with the brilliant and strikingly attractive Topham Beauclerk, the great-grandson of King Charles II and Nell Gwynn. Several years younger than her, he was amusing and generous with immaculate manners, a sharp wit and a growing reputation as an intellectual. He quickly became a regular visitor, and that summer the couple consummated the relationship during a holiday at the fashionable spa resort of Tunbridge Wells in Kent, where Lady Di was staying with her sister Lady Pembroke. The affair grew more intense when she returned to her London house at the end of August, where Beauclerk dropped in several times each day and always joined her for supper, sometimes staying until the early hours of the morning.

The servants were by now highly suspicious, particularly the footman William Flockton, who quickly realised that he could use the situation to his own advantage and began spying on the lovers. One evening he went up to the dining room to tell Beauclerk his chairman had arrived and was much surprised to find that the door was locked. Waiting outside for about two minutes to listen, he heard the couch creak and the rustling of clothes as if two people were upon it. He slipped away downstairs in case he was discovered, but after chatting to the chairman in the passage for a while, he heard a door open and shut, so went back up to the dining room, where the couple sat on the couch looking a little flurried and confused. Lady Di was in a difficult position, as a separated but still married woman, and knew as well as they did that she had to rely on the servants' discretion to protect her reputation. One day in December after Beauclerk had left around midnight, Flockton was clearing away the remains of supper in the dining room when she handed him a guinea, equal to almost a month's wages.

Meanwhile, Bully was depressed and struggling to cope with the separation. He lived nearby in Mayfair with their two sons and had anxiously taken 5-year-old George to start his first day at school, bribing an older boy to look out for him and leaving with tears in his eyes. Despite his blatantly libertine behaviour, he was deeply upset by his wife's departure and confided to his friend, the MP George Selwyn:

> I am so low, dejected, and miserable, that I cannot speak; I can only cry. The just parting with her … quite overcomes me; … If ever you happen to talk of me to Lady Di, represent me as appearing to you altered and unhappy. Excuse me plaguing you with my nonsense. You know too well the comfort it affords to an afflicted man to talk to his friends of his affliction not to forgive me.[83]

He was giving a different impression to his brother Henry, who informed Selwyn that Bolingbroke was:

> … not sunk into such low spirits as you seem to have heard. I think, on the contrary, though he laments the loss of a home, he does not whimper and whine after the object that has been these two years past the cause of his melancholy, and I fancy he at last sees that object in its true light. From a desponding lover and husband, as we have seen him, he is determined to become more a man of the world, and not to sacrifice his pleasure and interest in life to the indulgence of a grief, brought on by an accident originally, and afterwards continued by the foolish obstinacy of a woman.[84]

At least he still had a close circle of raffish friends to turn to including Selwyn, a well-known wit and colourful society figure, who had been sent down from Oxford for blasphemy after holding a mock holy communion pretending to be Jesus Christ. He had a reputation for necrophilia and was an avid spectator at public executions, which he went to disguised as a woman. Morbidly fascinated by corpses, he once paid a guinea for a severed head.[85] Their set also included the Earl of March, who had been described as 'the most brilliant, most fashionable, most dissipated young man in London' and later, when he became the Duke of Queensberry, achieved notoriety as Old Q, the old goat of Piccadilly, who even in his eighties hired a procuress to find young girls who would undress while he watched.

Lady Di hired a country house at Taplow in Buckinghamshire for Christmas 1766, where she stayed until the end of January, taking two of her own servants, Flockton and her loyal housekeeper, Mary Lees. Beauclerk booked into a nearby inn called the Orkney Arms at Maidenhead and later leased a house at Cookham 2 miles away, which was convenient enough for his daily visits. The two lovers continued their clandestine affair, which was as passionate as ever and included frequent close encounters on another handy large couch in the parlour, which were all carefully noted by the footman Flockton, who continued his spying and had by now come to bitterly resent Beauclerk's high-handed attitude. He was at Taplow every day until late at night, his horses were put into the stables to eat hay and he behaved in a great measure as if he was the master of the house, ordering the servants to do anything he had a mind should be done.

One afternoon the couple were together in the great parlour overlooking the garden when Beauclerk suggested they play a game of chess and ordered Flockton to close the window shutters and bring candles, even though it was not yet dark. On another occasion the footman went up to the same room to deliver a letter brought by the postboy from Lady Di's sister and realised the door was locked. He returned later to find the door had been opened and gave the letter to his mistress, who was sitting close to Beauclerk on the couch, her clothes and hair much rumpled and her cap almost off. In fact, nearly every night after the pair had been alone together in the parlour, they left the couch very tumbled and its cushions all in a heap. Flockton made it his business to check up on them to see when they locked the door and what state the couch was in later. Clearly things could not go on like this forever.

Inevitably, by January Lady Di was pregnant, despite relying on the popular herbal birth control method of taking medicine made from poplar tree bark. The servants had seen that she took regular deliveries that came by stagecoach from London, of small oval deal boxes containing phials of medicine, which Beauclerk then tore the labels off and burnt. They had also noticed her expanding belly, which was only slightly concealed by a new set of 'jumps', an unboned garment replacing stays which pregnant women laced up around the waist as tightly as they could. By living a quiet secluded life for the past few months, she had managed to hide her condition from family and friends, but with the birth approaching the utmost secrecy was now vital. In May both the housemaid Elizabeth Thomas, who had been caught gossiping to neighbours, and the troublesome Flockton were dismissed, followed by the cook. Only the housekeeper Mary Lees could be completely trusted to keep quiet and help with the necessary arrangements.

Lady Di had been consulting Dr William Hunter, the eminent Westminster man-midwife popular in society circles for his discretion, who made clandestine visits after dark and even arrived on foot in the rain to avoid the risks of his own servants knowing where he was going. They had also been exchanging letters carefully signed with feigned names to try and fool the meddling servants. The confinement was planned to take place in the rural privacy of Taplow, but in August Lady Di went into labour early one evening at the London house. Dr Hunter was summoned to assist at the birth and immediately took the baby girl away to a wet nurse. In a final attempt to cover up what had happened, the dirty bed linen was sent out to a different washerwoman. As Dr Hunter later told the court, 'every means were made use of to keep her being brought to bed a secret but the whole scheme was managed by her woman'.

Despite all the precautions the secret got out, and within a week news of the scandal was quickly spreading around the city through gossip and press reports. The *Morning Chronicle* was one of the first to break the story as George Selwyn wrote to Lord Holland on 28 August:

> The affair of Lord and Lady Bolingbroke is likely to become very serious, and a great amusement to the town when it fills, according as people's curiosity or sensibility is the most predominant. The *Chronique* says she is brought to bed. Servants are become evidencers, and the husband hopes by this imprudent management of her and her simple lover, to be freed *a vinculo matrimonii,* and in future times to marry a rich monster and retrieve his affairs. I hope you will not quote me.

A few months later Lord Holland wrote, 'I think poor Lady Bolingbroke's folly is likely to end better than I thought it would, though, God knows, I am sorry for it, very badly.' Lord March was relishing the more sordid aspects of the case and jokingly referred to a brothel run by Charlotte Hayes, 'I hear the house of Hayes in Chamber Alley is to make its appearance at B__'s trial. Are they to prove that Beauclerk, etc. etc? or has Bully called these witnesses to appear to his character?'[86]

In December 1767 the crim. con. action opened at Doctors' Commons and all the former servants were called to appear in the witness box to give accounts of what they had seen. The 35-year-old Mary Lees, who kept her position after the trial and pragmatically decided to remain loyal to her mistress, steadfastly denied most of the accusations against Lady Di, maintaining that the couple had rarely spent any time alone together. The court was told that two years earlier she had left her husband and refused to return home, but no mention at all was made of his own serial adulteries. The verdict was a foregone conclusion and Lady Bolingbroke was confirmed as the guilty party in the judgement which ruled that, 'unmindful of her conjugal vow, and not having the fear of God before her eyes [she] did commit the crime of adultery with Topham Beauclerk Esq.'.

It was obvious to most people that this was a deliberate case of collusion between the parties in which the real story remained hidden from the court. Bolingbroke had earlier reached agreement with his wife and her lover not to collect the damages and to conceal his own adultery from the court so that they could secure a Parliamentary divorce. All the evidence was reviewed again when the divorce proceedings were heard in the House of Lords, then in the Commons, and the marriage was finally dissolved in March 1768. Immediately afterwards Lady Di married Beauclerk. She had already been dismissed from her official court position as a Lady of the Bedchamber, but despite her public disgrace she was not disowned by her family and was still received by many of her society friends. Sadly, her second marriage did not turn out as well as she had hoped, when later on Beauclerk's morose temper and declining health made him increasingly difficult to live with, but she found consolation in a successful artistic career, painting, drawing and designing for Wedgwood pottery. All three members of the love-triangle got on with their lives, but the scandal also lived on and kept resurfacing in print.

Four years after the divorce, *Town and Country Magazine* published an article satirising the empty façade of the Bolingbrokes' typically fashionable marriage: 'Like people of fashion indeed, they lay separately; seldom met but at meals, conversed upon general topics; and seemed almost to have forgot that there was such a passion in love, at least in the marriage state.' It described how Bully the Battersea Baron had become notorious for his heavy drinking, reckless gambling and the pursuit of prostitutes as he 'administered to his pleasures and promoted his success with the first-rate demi-reps of this kingdom'. Readers were told that Lady Di had a brief affair with Lord Gower because Bully's 'irregularities excited her Ladyship to resolve upon retaliation, and the elegant and persuasive Lord G—r proved too powerful a suitor to sigh in vain'. The magazine went on to explain that it could not give the full sordid details, which were too unpleasant to print, when 'our hero deliberately sacrificed his own health to be revenged on his rival' by deciding to infect her with a venereal disease so that she would pass it on in turn to Lord Gower.

All the details of Lady Di's adultery, including the full transcript of the servants' evidence given in court, were published seven years later, in 1779, in the first volume of *Trials for Adultery: or, the History of Divorces*, a collection of salacious legal cases which proved so popular with readers that it eventually ran to seven volumes. The following year, in 1780, the notorious couple were again featured in a biting satire presented as the review of an art exhibition called *The Picture Gallery*, which described paintings supposedly created by a series of society figures. Lady Diana's adultery and unhappy second marriage was cleverly ridiculed in the review of her imaginary artwork entitled *Scylla and Charybdis*, showing a storm-tossed boat trapped between the monster and the whirlpool of Greek myth:

> How it ever escaped out of the jaws of the latter is worthy the attention of the curious ... after having escaped from the teeth of one lord and master, she was induced to try her success with another. The second gave rise to the English proverb Out of the Frying Pan.

Another issue of *The Picture Gallery* described Bolingbroke's picture *The Spendthrift and the Swallow* where 'the hero of the tale is depicted in a truly tattered condition ... having been born in the height of splendour, emblematical representation of cards, dice etc ... is very characteristic'.[87]

The old scandal did in time subside, until Bolingbroke died in May 1787 after enduring six years of madness, brought on by constant financial worries and possibly the final stages of syphilis. His obituary in the next issue of the generally sedate monthly *Gentleman's Magazine* referred to the earlier divorce, but it was restrained enough to acknowledge that 'to investigate the facts that produced this would be an office painful and improper'. It applauded his positive traits of affability and 'generosity and goodness of heart' but blamed Lady Di and their divorce for his tragic mental collapse and 'the miseries under which he laboured for the latter part of his life'.

Part Two

Vice and Virtue in Print (1760s–1770s)

'This vice, Adultery, is absolutely an outrage to *humanity*, to *good manners*, to *society* ... the more elevated the station of life in which the Adulterer is placed, the greater is the injury which he does to society.'

On Adultery, 1772

5

'THE FASHIONABLE VICE'

Infidelity among the aristocracy was a serious national problem because it eroded the institution of marriage as the foundation of society and the leadership of a class whose power was based on legitimate hereditary bloodline. Dr Johnson firmly believed that distinction of rank cemented social stability, and he dismissed gossip about elite immorality as just 'the malignity of women in the city against women of quality', where one scandal involving the aristocracy made 'more noise' than several cases in the lower ranks.[1] But few people shared this view, and in the 1770s adultery was being called 'the fashionable vice' because there was apparently such widespread promiscuity among the elite.[2]

King George III was extremely worried about the situation and asked the Lord Chancellor to do something 'that might be likely to prevent the very bad conduct among the ladies, of which there have been so many instances lately'. Divorce via a Parliamentary bill had been introduced in the late seventeenth century as a special privilege for the aristocracy, to ensure that ancient titles and estates were handed down safely only to legitimate male descendants. There had been very few cases up to the mid-eighteenth century, but the number of divorce bills more than doubled from fifteen cases in the decade 1751–60 to thirty-five cases in the decade 1771–80.[3]

One of the reasons why aristocratic adultery created such a public outcry was because it blatantly illustrated the gap between their public face of authority and their immoral private lives. Such revelations shattered trust in an aristocratic ideology based on assumptions that social hierarchy reflected a natural moral order. Ideas about morality had traditionally been shaped by religious beliefs and social frameworks, then enforced by the courts through legal sanctions. Lord Kenyon, who led what amounted to an anti-adultery crusade during his fourteen years as Lord Chief Justice, was a devout Christian who repeatedly emphasised that law and religion were tied together. Addressing the jury in the Duchess of Norfolk's adultery trial, he told them to carry out the duties owed to God and to society by deciding 'how far the morality of a libertine age could be corrected'.[4] He added, 'I have always had the satisfaction to find that Juries … had been desirous of lending their assistance to inforce the principles of justice, and render the law of the land subservient to the law of religion and morality'.

The word adultery is derived from the Latin root *adulterare*, meaning to corrupt. Disapproval of adultery, which was defined in the 1778 edition of *An Universal Etymological English Dictionary* as being 'the sin of incontinency in a married person', was framed as a contravention of both religious principles and social order. This link was highlighted in many of the annotated Bibles published at the time, such as *The Elegant Family Bible*, which noted on the seventh commandment 'Thou shalt not commit adultery' in Exodus 20: 14, 'Adultery is a crime of the deepest dye, because it is a violation of the most sacred bond of society … and has been stigmatized as an act of horror and enormity in all civilised nations'.[5]

Another stern Old Testament commentary in *The Protestant's Family Bible* declared that the sin of adultery was viewed with detestation because it would 'call down the wrath of Heaven upon their heads, and involve the whole nation in some terrible calamity'.[6] *An Illustration of the New Testament* believed that adultery 'beyond all Dispute is by far the most grievous Crime', and commented on the passage in Matthew 19: 9, which denounced re-marriage because it effectively meant committing adultery with the new spouse: 'Our Lord's Prohibition therefore of these Divorces is founded on the strongest Reason, and tends highly to the Peace and Welfare of Society.'[7]

Although illicit sex was seen as an understandable temptation for the leisured and wealthy classes, religious guidelines were put forward as both a safeguard against human weakness on earth and a threat of divine judgement to come. Such views were encapsulated in a letter from the devoutly religious Countess of Denbigh to her son serving in the army, which warned him against 'the Vices & Follies to which your Age and Rank would expose you' in the 'pleasure & Dissipation natural to Youth'. She advised him:

Obedience to God's Commands ... are the only foundations of Happiness even in this Life ... Young as you are, you are very capable of observing the Consequence of losing the command of our passions & Appetites ... for example, the Marquis in your Regt, and your Cousin the Colonel ... if once they plunge us into Guilt – the natural Consequence is that in order to subdue the stings of Conscience ... we employ that very Reason that would bring us back to Virtue in finding excuses for Vice.[8]

The numerous printed sermons and religious pamphlets denigrating adultery took a highly pragmatic stance by linking obedience to God with the promotion of social good. Peaks in the publication of such works reflected the periods of deep public concern about adultery in the 1770s and again in the 1790s. Many pamphlets followed a similar pattern, by setting out lengthy rational arguments for religious observance based on the twin pillars of morality (Reason and Virtue), supported by evidence from Biblical passages and references to the harsh treatment of adultery in many ancient civilisations. *Comments on the Ten Commandments* explained that adultery was punished by death under Mosaic law because it had 'the most fatal consequences for the welfare of society', while the author of *Sermons on the Most Prevalent Vices* argued that adultery 'makes us brutes ... because we indulge our animal nature at the expense of the rational. Adultery is a crime so odious and complicated, that it violates, at once, the laws of God, and the laws of man ... Adultery indicates the absence of every divine and social feeling.'[9]

Miscellaneous Essays, Divine and Moral. Designed to Discourage Vice and Promote Virtue, which went through several reprints, included dire warnings about the consequences of fornication and adultery, especially among fashionable men of pleasure and ladies of easy virtue whose follies might be aped by their social inferiors.[10] In a passionate tirade against seduction and its sister vice of adultery, another sermon lamented the 'torrent of vice and immorality' in which 'we see high birth licking the dust and grandeur mixed with littleness ... Poor Britain! how truly wretched is thy present situation!' Not only was the act of adultery 'an outrage to humanity, to good manners ... [and] resists the sacred voice of Reason', but 'the more elevated the station of life in which the Adulterer is placed, the greater is the injury he does Society. People in inferior walks of life fond of imitation, imagine that what superiors do must be right.'[11] Adultery was therefore a serious threat to social structure, but the damage was compounded when it became public knowledge through the publicity of trials and divorce petitions, and the nobility's façade of respectable authority crumbled to reveal the sordid truths of illicit sex with its furtive encounters, rumpled clothing and stained sheets.

Public indignation at the flagrant collusion in the scandalous divorce in 1769 of the prime minister, the 3rd Duke of Grafton, led to the introduction of a Parliamentary bill designed to curb adultery in 1771. All the details of his highly public liaison with a courtesan were omitted from the legal hearing in the House of Lords that allowed his divorce to go through, with the collusion of his wife who was eager to marry her own lover. In fact Grafton still remains the only English prime minister ever to divorce while holding office.

This was to be the first of four attempts to reduce the number of divorces via Parliamentary bills, by proposing legislation that would prevent divorced women from marrying their lovers.[12] Proponents argued that this would act as both a suitable punishment for offenders and as a deterrent for wives tempted by adultery. It would also remove the wife's motive for collusion, which was starting to emerge as the underlying factor in many divorce cases where both husband and wife had committed adultery and wished to remarry. Under English law evidence of a husband's adultery removed his legal right to take a matrimonial suit for separation in the ecclesiastical courts, followed by a private bill of divorce in Parliament, as the two crimes were considered to cancel each other out. However, many couples were surreptitiously getting round the problem by reaching an agreement before the initial trial for crim. con. that they would conceal all evidence of the husband's own adulteries, and he would not claim from the seducer any damages awarded by the court.

The 1771 Divorce Bill, which was presented to the House of Lords by the Duke of Athol, proposed a legal bar on remarriage after adultery and a declaration that any offspring would be disinherited. It passed through the Lords by a small margin but was eventually defeated in the Commons by twenty votes on 30 April.[13] The arguments in favour of the legislation were that it would cut the number of adulteries as women could no longer rely on the promises of a lover to marry them later. It would also 'put a lady on her guard against a false friend who, under the cloak of friendship, might insinuate himself into the family and … prevail over the lady's virtue'. Opponents of the bill argued that it would not actually stop the frequency of adultery, which was usually caused by 'present passions' and not by the distant promise of a future marriage. It would also be unfair to women who were unfortunate enough to be seduced, by leaving them 'in the worst situation possible', whereby they would either be forced to cohabit with their lover 'to the scandal of society, or else must be debarred society, and be deemed improper to marry at all, as none else would probably marry her'. Lord Strange was rather less sympathetic to women, and voiced the opinion of many people who blamed fashionable entertainment for corrupting morals, when he said that the only true system to prevent a vice of this nature was to reform the manners of the women. But whilst the Coterie, Cornelys's, Almack's and other public places of rendezvous for company, were so much encouraged, it would be impossible to have any reformation.

6

THE BLACK DUKE

'Were an angel from heaven to come upon earth, and be a prime-minister, the voice of the multitude would be against him', acknowledged the *Town and Country Magazine* in its popular 'Histories of the Têtes-à-Têtes' series featuring scandalous liaisons. Published in March 1769, the month the Duke of Grafton divorced, the article was overtly sympathetic to the prime minister, who 'as a statesman had many shining abilities', but swiftly went on to recount all the details of his notorious five-year affair with a beautiful courtesan. He was referred to throughout as Palinurus, after the helmsman in Virgil's *Aeneid* who fell asleep at the tiller and was washed overboard. This neat classical allusion summed up Grafton's tarnished public reputation, which had been irrevocably damaged when 'his domestic concerns were exposed to public view, and his separation from his lady was coloured with the darkest shades'.

As a high-profile public figure, enmeshed in a turbulent political scene of warring factions, he was a natural target for hostility. But it was his personal indiscretions and his wife's adultery that provided the best ammunition for his opponents to launch a politically motivated attack disguised as moral outrage, which generated extensive publicity. As *Town and Country Magazine* reported, 'his adversaries represented him as a gamester, one who squandered the treasures of the nation upon horses and women, and who, left to guide the helm of state, would soon plunge it into inevitable destruction'.

Augustus Henry FitzRoy was born in 1735, the elder son of a naval officer and his wife, Elizabeth, who was daughter of the governor of New York,

Colonel William Cosby. He was only 12 years old when he became heir to the dukedom following the early deaths of his father in Jamaica, while serving as the captain of a warship, and of his childless uncle. With the title went the family seat at Euston Hall in Suffolk, a plain and rather dilapidated red brick mansion set in extensive parkland, which had seen better days and the previous century had hosted a visit by King Charles and 200 guests. There was also Wakefield Lodge in Northamptonshire (a former hunting lodge set in 117 acres, once used by Oliver Cromwell), a substantial income of over £18,000 a year (more than a million today), together with a collection of public appointments including Lord Lieutenant of Suffolk, High-Steward of Dartmouth and His Majesty's gamekeeper at Newmarket.

After an education at Cambridge and the classical grand tour of Europe traditional for young nobles, at 21 he married Anne Liddell, the sole heiress of a wealthy Durham coal owner with a £40,000 fortune, who had been ennobled as the 1st Baron Ravensworth.[14] Later that same year, in 1756, he became MP for Bury St Edmunds in Suffolk but soon afterwards took his seat in the Lords on the death of his grandfather and earned a reputation as a good speaker in debates. His political career took off rapidly and he was appointed Secretary of State in 1765, First Lord of the Treasury in 1767 and then prime minister from 1768–70, and he remained as Lord Privy Seal until he resigned from the Cabinet in 1783.

It was the problematic overlap of public and personal life which was to prove the decisive factor in casting Grafton in perpetuity as the Black Duke who had neglected his country for personal pleasure. Explicit parallels were made between his lack of honour in private life and the poor judgement, inconsistency and corruption he displayed in office: 'public conduct, as a minister, is but the counter part of your private history'.[15]

Another commentator said that although Grafton's private life had 'not been entirely divested of human frailty', his adultery was a consequence of his wife's unruly conduct:

> … the husband who finds no consolation at home, will seek it elsewhere. A violent itch for play in his first duchess gave rise to their bickerings …. He has also been taxed with devoting himself to the turf, and being seen at Newmarket when he should have been at Whitehall; but these reports we consider as the little squibs of the day, let off by malice and ignorance. If a nobleman in office is to be deprived of every amusement, he must be considered as the galley slave, and not the minister of State.

> The public and private characters of great men are too often blended by
> the partial and interested, to form a character odious if not criminal in the
> eyes of the world … a statesman is sure to have his foibles represented in the
> most glaring light by members of the opposition, we are therefore not to be
> surprised that Junius and his adherents have bespattered this nobleman with
> all the filth they could cast upon him, in hopes that where so much is thrown
> some must stick.[16]

The Junius referred to was the author of a series of letters attacking the
government, and specifically Grafton himself, which were originally
printed over three years in the influential London newspaper the *Public
Advertiser* from January 1769 to January 1772, and then regularly reprinted in books published over the next fifty years. His immense popularity ensured that the anonymous Junius became the most notorious and
influential commentator on the political scene, noted for his 'invective,
ingenious and inflammatory; scurrility … impressive declamation, poignant and sarcastic malice … never was a political work more universally
perused'.[17] His classical pseudonym (taken from the republican hero
Lucius Junius Brutus) served as a theatrical prop which showed the audience of readers his chosen persona as a loyal friend of the people, opposing
the government.

The Grafton character presented in the letters was of course entirely the
imaginary and highly subjective creation of Junius, who declared himself to
be a high-minded historian of truth, writing with a moral purpose:

> … as for your personal character, I will not … suppose that you can wish to
> have it remembered. … but it is the historian's office to punish, though he
> cannot correct. I do not give you to posterity as a pattern to imitate, but as an
> example to deter; and as your conduct comprehends every thing that a wise
> or honest minister should avoid, I mean to make you a negative instruction to
> your successors for ever.

The chilling declaration of intent is all the more sinister in retrospect,
because Junius' wish did indeed come true and his printed words left a
deliberately distorted but lasting impression of the duke.

This was despite regular counter-attacks published in the press and pamphlets denouncing Junius' malicious attempts to create in the public mind
'the falsest, and most dangerous Notions of the Characters, and Conduct of

his Ministers' by 'the fascinating Powers of your infernal Pen ... the most subtle and penetrating Poison, that was ever invented'.[18] Another indignant letter from an opponent of Junius, which was published in the *Public Advertiser* on 30 March 1769, protested that since 'he made his appearance as leading the van, many other little ill-informed emissaries have started up, all of them echoing the same thing over again ... My only intention is to place the whole of this transaction in the clearest point of view ... [and] put the honest unsuspecting part of my countrymen more upon their guard against the artful address of seditious writers.'

The extraordinary popularity of Junius can be attributed both to his impressive literary skill and to the mystery about the writer's identity, which has never been solved conclusively. He was well aware of the power of anonymity, boasting, 'I am the sole depositary of my own secret, and it shall perish with me'. Of the sixty possible names suggested over two centuries, the most likely author was Sir Philip Francis, a clergyman's son who was chief clerk at the War Office and a prolific political writer who later purchased a seat as MP for Yarmouth. He never did admit authorship, but in a typically disguised symbolic gesture he gave a copy of the *Letters of Junius* to his second wife as a wedding present and inscribed another copy left for her after his death in 1818.[19]

Public debate about his identity from the beginning helped to boost the circulation of the *Public Advertiser*, and many other printers exploited his market appeal by publishing collected volumes of the letters, so that by 1772 there had already been twenty-eight unauthorised editions. At a time of immense political volatility, as shifting factions fought for power through a succession of transient ministries, there was naturally a public appetite for Junius' biting political satire. He cleverly manipulated readers by posing as a truth-teller who was the voice of the people and selected Grafton as the scapegoat for all his discontent, stating, 'You are the pillow upon which I am determined to rest all my resentments.' His authorised published collection of letters was arrogantly dedicated to the English nation, as 'written by one of Yourselves for the common benefit of us all', and he declared that 'the liberty of the press is the *Palladium* of all the civil, political, and religious rights of an Englishman'. This referred to the Palladium which was a sacred talisman of the Greek goddess Pallas Athena, believed to give protection.

The tone of the letters was spiteful and vindictive, attacking Grafton's neglect of 'a great country, driven by your counsels, to the brink of destruction', and portraying him as a weak, indecisive figure, acting out of personal interest, who was 'sullen and severe without religion, profligate without gaiety'.

The lengthy rants about Grafton's private sins condemned him not merely for indulging 'in all the fashionable excesses of the age' but for the careless public display of vice:

> There is yet a certain display of it, a certain outrage to decency … which for the benefit of society, should never be forgiven. It is not that he kept a mistress at home, but that he constantly attended her abroad. It is not the private indulgence, but the public insult, of which I complain.[20]

Grafton's liaison with Nancy Parsons was already well established in June 1764 when he openly took her to the races at Ascot in a controversial public gesture which clearly signalled she had become his official mistress. Nancy was an ambitious woman with arresting looks and a powerful magnetic appeal that men seemed to find irresistible. As a teenager she played bit parts as a dancer at the opera but soon found that work as a high-class prostitute was far more lucrative, reputedly charging a guinea per session and earning 100 guineas in one particularly busy week. She was taken to live in Jamaica as mistress of a West Indies slave trader and later came back to London where she attracted a stream of rich clients from the nobility.

By the time of his infatuation with Nancy, Grafton had been estranged from his wife, Anne, for several years. The couple had seemed well suited at the start, close in age and both with a lively intelligence. A portrait of Grafton as a handsome youth shows a thoughtful and sensitive man, with guileless kind eyes full of good humour. Anne was a tall and imposing brunette deemed to be 'not a regular beauty' but with an engaging, warm-hearted and impulsive nature. Despite the birth of three children, their differences gradually drove them apart as he became engrossed in his political career and she became addicted to card playing. He often returned home to the house in Bond Street, tired after a day in Parliament, to find his wife hosting rowdy card parties until the early hours and was forced to retire to his library or bed to get some peace.[21]

On her side, Anne felt unfairly neglected by her husband because of his frequent absences on political duties or social engagements: 'Your Gaming and going constantly to Arthurs was the original, I found myself night after night at home alone, this hurt me and I sought amusement abroad.'[22] The couple were constantly arguing, and the duke's valet later recalled that they usually quarrelled in French so the servants could not understand. However, on one occasion he overheard Anne say she was the most unhappy woman in the world, and her husband replied it was her own fault for he did all in his power to make her happy. To try and heal the rift they took an extended trip travelling around Europe in 1761, but it failed to bring them any closer and a formal separation took place after eight years of marriage in 1764.

Horace Walpole was a friend of Anne and took her side in the marital dispute. His initial assessment of the duke as a cold man 'of strict honour ... not particularly familiar, nor particularly good-humoured', later turned to antagonism when he damned Grafton's behaviour as being 'like an apprentice, thinking the world should be postponed to a whore and a horse-race'.[23]

For some time Anne had been ignoring gossip that Grafton was keeping a mistress, but shortly after the separation she found out that the rumours were indeed true. She dashed off a furious letter to him:

> Can it be that I have been thus deceived; that Lord Villiers's business and yours was what I ever feared; that you have a year and a half (the very time the Duke of York first told me was at Ranelagh and which you solemnly denied) had this person as mistress in constant keeping; that Lord Villiers introduced you to her, she having formerly lived with him ... that you have fitted up her house in the richest way; that her extravagance is without end ... that this person vulgar in her manner has acquired such an ascendancy as to try to make you break with all your family, and prevailed?

The duke replied in carefully measured tones to this angry tirade, although he was clearly upset at the unfair criticism of those who were unaware of their troubled marital history, 'I am most grossly injured by any one who can imagine that for any attachment of what nature soever I should have dissolved a Family Union of the kind ours ought to have been.' In the original draft of the letter he added two further bitter sentences:

> Whatever may be or may have been my failings, I never woud have been so unjust to anyone, as I find I am represented by you & by others ... I have often, I assure, passed over every thing that has occurred to us & between us since our Marriage, and if any thing surprises me more than the rest, is that it ever continued so long.[24]

But after further thought they were crossed out and not included in the final letter, as he obviously decided he was being too honest in expressing his feelings.

He voiced his long dissatisfaction with their marriage in a later passage, where his genuine emotional distress was clear, despite efforts to use a reserved and reasonable tone:

> You know (if you really think impartially) that this is not nor ever coud be affected for a Reason of the Sort you have lately insinuated. Recollect the Life we have led, which nothing but the Hurry & Dissipation of being in constant Bustling Company could ever have drove me so long to have endured. That like the Rest was to end, my eyes were opened on my Situation early & it was till repeated tryals & Expectations of a Change that I was drove by you to seek this last method of Redress.[25]

The couple's lengthy correspondence negotiating terms for the separation and subsequent divorce gives a fascinating insight into their difficult relationship. The duke's letters reveal him as a frank and serious man with a strong sense of duty, who found himself trapped from a young age in an unhappy marriage. His efforts to express himself as a self-controlled and honourable man are in marked contrast to the emotional outpourings of his wife's often incoherent letters.

Anne comes across as a highly strung and desperate woman in her long, barely legible rambling screeds, which had little punctuation and were covered with darkly-inked underlinings. She enlisted different tactics to try and influence her husband, and in one typical letter tried contrition, followed by flattery, then further self-abnegation, writing, 'As to my wretched self never was there a truer Mourner I own and lament my faults which were provoking to the last degree.' She then used emotional blackmail involving their children ('will you for ever continue obdurate against the Mother of three Dear Children who you love'), before briskly addressing practical matters by requesting household items and furniture. The next section resumed the tone of self-pitying repentance:

> I spend most of the day alone, indeed I am unfit for Company … I grow so thin and so weak … I hate myself for the past … but changed from the foundation as I am that rebellious spirit quite subdued save a Mother to Children you Love from despair you do not know my Agonies.

Finally, she again used the children as pawns to win some sympathy: 'my Dear Daughter … every day she begs me to be happy, and she says papa will take us all home'.²⁶ The letter was typical of dozens that she wrote to the duke over the course of several years, in which she fluctuated between being a lovingly dutiful wife deferring to his wishes and devoted to his children and a self-pitying discarded woman trying to manipulate him by emotional blackmail, with appeals such as, 'my daughter … called out to me indeed papa will love you one day don't fret yourself to death … it has almost broke my Heart'.²⁷

Eventually life settled down again for both of them, and while the duke was enjoying his new freedom to be with Nancy, in the summer of 1767 Anne met the 22-year-old John Fitzpatrick, Earl of Upper Ossory, during a stay in the fashionable resort of Brightelmstone (now Brighton) and fell in love. They began a discreet liaison and within six months she was carrying his child.

Repeated pregnancies were almost inevitable at a time when no effective methods of birth control existed, other than *coitus interruptus* and various natural herbal remedies, which were popular with women but unreliable. Linen condoms tied on with ribbon could be bought in three different sizes at brothels, but these were used by men purely for protection against venereal disease and not as a contraceptive. The tougher condoms made of sheep's intestine, which later became more successful as contraceptive devices, were originally sold at a Covent Garden sex shop in the 1740s.

Anxious to keep her condition hidden, Anne quickly retreated to a country house at Combe, 2 miles from Kingston in Surrey, to await the birth. Meanwhile Grafton had heard about the pregnancy and sent a note to Anne saying that he intended to obtain evidence for a divorce. He then wrote to his father-in-law Lord Ravensworth, struggling to find the correct words as he broke the dreadful news of her disgrace, 'I have for some time past dreaded this moment … I did not think it right to make publick every Reason I had for our Separation: but what I had harsh ground to suspect, her situation now has shown that she was Capable of committing.'²⁸ The duke arranged for her to be put under close watch by paid spies including some of the household staff, who reported what was going on to his agent, John Nuttall. The ever discreet and reliable society physician Dr William Hunter, who had attended the births of Anne's other children, was also put under surveillance.

On the morning of 23 August it was clear that the baby was on its way early, and all the servants were immediately sent back to the London house. Anne sent a post chaise to alert the doctor and collect her old nurse Martha Tyson, who had known her since childhood. The nurse reached Combe to find only two women in attendance, and when she entered the bedchamber Anne was already in labour and cried out, 'Tyson, I hope I am more to be pitied than blamed.' Dr Hunter arrived too late to help with the birth but collected the child to take away to a wet nurse, while hare-skins were put over the mother's breasts to dry up her milk.

The baby was dressed in a white satin robe with a red blanket over it, and it was quickly taken from the room by a maid before Anne could say goodbye. The small bundle was smuggled out of the house hidden under the maid's cloak and handed over to Dr Hunter, who had got into his waiting chaise and had hurriedly pulled up all the blinds. The coachman, who had been standing by a hedge eating blackberries with the postilion William Kenning, was ordered to drive as fast as he could, taking the route through a wood. When they reached London at twelve o'clock the men were both given half-crowns, with a promise that 'if it was not heard where they had been, they should have half-a-crown more'.

Now that the illegitimate child had been born, divorce was the only option for Grafton. He called twenty-four witnesses to give evidence in the collusive legal suit against Lord Ossory for crim. con., which was heard at the Court of King's Bench. Next the formal terms of the separation were negotiated, which allowed Anne an annuity of £2,000 a year for life (around £120,000 now). The divorce bill then went before Parliament where its smooth passage through both Houses was assisted by Basil, Earl of Denbigh, whose cousin Elizabeth married Grafton three months later. Writing with final instructions on the day the case was due to be heard in the Lords, Grafton advised Denbigh to follow 'your own Judgement on the spot' on the examination of witnesses and invited him to visit Wakefield Lodge 'in case we are *successful* today for otherwise, I should be too sulky to be company for anything but the Beast of the forest'.[29]

Soon after the divorce was granted Anne married Ossory and went on to enjoy a 35-year marriage, living quietly at his country estate Ampthill Park in Bedfordshire. But like most women who inevitably paid a high price for divorce, she was forbidden any access to her children. In a farewell letter to her husband, she said that when her adultery had become public knowledge she was 'abandoned and very justly by parents, friends and all mankind', and asked him, 'If it is not thought absolutely improper, I hope to be permitted some time to see my poor children, who are continually in my thoughts, and the loss of whom I can never forget; any other loss, God knows, is hardly felt in comparison.'

She sent a ring containing a lock of hair to her 8-year-old daughter Georgiana and a final letter saying she was an 'unhappy mother who dotes on you', who had always tried to 'cultivate your mind as much as lay in my power, and to instil precepts for your happiness and honour. This is my only consolation and no small one it is'. She requested 'a plain glass heart for the breast with yours and your two brothers' hair'. Anne never saw her three children again, until a brief visit by her eldest son on her deathbed over thirty years later.

While the divorce was going through in early 1769, Grafton finally ended the liaison with Nancy Parsons which had increasingly shocked society as they appeared openly together at public events and hosted lavish dinners at his house in London, apparently impervious to public disapproval. The split must have been a relief to some of his circle, who were beginning to worry that the relationship might become permanent. In July the previous year the *St James's Chronicle* had reported in its London news column, 'If an intended Divorce takes place between two great Personages, the friends of the Noble Husband are apprehensive, that from his fondness for his Mistress he will be unhappily induced to marry her.' Grafton was in fact planning to make a far more suitable match to the daughter of a baronet. He had also heard that Nancy had become the mistress of the much younger John Sackville, 3rd Duke of Dorset, who already held a reputation as a charming womaniser.

Several publications, including the *Public Advertiser* and the *Gentleman's Magazine*, printed what purported to be the former lovers' final letters. Although their authorship was never confirmed, Grafton's typically controlled tone and precisely articulated reasoning does suggest they were authentic. The duke's letter complimented Nancy, whose 'personal and mental Qualifications' and 'unearred assiduity to please me', had helped 'in a great measure alleviate my domestic Misfortunes'. But he reiterated his qualms about their affair:

> As I often told you ... such a course of life was unseemly both in my moral and political Character, and that nothing but the necessity could justify the measure. I am now to tell you that all our former ties are from this day at an end. I have taken care (my dear Friend, for I will now totally throw by the Lover) to make that establishment for you, as will make you easy in your circumstances for life, chargeable only with the proviso, that your residence be not in these Kingdoms; the rest of Europe lies at your Choice.[30]

Nancy replied calmly, in a letter signed 'the unfortunate Anne Parsons', that she was very surprised by his decision, but admitted, 'It is very true you did insinuate in our first Connection, that it did not totally agree with your Principles and Situation, as you was married.' Perhaps she had secretly entertained hopes of becoming his second wife, when she wrote 'Little did I think when that marriage was dissolved, and the odium which attended our connections consequently so, that your Affections could so mechanically abate, as in an instant thus to sacrifice the Lover to the sordid considerations of Interest or Public Opinion.' She protested at the cruelty of enforced exile abroad and insisted (rather unconvincingly given her new strategic liaison with the Duke of Dorset) that she still loved him. In a final bitter outburst, she added, 'May your future lady love like me, but never meet with such Returns.' A woman as ambitious as Nancy was bound to succeed in the end, and after a long relationship with Dorset, she at last secured a title in her forties by marrying the 24-year-old Viscount Maynard. Old habits are hard to break, and in her fifties she had a long affair with the 19-year-old Duke of Bedford, which was apparently accepted by her husband.

News about Grafton's political and social activities appeared regularly in the press, but many different publications also began to exploit the market appeal of scandal by cashing in on the sensational adultery trial at the centre of his divorce case. One of the first to appear was the *Town and Country Magazine*'s detailed exposé of the unhappy marriage and his liaison with Nancy, who 'presides constantly at his sumptuous table, and does the honours with an ease and elegance, that the first nobility in the kingdom are compelled to admire'. The article repeated allegations of corruption, which involved Nancy using her political influence to take thousands of pounds in bribes from those seeking court positions.

Soon after his marriage in June 1769 to Elizabeth Wrottesley, the Dean of Worcester's daughter, a satirical print entitled 'Fleet Marriage' appeared in the *Oxford Magazine*, featuring cartoon drawings of all the main protagonists as guests at the wedding, with speech bubbles giving their points of view. Anne is saying to her new husband, 'He made a Dutchess of me and I made a C-k-ld of him', while Nancy is pictured crying into a handkerchief and saying, 'I retire on a pension of 300 per an.m to make room for Miss Wr-y.' At the bottom of the print is a large pair of cuckold's horns with a label reading 'New Horns to Graft-on.'

The case was included in numerous printed collections of adultery trials, which usually portrayed Anne as the brazen adulteress and Grafton as the archetypal wronged husband who had always 'behaved towards her with true affection'.[31] *A New and Compleat Collection of the Most Remarkable Trials for Adultery* recounted the cases of both Grafton and of his father, Lord Augustus FitzRoy, who had in 1740 been the defendant in a trial for crim. con. with the wife of a baronet, Sir William Morrice, who won £5,000 damages plus 40*s* costs. It described how the lovers had met at Bath after the lady refused to accompany her husband home to his country seat, protesting that she 'would not be buried in the country with any baronet whatsoever'. Servants reported that the bed curtains and curtain rods had fallen down due to the vigorous crim. con. taking place at 4 a.m. one morning. Shortly after the affair began, FitzRoy was sent back to sea by the navy to captain a seventy-gun warship at the siege of Carthagena, and his love letters were produced in court as evidence. In one of them he declared himself 'bound in honour to defend her to the last, with his blood, life, and fortune', and in another he wrote 'I long for the expiration of the next five months, and then I hope to be with you. Adieu, my Angel.' But tragically he died of fever in Jamaica the following May, aged just 24, and never returned home to see her, or his wife and two young sons.

Many other literary spin-offs emerged to profit from the prime minister's scandal, including the spoof *Memoirs of the Amours, Intrigues and Adventures of Augustus Fitz-Roy, Duke of Grafton, with Miss Parsons* priced at 2*s* 6*d*, a poorly written book which made Grafton into a rakish fictional hero. Another was an anonymous short memoir laced with abuse, entitled *A First Letter to the Duke of Grafton*, which sold for 18*d* and commented that in previous years, 'Adultery, cuckoldom, and divorces were not at that time reduced to the easy and fashionable system at present so favourable to the caprices of the English nobility.'

It portrayed his life as a series of cunning roles acted behind a mask both in 'the political theatre' and 'in private society where your natural pride was concealed under the cloak of affability'. The writer told Grafton he would not, 'with the multitude, accuse your Grace of having pursued an adulterous lust with all the unguarded folly of boyish effeminacy', but sneered at him 'panting in the withered arms of your mistress at Newmarket'. He feigned shocked incredulity that:

> ... the English Prime Minister can, in a public theatre ... in the presence of the representatives of all the crowned heads in Europe ... sit with doting fondness by the side of an antiquated Figure-dancer, remarkable only for the sickened features of stale beauty, the artificial vivacity of hackneyed prostitution, and the infatuated adorations of a silly keeper.

A twenty-two page vicious satire, *An Epistle from N-y P-s to His Grace the Duke of G-n*, accused him of being sunk in an abyss of guilt over bribery and corruption. It cast Grafton as Phaeton, the son of the mythical sun god Helios who could not control his father's chariot and let the horses bolt so the earth was in danger: 'Phaeton, the emblem of his short-liv'd power, / The sport of chance, the bubble of an hour'. And another passage in *The Patricians*, published in 1773, which satirised government figures speaking in the House of Lords, presented him in the worst possible light:

> From White's, Newmarket, and those gambling schools,
> Where fools made sharpers, in their turns make fools,
> Where fickle fortune guides the wav'ring stocks,
> And Peer and pimp, by turns, command the box,
> Grafton stept forth his country to defend,
> He spoke it fair, and Chatham was his friend;
> But ah! What honour – what connections bind,
> Where interest only occupies the mind?
> That grasp for pow'r – that lust to rule alone,
> Which bear no rivals near their lawless throne,
> Fill'd all his soul – hence gratitude gave way,
> And ev'ry scoundrel maxim came in play,

The turbulent years around the divorce which created Grafton's lasting reputation in fact proved to be a personal turning point. In contrast to his earlier life, the remaining forty years were quiet ones when he enjoyed a stable marriage to Elizabeth which produced twelve children. His 1775 entry in *The Complete English Peerage* noted that:

> His grace's correspondence with the celebrated Miss Nancy Parsons is too well known for even the duke's best friends to attempt concealing it, but it is equally well known that since he has been married to a lady who makes it her study to please, he cannot be accused of any irregularities of this sort; and as her grace is emulous of being the best of wives, she finds in him the best of husbands.

In his *Biographical, Literary and Political Anecdotes* published in 1797, the London bookseller John Almon paid warm tribute to Grafton's honourable character, 'his virtues as a patriot, his talents as a statesman'.[32]

In later life the old duke devoted much of his time to horses and agriculture, while a deepening interest in theology made him reflect sombrely on the past. After the death of his first wife in 1804, Grafton explained to his son that he had planned to write to her, 'to let her know that I was sensible in our separation much lay on me to answer, as well as on herself; so that I wished to hear that she forgave any wrongs in me as frankly and fully as I did ... which declaration, at our time of life, I thought would lighten the remorses of both.'[33] He later confessed:

> I do regret with the most heartfelt sorrow that I turned not my thoughts more seriously to religion ... until I had lost so many of the best days of my life in the pursuit of every senseless dissipation of the times, or in an indulgence of the fashionable vices of the age ... In an advanced age I am enjoying so much more solid comfort by trusting to the mercies of God through the gospel of His Son, than ever I did in the days of my follies.[34]

His religious views found expression in two theological pamphlets, one of which called for better church attendance and reformed behaviour from the nobility and gentry, because 'in no country, at no time, the bad example of superiors has operated so rapidly, and so generally, through every class of the people, as it has done here of late; and that rank and character seldom now meet with a suitable distinction'.[35] The pamphlet entitled *Hints &c. Submitted to the Serious Attention of the Clergy, Nobility and Gentry* was printed anonymously by 'A Layman'. Its title page cited an apt and provocative quotation from Livy's history of Rome on the need for religious observance by those who command others, which summed up his argument and enlisted classical authority to underpin it. Grafton's use of Latin to come across as a learned layman did not impress another writer who published a ninety-nine page response, dismissing the classical phrases as a poor attempt 'to impress on your readers ... an idea of your learning'.[36] Another lengthy reply to the duke's pamphlet published in 1794 used the opportunity to reiterate past scandal and reaffirm the opinion of Junius, 'who seems to have understood your character'. It declared, 'To come forward in your declining days, and brave the public opinion, is effrontery, not courage.'[37]

Grafton's final self-portrait as 'a public man' appeared in his memoirs, written at the age of 70, where he recounted political events in which he had been a major player.[38] The master of his old Cambridge college, John

Symonds, advised him that memoir 'seems preferable to any other kind of narrative'.[39] The memoir's tone was the frank and thoughtful one of his earlier letters, but it ignored the unpalatable domestic incidents of his first marriage and carefully omitted any reference to Junius. His intention was to make a definitive public record in which, 'the relation of facts I have known and observations I have made are to be the main subjects for my purpose'. He warned readers that 'you are not to look into this memoir, for a general history of the times, but of those transactions solely, in which I was more immediately concerned; and of which I can give the best authenticated accounts'. He referred to his diary made at the time, and although concerned that 'a narrative taken from a journal so closely as this I fear will appear tedious', he believed that it would still be valuable 'if it lets us often into the ways of thinking, dispositions and manners of men, whose characters we wish to know'. The greatest insights of the memoir were, of course, into the mind of its author. But Grafton's own published works, which reflected his mature character, could not alter a public image tarnished by his past conduct, which kept stubbornly resurfacing in print for years afterwards.

7

NOBLE
REPUTATIONS

The tradition of hereditary power demanded that rank was allied to personal virtue, a position outlined by the clergyman Thomas Gisborne in his popular *Enquiry into the Duties of Men in the Higher and Middle Classes of Society*, specifying the duties of peers in their public function as legislators and judges in the Upper House, and their conduct in private life. He urged each peer to 'constantly recollect the power which he possesses of influencing the conduct and manners of others', because the pattern exhibited by peers was 'the most alluring and efficacious', spreading throughout the country to influence 'whether industry, morality, and religion shall flourish, or decline'. Members of the aristocracy had a clear obligation to act as moral exemplars and were held responsible for shaping the moral tone of the nation, as the Lord Chief Justice, Lord Kenyon, often pointed out when presiding at crim. con. trials. Speaking at the trial of Lady Valentia, he said peers should be vigilant in their conduct so as 'not to corrupt the lower order; the morals of the higher rank are of great importance to themselves, and ought to be adapted to keep the lower rank impressed with a respectful opinion of them, who look up to their superiors for example.'[40]

In similar tone, a 1s pamphlet addressed to the Duchess of Devonshire, as a leading figure in fashionable circles, observed that, 'they of high station are bound to consider the model of conduct they hold forth to the inferior world ... these times stand in particular need of virtuous example among Women of Rank and Distinction'.[41] This was an opinion shared by many, including the Evangelical writer Hannah More, who argued that those 'filling the higher ranks of life, are naturally regarded as patterns, by which the manners of the rest of the world are to be fashioned'.[42] The idea of a natural entitlement to rank was increasingly being called into question, and public debate about the example of the higher classes intensified as part of the moral reform movement that began to emerge later on in the 1780s.

For an elite who were now increasingly coming under scrutiny, aristocratic life was like a continual public performance of prescribed roles enacted before a highly critical audience. Public life in the late eighteenth and early nineteenth century had an intrinsic theatricality about it, which made it a place where ambitious men competed by negotiating which roles they would play. Stars of the stage could become public figures (like the actress Mrs Jordan who was the long-term mistress of the future King William IV), and politicians could achieve celebrity on the dramatic stage of public life.[43]

Throughout this period the theatre was a popular leisure venue which held a unique place in the national consciousness and became an iconic symbol of Georgian life itself. It exerted a powerful influence on society, and writers of the time often referred to the idea that people perform different roles on the stage of life. Young couples forced into arranged marriages were described as 'actors who have parts given them', and Lord Chesterfield commented to his son, 'I am going off the stage, you are coming upon it.'[44] The Shakespearian metaphor 'All the world's a stage, and all the men and women merely players', was a very familiar concept that the age was entirely comfortable with.[45] The playwright Arthur Murphy said that theatre 'engrossed the minds of men to such a degree, that it may now be said, that there existed in England a *fourth estate*, King, Lords, and Commons, and Drury-Lane play-house'.[46] And the Georgian era has been described as 'preoccupied to the point of obsession with the theatre as an institution and with the theatricality of social, political and personal behaviour. The discourse, practices and images of the theatre pervaded all aspects of the culture.'[47]

This theatricality was especially pertinent for the aristocracy. In his influential *Theory of Moral Sentiments*, published in 1759, the moral philosopher and economist Adam Smith saw social interaction as underlying the formation of an individual's moral identity. He argued that the act of putting on a public performance was the essence of nobility, because peers were aware that they lived under perpetual scrutiny:

As all his words, as all his motions are attended to, he learns an habitual regard to every circumstance of ordinary behaviour, and studies to perform all those small duties with the most exact propriety ... His air, his manner, his deportment, all mark that elegant and graceful sense of his own superiority ... these are the arts by which he proposes to make mankind more easily submit to his authority ... and in this he is seldom disappointed. These arts, supported by rank and preheminence, are, upon ordinary occasions, sufficient to govern the world.[48]

A class that found itself permanently on public display needed some basic training for the part and advice on how to perform as a good peer. This was derived from the pages of classical literature, which outlined the ideals of manly virtue and dutiful leadership as the basis of the aristocratic role. The classics not only shaped notions of appropriate behaviour, but they also had a far wider influence on the perceptions of life and personal identity held by peers, who had invariably been steeped in classical literature from boyhood.

The benefits of classical learning to promote the development of virtuous manhood were well known. The poet Jonathan Swift had even argued that studying role models from ancient fiction and history was essential for continuation of the aristocracy, by inculcating sound morality in young nobles.[49] Lord Chesterfield said that he had left Cambridge believing the classics contained everything needed for life and were 'a most useful and necessary ornament'. However, he advised using them only in moderation and criticised those boring pedants who 'draw all their maxims, both for public and private life, from ... the ancient authors', or adorned their conversation with Greek and Latin quotations to impress.[50]

The preface to *Observations on the Greek and Roman Classics. In a Series of Letters to a Young Nobleman*, published in 1753, emphasised their practical importance in meeting the demands of public life: 'The Classics are not introduced here as subjects of empty panegyric, they are proposed as patterns of imitation.'[51] It explained how classical orators, historians and poets could all give useful templates of 'manly eloquence' and 'the arrangement of thought and form of argument' which would be particularly valuable as preparation for a Parliamentary career.[52] In similar vein, another writer argued that the advantages of reading ancient Greek authors were 'too many and too great to be described', because they 'furnished the brightest examples of every virtue and accomplishment, natural or acquired, political, moral, military', and from them 'posterity may learn all that is elegant, magnificent and glorious'.[53] The many ways that literature influenced behaviour in everyday life were detailed at length in *Elegant Extracts: … for the Improvement of Scholars … in the Art of Speaking, in Reading, Thinking, Composing; and in the Conduct of Life*, which was published anonymously in 1784. It said that a classical education was needed to fashion the raw material of the young mind because the 'fairest diamonds are rough till they are polished'. The true use of knowledge was 'to lay up a store of good sense, and sound reason, of great probity, and solid virtue', and to learn 'a beautiful System of Morals'.[54]

There were vast numbers of books offering guidance in selecting and reading the classics, such as *A Dissertation on Reading the Classics, and Forming a Just Style,* and *An Introduction to the Classics: Containing a Short Discourse on their Excellencies; and Directions how to Study them to Advantage* which was printed in 1746. Other titles promoted the practical utility of literature in life, such as *Directions for a Proper Choice of Authors to Form a Library, Which May Both Improve and Entertain the Mind, and be of Real Use in the Conduct of Life.* Beliefs in the social impact of literature date back to Aristotle's *Poetics*, which said that all forms of art, including poetry, not only imitate life but also help us understand it better: 'poetic enactment is … the vehicle of a structure of meaning which … can nourish the understanding and move the emotions'.[55] By the eighteenth century Horace was more widely read than Aristotle, and his *Ars Poetica* had a section on the social uses and value of poetry, describing how 'honour and renown came to divine poets' who 'sharpened masculine hearts for war by their verses. Oracles were uttered in verse. The path of life was pointed out in verse.'[56]

Such classical theories of literature as an active force that could profoundly affect the lives of its readers underpinned the thinking of many Georgian writers. But the wider influence of the classics on eighteenth-century thought cannot be underestimated, and classical authors were routinely cited in all genres of writing as a frame of reference to understand modern experiences. The satirical *A Modest Apology for the Prevailing Practice of Adultery* printed in 1773 was liberally sprinkled with quotations from Juvenal, Ovid and Horace to emphasise its points. Quotations used in speech, letters and published writings were also intended to invoke classical authority and acted as a form of shorthand code which enabled others to unlock deeper meanings. The verses of Horace were cited more often than any other classical writer and could often be found heading periodical essays. Satirists and poets imitated his style, and references were made to his maxims by novelists and other writers. His lines were quoted 'as familiar vehicles of thought' by letter writers such as Horace Walpole and Lord Chesterfield and also in Parliamentary speeches by renowned orators, including Charles Fox and William Pitt.[57]

From an early age, the sons of the nobility and gentry were coached in Latin and Greek by tutors, schoolmasters and finally university dons. Many peers attended Eton College, where they were known as Oppidans, or non-scholars.[58] The Classics syllabus for boys was very demanding and centred on the works of Homer, Virgil and almost the whole of Horace, with lessons in speaking, repetition and construing, although not in written translation. After eight to ten years of such intensive study, it is not surprising that classical literature played a part in shaping boys' outlook. It provided a frame of reference for life, behaviour and attitudes, influencing ideas of masculine identity and giving them role models for the conduct of life. It also taught the practical skills necessary for public duty including oratory, rhetoric, persuasive argument and an elegant writing style. Such guidance was seen as invaluable for a class distinguished by the experience of having its behaviour constantly under public observation.

With the advent of the commercial press, an important stage on which members of the aristocracy performed was in print, where peers were portrayed as entertainers by newspapers and periodicals. One of the first to seize the opportunity was *Town and Country Magazine*, with its popular 'Histories of the Têtes-à-Têtes' series of articles, each exposing the intimate secrets of a notorious couple with a scandalous sex life. The feature was an early form of modern tabloid journalism and dug up all the old dirt and gossip it could find, without attributing any of it to named sources. Each case was illustrated by two oval-shaped portraits of the man and woman 'head-to-head', and described their sexual histories before reporting all known tit-bits about their present relationship. The identity of victims was thinly disguised by pseudonyms, but enough clues were given to allow readers to make an accurate guess. Viscount Falmouth was dubbed Lord Pyebald in the article describing his liaison with a young milliner. The series started in 1769 when the public was riveted by the sensational adultery trial involving the Duke of Cumberland (the king's brother) and Lady Henrietta Grosvenor. Perhaps because of the royal connection, the magazine decided it was wiser not to publish an article explicitly linking the guilty pair, so it ran separate ones on each of the three members of the love-triangle in September 1769, August 1770 and September 1778.

The risqué series proved so popular with readers that it ran for over twenty years until 1792, reaching a national circulation of 14,000 copies. The *Town and Country Magazine, or Universal Repository of Knowledge, Instruction and Entertainment* was an ambitious monthly periodical, containing serious foreign and domestic news alongside a bizarre mix of articles written by various 'correspondents'. One typical issue included pieces titled 'The Gardener's Kalendar', 'On Matrimonial Happiness', 'Oddities of the late Earl of Uxbridge', 'History of the French Theatre', 'Fame Often Owing to Chance', 'Curious Natural Caves in Ireland', 'Anecdotes of Lord Camden's Brother', and 'Terrible Consequences of Modern Hair-dressing'.

But it was 'that leading feature, which has so peculiarly distinguished this Magazine, the Department of the tête-à-tête' which secured its reputation. The feature was especially clever in the way it disguised blatant character attacks by using a gentle tone of sorrowful regret to dutifully rehash gossip, which it insisted the public had a right to know. The publishers proudly boasted of their fearless campaign to expose and put an end to vice, declaring in one editorial of 1772, 'To those few who seem to be hurt at the freedom of our pens, we reply that the Liberty of the Press is an object with which the rights of Englishmen are so intimately connected, that its advantages cannot be too frequently insisted upon, nor too forcibly inculcated.'

Dismissing complaints by 'a few snarlers', the article declared that, 'our object has constantly been the vice and not the man; and characters that are publickly reprehensible are certainly fair game for public satire'. The piece concluded with some self-promotion, saying that the magazine was now read throughout the British Isles, in most capital cities on the Continent and was being translated into several languages. Another editorial a few years later said some readers had been surprised that it was able to find a constant supply of amorous couples to feature over so many years, 'but the truth is, the only difficulty we labour under … is to make a choice'.

One aristocratic pair chosen as obvious victims for attack was William Stanhope, 2nd Earl of Harrington, and his wife, who appeared in separate profiles in 1771 and 1772. Lord Harrington, amusingly dubbed Lord Fumble, was one of the most notorious rakes of his day, known for bouts of debauchery and a voracious appetite for prostitutes, including the famous Kitty Fisher. Lady Harrington was known as a promiscuous and vulgar woman, who at George III's coronation had been decked out in as many diamonds as she could borrow or hire. Her nickname of the Stable Yard Messalina came from her address in Stable Yard by St James' Park, London.

The magazine said of them:

> The Tête-à-Tête with which we shall open this annual campaign, has long been the subject of private animadversion, and we think it now so well corroborated as to be transmitted to the public. The hero has been as celebrated in the annals of politics, as the heroine in those of gallantry; their conduct has constantly been superior to vulgar censure or prudish criticism.

Lady Harrington was then portrayed as a nymphomaniac of highly 'refined salaciousness' who had enjoyed illicit sex with dozens of men, including her footman. The article said there were many reports of her amours with 'lovers from a monarch down to a hairdresser, and every member of the diplomatic body', to a northern potentate and several of her own servants. She had many children but 'it was often intimated that his L—p has some doubts of their being his offspring'.

The Harringtons were perfect for lampooning as appalling stereotypes of vice. And of course striking caricatures like this provided great entertainment, just like the stock characters of villains and heroes who had always appealed to audiences of stage drama since the earliest plays in Ancient Greece. The periodical press was starting to flex its muscles and subtly beginning to influence public perceptions of nobility. In articles like this, original prototypes of real aristocrats were being cleverly manipulated by writers to form a fixed mental impression – what we would now call a stereotype. The word was derived from the Greek 'solid' and 'impression' to denote a new method of printing invented in revolutionary France in 1794 to prevent forgeries. Stereotype printing was introduced to England in 1803 by the 3rd Earl Stanhope (son of the old rake), who invented a new printing press which was soon in use at *The Times* and Oxford University Press.[59] Significantly, it was the process of printing that literally and metaphorically cast the type of the aristocrat, permanently fixing impressions onto the page in ink and in the minds of readers. So fixed notions of aristocratic roles can be seen developing from the time stereotype printing was invented, which heralded an era of cheaper mass publishing. It took many years for the word 'stereotype' to enter common usage. The meaning gradually evolved from a printing term to a fixed, unchanging form of speech in the early 1800s and finally to the modern sense of a 'preconceived and oversimplified idea of the characteristics which typify a person'.[60]

For many people it was publicity and open public discussion of adultery, rather than the crime itself, that posed the greatest threat to society. Speaking in a debate at the House of Lords on one of the later adultery prevention bills, Lord Auckland stressed the dangers of making the private public when he pointed out that divorce 'tended to expose to public remark and discussion, the weaknesses and vices of men of rank and opulence … who ought to give examples of good order and of morality'.[61] In fact, adultery was the most serious of several vices supposedly favoured by the aristocracy which was highlighted as part of a wider political attack on aristocratic privilege. Stories of sexual scandal naturally held the greatest public fascination, by offering the titillation of prurient detail combined with the satisfaction of moral judgement on social superiors.

Publishers fuelled the notion that the public was entitled to know the whole truth about those in authority and indeed that revelations about their personal lives were for the good of society. *The Complete English Peerage* denounced other guides to the nobility for distorting known facts and creating fictitious virtuous characters for peers:

> Instead of being faithful historians, they have been little more than mere panegyrists, who thought it their duty to varnish the characters of the living with adulation … and burying those vices in oblivion, which even the advantage of high birth could not hide from the knowledge or detestation of their contemporaries.[62]

In contrast, this book was intended for 'admirers of *real* nobility', and the preface proclaimed, 'We shall not be afraid to pull aside the ermine, to shew the corruption which lies hidden behind … to disclose the weakness of the head, even when encircled by the diadem.' Superficial appearances were no longer to be accepted without question. The growing power of the press meant that peers' lives had now become public property, and there was no shortage of writers willing to sharpen their quills and jump on to a highly lucrative bandwagon. The barbed wit of satire proved particularly popular, such as the political verse *The Patricians* which explicitly linked marital fidelity with conscientious public duty:

Learn then ye shameless Nobles of the age,
Who deaf to truth – in ev'ry vice engage,
Your vows forgot – who wanton in *divorce*,
And stab domestic honour in its source,
Learn from this bright example, to improve
In all th'endearments of connubial love,

...

That he who doth his heart-felt duty here,
Shall act with honour in a wider sphere.

The bright example referred to was that of George, 1st Baron Lyttelton, whose honourable character, public standing, literary output and virtuous domestic life cast him in the role of archetypal exemplary peer, whose 'virtues make the Peerage shine'.[63] Popularly known as the Good Lord Lyttelton, he was credited with a discernment drawn from 'books, from business, and mankind' which had made him 'Though learn'd, polite, and though polite, sincere'.

The way stereotypes evolved in print was illustrated in the very different public opinions of Lyttelton and Philip Stanhope Dormer, 4th Earl of Chesterfield, who both died in 1773. The following year the published *Works of Lord Lyttelton* and *Lord Chesterfield's Letters to his Son* were both reviewed in the *Monthly Review*, which commented on their respective characters that 'The contrast between the spirit that breathes through each is striking ... and we hope we may venture to prophesy, that the virtues of a LYTTELTON will be remembered with respect, when the *graces* of a CHESTERFIELD shall be forgotten.'[64]

This prediction about their standing in posterity was in fact completely reversed. The superficial false graces 'calculated to inspire distrust, and an artful conduct' shown in Chesterfield's letters, drew widespread condemnation when published for advocating the amoral court code of polite role playing, self-interest and adultery. The adverse publicity ensured the book went through eleven editions by 1800, spawning dozens of commentaries and proving to be one of the top ten titles borrowed from circulating libraries.[65]

The letters revealed the hypocrisy of enacting politeness with calculated deception, and it was this revelation of false role play on top of their perceived immorality, which caused the outcry. 'Lord Chesterfield has let us all behind the scenes: he invites us to see the peer dress for public exhibition,' wrote one critic, rather unfairly, for the *Letters* had been written as personal advice to his son Philip for a successful diplomatic career and were never intended for publication.[66] When printed after Chesterfield's death by his daughter-in-law, they made the private public and cast him in perpetuity in the role of a bad peer. Although his executors served an injunction on the printers to stop publication, Chesterfield's widow apparently supported the circulation of letters she saw as elegantly written and educational.

Readers took a different view of 'lessons of lewdness, of avarice and ambition', in which 'the true character of the noble Lord is given us, by himself, in colours too striking to be mistaken'. The contradictions revealed between the public man and his personal life were used to make a wider point about the moral example of the aristocracy. Clergyman Thomas Hunter's lengthy critique observed that 'the very name and example of so accomplished a Nobleman, may have a very unhappy effect upon the morals of Britons … We have only to lament, that a Nobleman of such eminent abilities, should … adopt and recommend principles subversive of public and private virtue'.[67]

In complete contrast, Lord Lyttelton's *Works* placed him 'before the public view, under the several characters of the judicious critic, the entertaining traveller, the wise and upright statesman, and the good man'.[68] Various commentators drew conclusions about the private characters of the two peers from their published writings. A letter-writer to the *Gentleman's Magazine* noted the contrast between Chesterfield's letters to his son and Lyttelton's letters to his father, which were 'an admirable contrast, and well-timed antidote … since the lurking poison of the one fell from the pen of an artful profligate father, while the wholesome instruction of the other flows from the heart of a virtuous and dutiful son'.[69] Chesterfield himself had earlier written a waspish caricature of Lyttelton as ludicrously absent-minded and physically awkward, concluding, 'I sincerely value and esteem him for his parts, learning and virtue; but for the soul of me I cannot love him in company.'[70] But these less appealing personal qualities were buried under a torrent of positive words from other writers, which built a lasting edifice of virtue around George Lyttelton.

'The Good Old Peer'

Born two months premature as a baby, George Lyttelton was baptised on the same day as no one expected him to survive. But what he lacked in physical strength, he more than made up for in character, growing up to be a frail, thin and pale man, with a solid reputation as a wise statesman, talented scholar and genuinely good man. Despite caricatures in the press joking about his tall and skinny frame, almost everyone seemed to agree about his merits. Nearly thirty years after he died, the preface to a new printed edition of his poems said:

> The character of George Lord Lyttelton, was held in universal estimation during his life, and his memory has been revered every since his death … his reputation is so decisively fixed, and so firmly established, that it can receive little additional lustre from panegyric; and is in no danger of suffering from the attacks of criticism or censure.

The radically different reputations of George (known as the Good Lord Lyttelton) and his son Thomas (known as the Wicked Lord Lyttelton) were so fixed in the public imagination that they became enduring role models of aristocratic vice and virtue. It was this striking family contrast that magnified Thomas's bad repute more than his actual behaviour warranted, as by many accounts it was no worse than other privileged youths before or since. The personal conduct of both men, and their experiences of marriage and adultery, were inextricably linked to their public image. And in both cases mass circulation of their own writing and other published narratives played a big part in creating a lasting reputation.

The eldest son of a Worcestershire baronet, George combined his literary and scholarly interests with a political career that included a year as Chancellor of the Exchequer. He entered Parliament as a member of a young political group of cousins, including Pitts and Grenvilles, under the influence of their uncle Viscount Cobham. He was close to Frederick, the Prince of Wales, and became his private secretary in 1737. After being created Baron Lyttelton of Frankley in 1756 he became an active member of the House of Lords but consistently refused to take office. He was also influential as a literary patron or friend of leading writers, such as Pope, Thomson, Fielding, Voltaire and the bluestocking Elizabeth Montagu. At 19 he published his first poem, the earnestly patriotic *Blenheim*, and went on to write numerous essays, pamphlets, poetry, and the religious commentary *Observations on the Conversion and Apostleship of St Paul*. His two major works were *Dialogues of the Dead*, which was well received and often reprinted, and the *History of the Life of Henry the Second*, which took him thirty years' work and drew mixed reviews. His first brief but happy marriage to Lucy Fortescue, producing a son, Thomas, and daughter, Lucy, ended with her early death in childbirth.[71]

Lyttelton's name had already become synonymous with virtue by the time he reached his thirties, and even his daughter Lucy playfully referred to him in letters as 'the good old peer'. The author Henry Fielding had been a friend since their schooldays at Eton College and dedicated his first novel *Tom Jones* to Lyttelton, who had read the manuscript and helped to promote his career. In the dedication, Fielding confirmed he had based his fictional character Squire Allworthy partly on the real-life example of Lyttelton:

> If there be in this work … a stronger picture of a truly benevolent mind than is to be found in any other, who that knows you … will doubt whence that benevolence has been copied? The world will not, I believe make me the compliment of thinking I took it from myself; I care not; this they shall own – that the two persons from whom I have taken it … two of the best and worthiest men in the world, are strongly and zealously my friends.[72]

Fielding's relative Basil, Earl of Denbigh, was believed to be the model for the novel's jovial Squire Weston.

Ideas of what constituted the correct behaviour for peers were drawn from many past prototypes and literary influences, including poetry and characters in novels, which continued to shape the beliefs of future generations of readers. Lyttelton's identity as a 'good peer' was also created by his own prolific writings, which were widely read during his lifetime and afterwards.

Dr Johnson noted in his *Lives of the Poets* that *Dialogues of the Dead* was 'very eagerly read' and 'kindly commended by the critical reviewers', but he dismissed it as the product rather 'of leisure than of study'. A schoolboy quarrel apparently caused Johnson's lifelong prejudice against Lyttelton, and he was equally patronising about the amateur nature of Lyttelton's poems, of which he wrote that 'They have nothing to be despised, and little to be admired … His little performances … are sometimes sprightly, and sometimes insipid', but he conceded grudgingly that one poem did show 'a power of poetry which cultivation might have raised to excellence'.[73]

Lyttelton's best-known poem, *To the Memory of a Lady Lately Deceased. A Monody*, was inspired by grief at the death of his beloved first wife, Lucy, in 1747, and it drew both criticism and praise. Poetry was very widely read at the time and ranked second only to religious sermons as the most published type of literature. It was especially suitable as a stage where public men could express their private feelings in a socially acceptable way. In *Monody* Lyttelton used the pastoral mode, a poetic form devised by the Greek poet Theocritus and later imitated by Virgil in his pastoral *Eclogues*, which evoked an idealised rural life. Pastorals had been popular in the Renaissance and were revived in the early eighteenth century as a means of expressing nostalgia for the natural moral values of the countryside.

Monody was written in nineteen verses, with a poignant tone of wistful longing and the traditional poetic conventions of rhetoric, classical allusion and nature imagery to recreate a golden age of the past. Recurring nature motifs conveyed a blissful Miltonic vision of pure married love in the idyllic rural setting of Lyttelton's country home, a refuge from the 'pomp of cities and the pride of courts'.[74] Critics of the poem, such as Horace Walpole, disliked its artificial pastoral sentimentality, and the poet Thomas Gray admitted, 'I like kids and fawns as little as you do' but praised the fourth verse.[75] In fact, the poem was most affecting when Lyttelton's genuine emotion burst out to describe touching details of his everyday life:

My dear, departed Love, so much was thine,
That none has any Comfort to bestow.
My Books, the best Relief
In ev'ry other Grief,

Are now with your idea sadden'd all:
Each fav'rite Aurthor we together read
My tortur'd Mem'ry wounds, and speaks of
LUCY dead.

This outpouring of private feelings in poetry was greeted as a laudable example of manly sentiment, and the verse satire *The Patricians* used it to illustrate Lyttelton's model conduct as an exemplary peer, noting approvingly how his 'elegant and pathetic *Monody*' elicited reader sympathy:

When fix'd in grief I see thee, widow'd, mourn,
And drop the tear o'er Lucy's envied urn,
O! where's the breast, not petrified as stone,
But what will judge thy sorrow by his own,
Catch ev'ry sigh, just issuing from the heart,
And share with thee, the sympathetic smart.[76]

Another writer believed the poem would always 'be read and admired while such an interchange of reason, sentiment, sympathy, and affection … is experienced or understood'.[77]

The role of the loving husband revealed in Lyttelton's *Monody* helped to confirm his positive public reputation. But what remained unpublished was equally important for shaping his image. In 1749, two years after Lucy's death, he married a baronet's daughter called Elizabeth Rich. The couple were apparently ill-matched from the start, and the marriage became increasingly strained following her indiscreet liaisons with George Durant, son of the rector of Hagley, and with another man. Lyttelton arranged a formal separation in 1759 after Elizabeth's love letters to an Italian opera singer became public, but despite allegations of her adultery the couple never divorced.

He wrote bitterly to his brother William, the governor of South Carolina:

Had I known two years ago all that I know now I should have parted with her then and been Deaf to her entreaties for a Reconciliation: but besides her ill conduct before that time, of which I have now received more full information, she has again made herself the talk of the Town by writing Love Letters to Signor Tenduchi, one of which has been shown to several people. I have therefore determined to separate from her, that my Honour may suffer no worse by her Shame.[78]

The forceful, darkly-inked handwriting with lots of underlinings expressed his strength of feeling and determination to protect the family honour. The letter was very different from the relaxed, urbane and witty style of his other letters, which were usually scattered with apt quotations and classical allusions. For a man very aware of his own public image, this personal letter to a trusted brother was a safe place to reveal the depth of his emotion about a humiliating situation.

The marital split was triggered by public gossip and Lyttelton acted quickly to stop the scandal from developing. Because he had not been able to get 'convincing and convicting proofs' of Elizabeth's adultery, he was forced into an amicable separation using their friends as mediators. He agreed to pay a generous maintenance, equal to her jointure, of £600 a year plus £200 pin money, to prevent further tittle-tattle and safeguard his reputation. He was frank about his motives with his brother and clearly anxious to retain the good opinion of his social circle:

> In short, my dear Billy, I found no way to get rid of her, without a quarrel with all her friends … rather than take any violent methods of forcing her out of my House … I have the satisfaction to find that Ld Hardwicke and others of my most judicious Friends, much approve, both of my parting with her, and doing it in a manner so handsome, as to stop every mouth.[79]

He admitted the payments would be a difficulty but one 'that bears no proportion to the Advantage I shall gain by it in Honour and Quiet. My House will now be agreeable both to me and my Friends'. Although Lyttelton wanted a public vindication and the legal proof needed to divorce Elizabeth, the fact that his wife's adultery never came to trial effectively hushed up the domestic scandal and kept it out of the newspapers. As other peers found to their cost, it was the publicity given to crim. con. trials that dented their reputations more than the fact that adultery had been committed.

Another potentially damaging incident was the publication in 1775 of the epistolary novel *The Correspondents*, telling in a series of letters the story of Lyttelton's allegedly adulterous courtship of Mrs Apphia Peach, three years before she married his son Thomas. At the time George Lyttelton was still legally married to, though separated from, Elizabeth. The novel claimed to contain genuine letters, and uncertainty about their authenticity ensured it received wide publicity through four editions. The *Monthly Review* suggested that the letters contained 'touches relative to time, place and circumstance, not likely to be founded on fiction', but also noted 'a similarity of style that runs through the whole series'.[80] Six pages were devoted to the review and excerpts from the novel, in which the hero appeared to be 'a Noble Poet and Historian lately deceased … *a widower bewitched*'.

Readers were given plenty of clues so they were left in no doubt about the identity of the pair:

> The groves of H—y have often been made vocal by the Peer's elegies on the loss of his LUCY, and the press has long since groaned beneath his sorrows. His fair Correspondent was at that time a real widow, a young widow however, with the bloom on the PEACH.

The reviewer pointed out that the sentiment revealed in the letters was difficult to characterise ('We *cannot* call it so little as mere Friendship; we *must* not call it so much as Love') but concluded, cryptically, 'We do not infer any sensual intercourse, yet we must class them – botanically – by a sexual arrangement.'[81]

Horace Walpole, not usually someone given to expressions of empathy, was initially shocked to see the publication of letters he believed were real. He wrote to his friend the Countess of Upper Ossory (the disgraced ex-Duchess of Grafton):

> I think one cannot doubt the letters to be genuine; but who has been so cruel as to publish them? and yet, except a little weakness … there is nothing that can reflect but on the publishers … Merciful! If all the foolish things one writes in confidence were to be recorded![82]

However, a month later he was beginning to change his mind: 'Now it seems the executors deny their authenticity so I do not believe it any longer, because anybody is at least better authority than everybody, for one person *may* speak truth, which all the world rarely does.'[83] The executors' denial was never actually found. Walpole's rather ambiguous sentence, with its ironic undertone, makes it unclear whether he really accepted at face value the predictable official denial intended to prevent family scandal. But as someone who knew Lyttelton, and was himself a sophisticated literary judge, his first instincts were probably accurate.

It is impossible now to be sure if the letters reproduced in the novel were faked or genuine ones cleverly packaged as one of the 'novels of sensibility' popular at the time. A warm friendship did exist between Mrs Peach and George Lyttelton after her marriage to Thomas, and it would be understandable if the lonely widower had earlier entertained hopes of a relationship with the attractive young widow, who lived only a few miles from his country estate Hagley Hall and who was certainly flattered by the attentions of a peer.[84] Some genuine letters may well have been handed over to a publisher who realised their commercial potential and copied the writing style to produce a novel. The intriguing uncertainty about their authenticity was undoubtedly good for sales.

There were several other potentially damaging portrayals of Lyttelton in print, including a political satire and attacks on his literary patronage, like the savage caricature of him as Sir Gosling Scragg in Tobias Smollett's 1751 novel *Peregrine Pickle*, which was deleted with an apology in the second edition. But despite these, his solid reputation for virtue remained untarnished. A poem published shortly after his death cast Lyttelton in the role of the classical hero Lycidas, a traditional figure in pastoral elegies based on a goatherd poet of ancient Greece. The elegy praised his many good qualities and mourned that 'The Pride of Virtue, Lycidas is dead'.[85]

It was not only Lord Lyttelton's conduct that cast him as 'good' but the fact this was repeatedly confirmed in print during his lifetime and long afterwards. His behaviour and the literary portraits formed a positive image too strong to be damaged by potential scandals like his wife's adultery or his close friendship with a young widow. His reputation was firmly fixed as 'our departed, truly Virtuous Friend'.[86]

9

WICKED
LORD LYTTELTON

A ghostly figure in a dream warned Thomas Lyttelton he was about to die, and three days later the premonition came true. His sudden death at the age of 35 immortalised him as the original hellraiser whose wickedness shocked the nation. And although his behaviour was no worse than many other men of the time, this intervention of fate cast him as the villain in a morality tale of divine retribution which fascinated generations of readers.

The handsome and spirited youth had quickly won notoriety for his leisure pursuits of gambling and fornication. 'A Character so full of Fire as his' was destined for trouble, and his exploits in Europe on the Grand Tour were only the start of a short life full of debauchery.[87] He later admitted, with typical frankness, 'my character is divided between an ardent desire of applause and a more than equal love of pleasure ... I will freely own that my life has been marked with an extravagance of dissipation'.[88]

Thomas's letters to relatives revealed a likeable, even endearing character with a natural charm and sense of fun. Penned in a bold, careless hand, they were full of extravagant phrases of gratitude and affection. Writing to his uncle from Naples, he promised:

> I do give you the most solemn and sacred assurances that you have nothing to fear ... Gaming I hold in detestation, and if again I ever relapse in that most absurd Vice I will forfeit my Life and my Estate, or what is as dear to me as either the good opinion of Men, and will allow myself patiently to be treated with universal Contempt.[89]

Such dramatic avowals of reform were obviously destined to failure, and he had soon lost so much money at gaming that his father ordered him to cut short his European tour and return home immediately, but he acknowledged that Thomas's 'faults are only those of most of our Young Travellers'.[90] The debts apparently prompted a hasty marriage in June 1772 to secure the hand of Apphia Peach, the wealthy widow of the governor of Calcutta, with her fortune of £20,000 (roughly £1.2 million today). Accounts of the match in Thomas's letters presented it as a calculated two-way deal in which he gained her money, while she fulfilled her ambitions in 'the expectation of a coronet'. As they left the parish church of Hales Owen after the wedding ceremony, he strode back to the carriage alone, oblivious to his new bride. Recollecting himself just as he mounted the step, he turned back to apologise but compounded the mistake by addressing Apphia as Mrs Peach instead of Mrs Lyttelton. He later told a friend, 'This fit of absence was as strange as it proved ridiculous – an omen, perhaps, of all the ungracious business which is to follow.'

Thomas expressed his pragmatic view of marital fidelity in a letter to his sister Lucy, in which he counselled her to ignore the libertine behaviour of her husband, his close friend Arthur Annesley, Lord Valentia. He wrote, 'Never had man more deep or settled affection for a wife than he has for you' but warned against 'your romantic ideas of conjugal happiness perhaps arising from splendid descriptions of it in the fashionable novels of the age'. Novelty and desire, he said, naturally faded over time but 'unconquerable affection remains together with ... sympathetic friendship', and he advised, 'Believe me, you must wink at these little sallies of youthful fire and that disposition to gallantry ... If you banish one fair one, another and another will occur.'[91]

In an amusing letter to a friend, full of literary allusions to well-known stories, including *Don Quixote* and *The Odyssey*, Thomas ironically compared the classical ideal of blissful wedlock with the mundane reality of his own marriage:

Assiduity without love, tenderness without sincerity, and dalliance without desire, afford the miserable, the hopeless, but faithful picture of my sluggish journey to the temple of Hymen ... the reality will offer to your compassionate experience the marriage of infatuation and necessity, whose legitimate and certain issue will be a separate maintenance, and perhaps a titled dowry.

Shortly afterwards he wrote to another friend, 'I am already married, and what is to follow, God alone knows … Suffice it to say at present – *Quaedam parva quidem, sed non toleranda maritis*'.[92] The Latin quotation ('Some things are indeed small; but not to be borne by husbands') was a line from a harshly satirical passage against women in Juvenal's *Satires*, Book Six. By quoting one line from a work which would have been well-known to any classically educated man, he knew the reader could pick up the implications of the passage as a whole which complained about female affectations and the irritants of marriage.

In a letter to his father, he managed to give a very different picture of the match, writing, with characteristic enthusiasm, 'I am as happy as it is possible for me to be … My dearest little woman is every thing to me, the sweetest Companion and the most sensible friend, and will make the best of wives.'[93] Perhaps this was a spontaneous expression of real (if fleeting) passion. A hasty note scribbled on the back by Apphia to her father-in-law expressed her 'tender and unutterable affection' for her new husband and noted, ominously, 'the ten thousand dormant virtues of his heart' and vowed that 'it will be the delightful employment of my life to preserve his love and enlarge his happiness – fortunate beyond expression should I succeed'. In spite of her good intentions, Thomas was already losing interest after only three months and had gone away to London when his father reported the marriage was 'in a very uncertain and dangerous state'.

The socialite Mrs Mary Delany blamed Thomas:

> *The adventurous widow*, I am afraid, at Hagley, will fail in her hopes of reform-ing a rake, and dearly pay for her presumption. Everybody is sorry, as she is well spoken of and much liked; but it is manifest that his whole scheme was to cheat her of her fortune … he has no doubt already sunk it.

Others were more generous in their assessment, such as the bluestocking Mrs Montagu, who approved of the handsome settlement Thomas had made to pay off his long-term mistress:

> I daresay Mrs L will derive much satisfaction from this honourable proceed-ing of her husband's. This act shews that there are latent virtues in his heart, and I believe she will find him upon the whole, a much better man than she had any reason to expect from the character she had heard of him … the woman who marries a rake is fortunate if in any instance he deviates into virtue. There is much to be hoped from time.

But the marriage deteriorated fast as Thomas carried on regardless with his usual shocking behaviour which was described by a family friend:

> He has lived for these last two months with only laying at home now and then, at the gaming table, at the Savoir Vivre, and with women. His treatment of his wife upon many occasions has been harsh and brutal. I think there is a mixture of insanity about him that drives him to perdition.

By February 1773 the couple had separated, and in the spring Thomas eloped to Paris for a wager of a hundred guineas, with the barmaid of Bolton's Inn at Hockerell. The escapade was quickly immortalised in print as a ribald poem *The Rape of Pomona*, followed soon afterwards by press reports in the *Morning Post* of another prank in July when he got into a brawl over an actress in Vauxhall pleasure gardens.[94] Although the incident involved several other youths, Lyttelton was blamed as the ringleader and a heated debate ensued among correspondents to all the leading London newspapers, about the rowdy behaviour of fashionable young men, known as macaronis. A popular 120-page pamphlet titled *The Vauxhall Affray; or the Macaronis Defeated* went on sale, which recounted the whole story and described Thomas as 'a man rendered a glaring phenomenon throughout Europe'. The affair was the talk of the town that summer, and Thomas retreated to the Continent until the scandal had blown over.

Then in late August his father died, and elevation to the peerage as the 2nd Baron Lyttelton seemed to mark a turning point in Thomas's life which promised a better future:

> I awoke, and behold I was a Lord! It was no unpleasant transition … from insignificance and dereliction, to be a Peer of Great Britain, with all the privileges attendant upon that character … My consequence, both internal and external, is already greatly elevated; and the *empressement* of the people about me is so suddenly increased as to be ridiculous.[95]

Despite this playful mockery of the superficial display of deference to a title, his letters revealed an underlying seriousness and acute grasp of his new social role. He was clearly well aware of the elements of role play in the possession of a peerage, but enthusiastic about a more fulfilling life where public duty would replace aimless womanising:

I have now succeeded to the possession of those privileges which are ... perhaps the best part, of my inheritance ... My exterior of things is totally changed ... No longer forced to drown sensibility to public disgrace and private inconvenience in *Circean* draughts, my character, I trust, will unfold qualities which it has not been thought to possess ... My natural genius will now have full scope for exertion in the line of political duty; My amendment must be slow and progressive, though, I trust, in the end, sincere and effectual. But be assured that ... I am perfectly sensible that there is something necessary besides title, rank, and fortune, to constitute true honour.[96]

He moved into the grand Palladian mansion Hagley Hall in Worcestershire, built for his father in 1760. But the magnificent rooms, decorated with ornate rococo plasterwork, and the vast 350-acre landscaped park held little charm for him. After his riotous London existence he found country life boring and the vast estate far too expensive to run. He confided to a relative that his father's extravagance had meant the estate was always in debt and unable to cover all the bills from its rental income:

I have suffered great *ennui* at seeing the vast expense that Hagley runs me into, and the little pleasure it affords me. I love the country at times, but I consider it a place for retirement, and am surprised to find myself 130 miles from the metropolis in an immense palace without company, and surrounded, like a deposed nabob, by a set of blackguards ... But jesting apart, Hagley is to me a gulph that swallows up all my estate.

He especially hated the intrusion of gawping carriageloads of tourists who flocked to admire his country estate, complaining that the summer visitors 'are hourly chasing me from my apartment or, strolling about the environs, keep me a prisoner in it. The Lord of the Place can never call it his during the finest part of the year. Nor am I proud, as others have been, of holding myself forth to the complimentary envy of those who come to visit it.' More to his taste was a small villa called Pitt Place, which he had recently won as payment of a wager with Lord Foley and for which he commissioned a set of drawings of female nudes to decorate the dressing room. It was set in a wooded hollow near Epsom in Surrey, and he often stayed there to enjoy its peaceful seclusion not far from the city.

Inheriting the estate and title did nothing to reduce his notoriety, and in October 1773 he was again the subject of a press attack, this time in the

Town and Country Magazine's scandal serial. His name was coupled with the actress and courtesan Mary Robinson, known as Perdita, who achieved celebrity as a mistress of the Prince of Wales. After several weeks trying unsuccessfully to seduce her, Thomas was said to have paid off some of her debts and, 'fearful to offend her benefactor, she suffered him to take such liberties as soon led him to the ultimate point of his wishes'. Their affair had then apparently included amorous frolics inside a closed carriage while Mr Robinson rode behind on horseback. The article hoped that his recently acquired title would make him review his conduct and follow his good father's example, to 'make every reparation in his power to society for the perversion of talents which would otherwise do so much honour to himself and country'.

Thomas was well aware of the distorting effects of bad publicity and the difficulty of changing a fixed public image, whatever he did now:

> Examine the world upon my subject, and you will know what confirmed prejudices it possesses against me, – that I am the continual victim of its injustice, and that, not contented to blazon forth my defects and follies into a false, unnatural magnitude, it seems pleased with the malignant task of fabricating tales to my dishonour.

His legendary wickedness ensured an inclusion in the satirical poem *The Diaboliad*, published anonymously in 1777 but written by an Eton schoolmate, William Combe. Lyttelton featured as one of the candidates considered by the devil, seeking a successor to the throne of Hell. But the verse also noted his public abilities since entering the House of Lords, describing him as a 'Peer of words,/ Well known, and honour'd in the House of Lords,/Whose Eloquence all Parallel defies!'[97] Thomas had been studying the language and imagery of Milton's poetry to help carve out a fresh identity for himself and win public applause as a respected orator:

> To attain a reputation for eloquence is my aim and ambition: and if I should acquire the art of clothing my thoughts in happy language ... or enforcing them by commanding words, I shall be indebted for such advantages to the study of our great British classic.[98]

Despite such promising indicators of maturity, his sudden demise in November 1779, and the fact that it came following the appearance of a female apparition predicting his death within three days, cast him forever as a prototype of aristocratic vice.[99] Many different published accounts of this premonition, and strange tales of his ghost being seen by a friend, intrigued the public. The avid society gossip Hester Thrale reported in her diary, 'Lord Lyttelton's Death & Dream fill everybody's Mouths ... Johnson considers the whole as false, for my own part I feel rather too disposed to believe'. Dr Johnson described it as 'the most extraordinary thing that has happened in my day'.[100]

The *London Magazine* devoted a lengthy commentary to the implications of Lord Lyttelton's death for 'the existence of a superintending Providence'.[101] It discussed alternative interpretations, including the possibility that a supernatural apparition had intervened 'to promote the reformation of a hardened sinner' but concluded that death was caused by a stomach disorder or heart disease, aggravated by a heated imagination. In an effort to prolong the mileage of a popular topic, the magazine urged readers to continue the debate by writing in with their opinions.

The commercial press was quick to cash in on the appeal of this ultimate morality tale of aristocratic corruption by publishing his collected poems and *Letters of the late Lord Lyttelton*, which reached a sixth edition by 1783, though the authorship of both works remains disputed. William Combe later claimed he had written the letters, but it seems more likely he was actually the editor as they referred to family matters of which he could not have been aware. Books of collected correspondence were very popular with readers at the time, and the introduction to Lyttelton's *Letters* commented that such private writings were, 'the most unequivocal authorities of real sentiment and opinion. Conversation is too fugitive to be remembered; public declarations may be oftentimes suspected; but the epistolary communications of friendship may be depended upon as faithful to the mind from whence they arise.' As a means of making the private public, published volumes of letters could have a substantial impact on reputation, as they did in the case of Lord Chesterfield.

The frank and charming persona which emerged from Thomas Lyttelton's letters was far from being the iconic evil rakehell of popular opinion. As a natural chameleon, he was adept at acting out different roles depending on the effect he wished to produce. And there seemed to be every hope that his early attempts to re-invent himself in the role of dutiful public figure and accomplished orator would eventually have superseded his youthful reputation. His poems were edited by a friend and executor who inherited the manuscripts. The preface to a 1780 edition of the collected verse noted 'no wonder that he attracted the censure of the age', but pointed out that:

> ... though his love of women, and of play, rendered him less attentive to the discharge of those important duties which his exalted rank in the state had imposed upon him; yet his passion for both was on the decline, when a premature death ... terminated his existence.[102]

The key factor in casting the stereotype of wickedness was his early death. Thomas died too young to change his image, which had been set firmly in print, and there was not enough time for his own hopeful forecast to come true: 'The circumstances of my past life have produced the colour of the present moment; a future period may receive another hue ... Experience may do something in my favour ... the calls of public duty may have their effect.' The conflation of real and fictional identity in the public imagination was confirmed by the memoirist Sir Nathaniel Wraxall, who wrote of Thomas:

> By the profligacy of his conduct, and the abuse of his talents, he seemed to emulate Dryden's Duke of Buckingham, or Pope's Duke of Wharton; both of whom he resembled in the superiority of his natural endowments, as well as in the peculiarity of his end.[103]

The prototype of aristocratic vice created by Thomas remained in the public imagination and in print to achieve a legendary status, which influenced another notorious hell-raiser, George Gordon Noel, 6th Baron Byron, who was born nine years after Lyttelton's death. Parallels between their lives were striking. Both were heirs to a barony, precocious and rebellious boys, over-indulged during a childhood spent living with distant relations. As youths they ran up huge debts in lives of dissipation, sexual adventure and European travel before making a disastrous brief marriage followed by adulterous liaisons. They were highly intelligent men showing early promise, with ambitions to become respected orators, but both found lasting fame as quasi-mythological figures partly as a result of an early death (Lyttelton at 35 and Byron at 36).[104]

Thomas had already created the prototype of 'the wicked Lord Lyttelton' and Byron's correspondence shows that this role had already been brought to his attention as an appealing identity which he deliberately chose to re-enact. His youthful relish at having a reputation as a rogue was clear, in a letter written from Cambridge, aged 19:

My pretensions to virtue are unluckily so few, that though I should be happy to merit, I cannot accept, your applause in that respect. One passage in your letter struck me forcibly: you mention the two Lords Lyttelton in a manner they respectively deserve, and will be surprised to hear the person who is now addressing you has been frequently compared to the *latter*. I know I am injuring myself in your esteem by this avowal, but the circumstance was so remarkable for your observation, that I cannot help relating the fact. The events of my short life have been of so singular a nature, that, though the pride commonly called honour has, and I trust ever will, prevent me from disgracing my name by a mean or cowardly action, I have been already held up as the Votary of licentiousness, and the disciple of infidelity. How far justice may have dictated this accusation, I cannot pretend to say; but … I am made worse than I really am.[105]

He was again trying out this thrillingly villainous persona as he concluded another letter the next day, 'you have here a compendium of the sentiments of the *wicked* George Lord Byron'. The editor of the 1835 edition of Byron's works noted:

There is here, evidently, a degree of pride in being thought to resemble the wicked Lord Lyttelton, and, lest his known irregularities should not bear him out in the pretension, he refers mysteriously, as was his habit, to certain untold events in his life, to warrant the parallel.[106]

Byron's letter, with its youthful self-dramatisation, disarming frankness and faintly ironic charm, strongly echoed the style of Thomas's correspondence, which had by then been continuously in print for almost thirty years (the sixth edition was published in 1806). There were also parallels in his enjoyment of public notoriety for sexual adventures, the assertion that reality has been distorted by gossip, and a more serious underlying awareness of his noble heritage and personal honour. It revealed how Byron was already beginning the process of creating his image as a wicked but irresistible aristocratic villain by choosing to copy the wicked prototype of Lyttelton.

What he could not foresee, of course, was his own tragic early death that would cast him permanently as the mythical Byronic hero. His legendary status developed further through his writings, which had a substantial influence on later European literature. Soon after his death in 1824, admirers began copying aspects of his dress, manner and sexual reputation, and visiting associated places and people, as a means of enhancing their own celebrity. The imagined characteristics of the bad and dangerous Byronic hero have continued to exert a vicarious thrill on successive audiences of readers. Sexual scandals and stereotypes of aristocratic vice were guaranteed to be lucrative for publishers, especially when God seemed to intervene by punishing sinners like Lyttelton and Byron, and Lady Abergavenny before them, with a dramatic early death.

Part Three

Staging Adultery (1770s–1780s)

'Conjugal infidelity is become so general
that it is hardly considered as criminal;
especially in the fashionable world.'

Trials for Adultery, 1779

10

Courtroom Dramas

An amusing article in the *London Magazine* reflected a general public unease about the perilous state of matrimony. It listed spoof national statistics on wedlock which included 5,000 wives eloped, 500,000 married pairs 'living in a state of open war', 100,000 pairs 'living in a state of inward hatred … though concealed from the world', 10,000 separated, and only 100 couples 'absolutely and entirely happy'.[1] There was no doubt that the number of divorces and actions for crim. con. were growing every year, but those few cases which became common knowledge were seen as evidence of a much larger hidden problem.

Recorded crim. con. suits in England increased rapidly from 1770, reaching their height in the period between 1790 and 1830. However, numbers were still relatively low due to the exorbitant costs of litigation, which meant that around half of all cases were brought by members of the gentry and aristocracy. The widespread publicity given to crim. con. trials and Parliamentary divorces involving peers added to the perception that adultery was rife in aristocratic circles. In fact only a tiny minority of around eighty peers, which was less than 4 per cent of men holding a title during the period, were participants in such cases.[2]

The rising number of crim. con. suits was partly attributed to the huge growth in monetary damages being awarded by courts from 1780 to 1830 and the requirement of a successful crim. con. action in order to obtain a divorce in Parliament. The amount of damages awarded by juries was based on the wealth and rank of the plaintiff and defendant, and legal arguments in cases reflected the changing moral values of each period.[3] A woman's body was legally her husband's property, as were any material possessions she had and even her children. In the century up to 1770 prosecutions emphasised the defendant's trespass of the husband's property rights over his wife's body, but later the focus changed to compensation paid for the loss of the comforts of matrimony. By 1800 a moral reaction had set in against the payment of enormous damages, which could exceed £10,000 (roughly £600,000 today). This had encouraged deliberate collusion between the parties, where the majority of husbands did not accept the monetary award but in bringing the action enabled both themselves and their wives to divorce and remarry.[4]

The only way to get divorced was by a special Act of Parliament, which was granted to men and only very rarely to women. Wives seeking a divorce had to prove that additional acts of serious cruelty or sodomy made the marriage unsustainable, as evidence of a husband's adultery was not by itself accepted as sufficient grounds for a case. Adultery cases crossed the threshold from private life into the public domain when they reached the courtroom, either at the Courts of King's Bench or Common Pleas in London for crim. con. cases heard under common law, or the ecclesiastical courts in matrimonial suits for separation and restitution of conjugal rights under canon law.

The physical space of the courtroom had many similarities to the structure of the Georgian theatre, and it too was the venue for a public show. The *dramatis personae* of defendants, witnesses and costumed lawyers recited their set speeches in the enclosed performance area while the jury sat listening in a side box and the robed judge presided from his elevated bench. Looking down on these performers were spectators watching from the public gallery, who interrupted the production with shouted comments when roused by what they had heard. In contrast to the theatre, of course, the main legal action took place in the central 'pit' area and not on a raised stage, but the courtroom was just as much a dedicated space designed for acting and viewing dramatic performances.

The outcome of adultery cases largely depended on the ingenuity with which stories of infidelity were shaped and acted out in the courtroom, where the complexities of personal behaviour over many years were simplified into an apparently straightforward moral tale hinging on the actions of the sinning wife. The offence was doubly serious in the case of peeresses who were expected to set a good example:

When a woman (especially of the superior class) has lost that inestimable jewel, virtue; alas! how is she fallen! her nobility no longer claims our reverence; her coronet ceases to be enviable; her birth (which she has disgraced) but adds to her offence; as … it was incumbent on her to have been an example of purity to the rest of her sex: she is indeed become the object of the scorn, pity, and derision of her relations, her former associates, and the public.[5]

Courtroom narratives, composed ostensibly of objective legal fact, were devised to deliberately mould the truth into a fictitious script featuring the familiar stock parts of seducer, adulteress and wronged husband. A cast of witnesses was called to narrate this version of the adultery tale by giving evidence, which usually managed to conceal the husband's own adultery with the selective use of truth and omission of key facts. In these false narratives, laying bare the sordid details of illicit sex, the shameful figure of the unfaithful wife, her callous seducer and the sympathetic persona of the innocent deceived husband were revealed. In the public theatre of the courtroom such roles were enacted for those present at the hearing but then played to new audiences in published pamphlets and adultery trials, which were widely read and influential in shaping public opinion.

These legal stories of adultery showed the different gender roles acted out in public and in the hidden domestic lives of the aristocracy. The meaning of male and female roles in society was much debated at the time, partly as a result of expanding options in the newly commercial culture. Enlightenment philosophy influenced ideas about 'natural' male qualities of rationality and intellect, while femininity was also redefined to embrace an idealised vision of virtue and piety. In the domestic ideology of the emerging middle classes, masculinity was 'decisively equated with the public sphere of "work, politics and power", femininity with that of the private sphere of the "home, family and emotion".'[6] This reassessment of gender roles was discussed widely in newspapers and periodicals, fiction and polemical texts, such as the radical writer Mary Wollstonecraft's ground-breaking *Vindication of the Rights of Women*, which argued for female education and independence, and intellectual and moral equality with men, but still viewed a woman's main role as motherhood.

The issue of maternity was inevitably at the heart of most aristocratic adultery cases, and courtroom narratives portrayed pregnant adulteresses as especially repugnant because they so flagrantly subverted ideals of virtuous womanhood. For a peer's wife the moral dimension was coupled with the more important aspect of property claims by illegitimate offspring, with the consequent threat to the family's hereditary rank and fortune.

Many cases were precipitated by the public knowledge of a wife's pregnancy by her lover, which forced the husband to act quickly in order to protect his legitimate bloodline. This happened in both civil suits for crim. con. and matrimonial suits for separation. The main task of witnesses called in court was to establish the presence of the wife alone with her lover on one or more occasions and to confirm that the husband had no private access to her body during the timespan of possible conception. In these trials the wronged husband was mentioned only fleetingly, as a powerful figure in the background of the adultery tale who commanded the moral high ground. He had in fact masterminded the creation of a story, told entirely from his viewpoint by the prosecution and a succession of witnesses. In crim. con. actions the wife's lover could of course employ his own defence counsel and witnesses, but in no case was the adulteress ever allowed to speak out publicly in her own defence.

Exposure of the adulterous wife's pregnancy was the catalyst for legal action which brought disgrace on women such as Lady Abergavenny, Lady Bolingbroke, the Duchess of Grafton and the Marquis of Granby's daughter, Lady Frances, who eloped from the Surrey home of her husband, the Earl of Tyrconnel, and at the time of the trial was six months pregnant with her lover's child. Wives like this, who stepped outside the female ideal of virtuous motherhood for whatever reason, effectively relinquished their place in society and could expect little sympathy, even from other women. Commenting on the Parliamentary anti-adultery bills with characteristic bluntness, the diarist Mrs Thrale believed there could be no excuses for adulteresses and harsher punishment was the only deterrent:

> Was a Woman to have her Ring Finger cut off, her Lover would hesitate a
> little in marrying her I'll warrant him; & She well deserves a Punishment
> as severe as that at least, for thus madly transgressing – however provoked –
> the great Laws of both God and Man.[7]

Such assumptions that virtue was the mainstay of a woman's identity were reflected in a newly popular type of drama known as 'she-tragedy', with its theatrical role models of virtuous heroines who chose to die defending their chastity. A dramatic speech by Calista, the tragic heroine of Nicholas Rowe's play *The Fair Penitent*, was actually quoted in court by the defence lawyer

Thomas Erskine during the adultery trial of Lady Elizabeth Howard to try and win sympathy for a fallen woman. Many of these stage melodramas featured a devoted mother as the heroine, such as Isabella in David Garrick's adaptation of Thomas Southerne's *The Fatal Marriage*, a play that appealed to contemporary sensibility and proved to be a big crowd-puller. Believing her husband to be dead, Isabella was forced by debts to marry a rich suitor in order to care for her child, but she killed herself in remorse when the missing husband reappeared.

In real-life cases, the adulteress almost invariably became invisible to society both metaphorically and often quite literally by exclusion from fashionable circles, being exiled to a quiet life in the country or even disappearing to Europe. This was the fate of Lady Penelope Ligonier, who was divorced by her husband following a passionate affair with an Italian count, and escaped the scandal to live in France.

Penelope, the eldest daughter of the diplomat George Pitt, 1st Baron Rivers, was just seventeen when she married Edward Ligonier, a tall and handsome army colonel who was heir to an Irish viscountcy and the King's aide-de-camp. Within five years she became involved with an Italian nobleman, Count Vittorio Alfieri, whom she had met in London society circles, and the couple began meeting openly for walks alone in St James' Park and Hyde Park. Despite warnings from her husband about her conduct, the affair continued and soon the lovers were holding secret assignations at her country house in Cobham, Kent, where she would let him in after dark while Ligonier was away on military duties. On several occasions there had been reports of a foreigner seen in the grounds and footprints left by the garden gate, which were making the servants suspicious about what was going on.

On one evening Count Alfieri arrived by post chaise from London disguised in an old blue coat but was spotted by the postboy, who noticed his unusual foreign-looking appearance and striking 'very red carrotty hair'. Penelope had earlier asked the gardener for the key to the gate and went down to let in her lover, but they were seen by the footman William Pepper and the groom. The next morning, William checked one of the shuttered bedchambers, which had been left unoccupied and without a fire for three months, and found the bed had obviously been used. The bedclothes were rumpled, there was hair powder on the pillows and two telltale hollow dints were impressed into the feather mattress.

With such clear evidence of guilt, the house steward felt it his duty to report what was going on when his master got home. Lord Ligonier was furious. He immediately ordered a chaise to send his wife back to her father's house, then hurried to London intent on revenge. Afraid for her lover and desperate to avoid a scandal, Penelope dispatched a letter warning that her husband was on his way, writing, 'My Lord knows the whole. A servant saw you in the garden. Think of the consequences for him, you, and for me.' But it was too late. Ligonier was intent on preserving his honour, so he collected a sword in Bond Street and went to find the count at the Opera House, where he challenged him to a duel. The sword-fight took place in Green Park, and with his military training Ligonier was more than a match for the count, who was quickly wounded and confessed to the adultery.

At the trial for crim. con. in the late autumn of 1771, the court heard all the sordid details of the illicit affair, which had included a furtive tryst in a rented room in The Rose at Dartford. The country house servants were each called into the witness box to give evidence about the count's overnight stays during Lord Ligonier's absence. The French lady's maid described how she had tried to avert disaster for her mistress and conceal proof of the affair by lying to other servants about a stained bedsheet that had gone missing, saying she had burnt a hole in it.

The case caused a sensation and was avidly followed by the press, with regular updates about the notorious couple's activities and social engagements. A column of brief news reports in the *London Evening Post* of 14 May 1771 noted, 'Count A---i, who was wounded in a duel with Lord L---er, is nephew to the Spanish A---r', followed by an ostensibly separate sentence clearly intended as a clue for readers, 'On Monday Lady Ligonier set out for France.' The *Middlesex Journal* of 7 September joked that 'Lady Ligonier will speedily be preferred to an Italian regiment', while the *London Evening Post* reported playfully on 10 October: 'Lady Ligonier is now pensioned at a little farmhouse near Ardres, a town between Calais and Boulogne, where she leads a life of great regularity and example.' And most of the main London newspapers, including the *Whitehall Evening Post* and the *Gazetteer and Daily Advertiser*, carried progress reports of the Ligonier Divorce Bill through Parliament, where it was finally granted early in 1772.

Several books of collected adultery trials included the case, publishing full transcripts of the crim. con. hearing and the guilty couple's long and melodramatic love letters, which would not have been out of place in a popular romance novel. Count Alfieri's letters to Penelope were urgent declarations of love and despair at 'the precipice I am dragging you towards'. In one note he threatened suicide when they had not been able to meet and he had only snatched a fleeting glimpse of her through a window.

Penelope also wrote of her despair and thoughts of dying, telling him to go away travelling for a year to try and break their bond, and exclaiming, 'Why should you be so much above the common rank, why was I not contented with some common lover such as is every day to be met with?' These overblown histrionics were ridiculed in the press, and the *Middlesex Journal* mockingly paraphrased one of the count's effusive declarations that, 'when he is in her company his blood is all milk, but when he is absent from her it is all gall'. It added, 'The lady's letters do not discredit her understanding and prove that her disorder was not in her *head*.'

The whole dramatic affair was more enthralling than fiction, and in fact the story was seized on and re-written as a novella called *The Generous Husband; or, The History of Lord Lelius and the Fair Emilia*, which was published the same year of the adultery trial. It described the heroine as 'not a first rate beauty' but 'witty, and well-tempered' with 'a certain degree of simplicity and native innocence'. In the foreword, the anonymous author explained:

> The materials for the following memoirs are, for the most part, genuine and authentic, wherever there is the least deviation from truth, it is solely with a view of exposing vice, promoting virtue, innocently entertaining the reader, conveying instruction by example. Nevertheless, I have not dared to varnish over crimes for which no possible reparation can be made, though they may have some claim to our forgiveness.

Both the Ligoniers eventually remarried, but Penelope's notoriety continued. Several years later she appeared alongside other well-known adulteresses in a satirical poem and print in the *London Magazine* of April 1777, entitled *The Diabo-Lady*, where various depraved women competed for the devil's attention.

Noblewomen who had relinquished the only role society allowed them, as wife and mother producing legitimate heirs, were left facing a miserable future. The consequences of adultery were often catastrophic for women, who faced social disgrace and total estrangement from friends, relatives and, worst of all, their own children. Remarriage might bring the prospect of partial social rehabilitation, but in cases of separation without divorce in which there was no prospect of remarrying, the situation was even bleaker. Lady Henrietta Grosvenor was forced to live retired from society for over thirty years after her husband's crim. con. action against the king's brother, the Duke of Cumberland, following their nine-month affair. Although she took the highly unusual step of counter-suing Lord Grosvenor for prior adultery with a series of prostitutes, and was granted a separation and join-ture settlement by the ecclesiastical court at Doctors' Commons in 1771, her legal action permanently precluded divorce. In the eyes of society she became thereafter *persona non grata*.

Adultery naturally had implications for the wider aristocratic kinship network, and relatives of the guilty culprits often tried to intervene before it was too late to prevent a family scandal. When Lady Elizabeth Howard's affair became known, her husband suggested that to avoid meeting her lover she should leave London and go to visit her parents, so he exchanged letters with her father to enlist his help in an attempt to resolve the situation. Baroness Percy openly conducted her liaison while she was living at her sister's country house while her husband was away with his regiment. She invited her young lover to stay for three weeks as a guest in an adjoining bedroom, shocking her family, who condemned the behaviour as injurious to her honour. When Anne refused to break it off, they left the house in order to safeguard their own reputations by distancing themselves from the scandal. After her indiscreet extra-marital affair became known, she was met with complete social ostracism when 'ladies of fashion and character declined [her] company'.

Such women who challenged the prescribed role of the aristocratic wife were usually shunned by their own families, who acted according to an unspoken code of conduct which effectively upheld the *status quo* and to some degree acted as a deterrent to other wives tempted to sin. In assuming the guilty persona of the adulteress, a woman was forced to give up her whole place in society. Virtuous motherhood underpinned the entire iden-tity of an aristocratic wife and when this was subverted, there was nothing else left for her to be. While domestic duty and the public role of wives were synonymous, for peers the male role was framed entirely as a public one. So although adultery could have an impact on men's public lives, it did not completely demolish their social position as it did for their wives.

11

ADULTERY TRIALS
FOR SALE

Shocking tales of cases heard in the criminal and civil courts became popular entertainment in the Georgian period. The ready-made plots and colourful characters in published trial reports proved to be compelling reading, as exciting short stories taken from real life. Collections of legal proceedings for adultery were being printed from the 1750s, and by the 1770s had developed into a highly lucrative literary genre for publishers.

Titles such as *Adultery Anatomized*, *The Cuckold's Chronicle* and the hefty seven-volume *Trials for Adultery: or, The History of Divorces. Being Select Trials at Doctors Commons, for Adultery, Cruelty, Fornication, Impotence &c* were cleverly marketed to appeal to readers as juicy scandals in the guise of educational morality tales. Referring to the latest Parliamentary anti-adultery bill, the preface to the first volume of *Trials for Adultery* published in 1779 commented that 'conjugal infidelity is become so general that it is hardly considered criminal; especially in the fashionable world'. It hoped the book would 'effect what the law cannot', by ensuring the details of illicit sex were 'publickly circulated', preserving others:

> ... from the like crimes, from the fear of shame, when the fear of punishment may have but little force ... It may, perhaps, deter the wavering wanton from the completion of her wishes ... it will shew to the world in general by what gradual steps affection sinks into indifference, indifference into disgust, and disgust into aversion: the consequences of which are but too apparent from the perusal of these volumes.[8]

Exposure of the secret lives led by the aristocracy was a clear selling-point, and the title page boasted that the book contained 'a complete History of the Private Life, Intrigues, and Amours of many Characters in the most elevated Sphere: every Scene and Transaction, however ridiculous, whimsical, or extraordinary, being fairly represented, as becomes a faithful Historian, who is fully determined not to sacrifice *Truth* at the Shrine of *Guilt* and *Folly*.'

Legal stories of adultery were in fact narratives constructed in a series of layers, each layer acting as a filter of subjectivity by presenting what happened from a different perspective. First the key facts were selected and shaped by the prosecution to secure the required outcome for the husband, then events were reinterpreted by trial witnesses and finally the entire case was summarised by a shorthand-taker and edited for publication in pamphlets, books and newspaper reports.

The Cuckold's Chronicle criticised the dull legal style of other rival published trials and announced its aim was 'to present to the Public, a series of circumstances of such mingled seriousness and absurdity … as must arrest every attention, and furnish food for every disposition; and this we shall convey in the easy mode of *Narrative*'.[9] The attraction of being an easy read was a point highlighted by the two-volume *A New and Compleat Collection of the Most Remarkable Trials for Adultery*, published in 1780, which presented roughly edited cases as racy tales that were flagged up on the title-page, 'Given in the Way of a Narrative; not in the Tedious Form of Depositions'.

Whether describing themselves as narratives or histories, such collections skilfully packaged amusing and salacious details of scandals which were bound to enthral readers. What they found particularly fascinating was the wealth of information, normally locked away from general public view, about life inside the Georgian country house. There could never be any secrets kept from the household staff, who were constantly on hand to ensure the smooth running of domestic routines. This meant that moments of being completely alone were rare for the family. The watchful eyes of the servants were everywhere.

Dozens of servants were called to give circumstantial evidence at adultery trials, each outlining their own version of events and revealing all the minutiae of everyday life, including the times and procedures of basic tasks such as serving meals, tending fires, lighting candles and closing window shutters. They often described the layout and furniture of rooms, the conversations and amorous activities of their employers and even the most intimate details of bodily fluids staining bedsheets or clothes.

Sometimes the love letters delivered by servants played a pivotal role as evidence of adulterous liaisons. This happened in the cases of the Duchess of Grafton, who sent daily notes to her lover via a footman; of Elizabeth Howard, who relied on a nursemaid; and of the Marchioness of Carmarthen, who wrote to a military officer via a chairman. The passionate outpourings of lovers in the throes of an affair could appear ridiculous to the scrutiny of observers, and their letters proved useful ammunition with which to humiliate their authors both inside the courtroom and in the wider public sphere of print. Trial reports often printed intimate love letters between the protagonists which were read out in court, and these proved especially fascinating for readers familiar with the epistolary novel, who enjoyed this privileged access to the lovers' feelings.

The rambling and illiterate epistles sent by HRH the Duke of Cumberland to Lady Grosvenor during their affair were widely mocked in the press and later reprinted as pamphlets, one of which ran to seven editions as the public clamoured for more and more copies.[10] Recounting his dreams in one note, the duke wrote, 'I then prayed for you *my dearest love kissed your dearest little Hair* and laye down and dreamt of you had you on the dear little *couch* ten thousand times in my arms kissing you and telling you how much I loved and adored you.'

Another letter said:

> My Dear little Angel I am this instant going out of Town ten thousand thanks for your kind note I am sure nothing could make my aking [sic] heart to night bearable to me than when you say you are sensible how much I love you … dont [sic] mention to D that I wrote by her servant to you for I have ordered him not to tell – Adieu Good night God bless the Angel of my Soul.

But despite this apparently heartfelt, if transitory, passion for his 'dear little angel', he abandoned her for a courtesan shortly after the court case and married another woman the following year in October 1771.[11]

The Grosvenor case illustrated how various personae were presented through a series of different stories, which overlapped and gradually altered after each re-telling. The initial crim. con. action at King's Bench in July 1770 set out the familiar principal parts of the sinning wife, wronged husband and cunning seducer. The second court case at Doctors Commons (which included Lady Grosvenor's countersuit proving prior adultery by her husband) re-framed the action to reveal him as an unsavoury character with a predilection for the lowest type of dirty street girls.

This countersuit meant that it was one of the few cases where the adulteress's side of the story was fully told in public, through the witnesses called to give evidence on her behalf. The royal connection and explicit descriptions of illicit sexual encounters given during these trials ensured enormous publicity for the case and spawned many different publications, including 3s pamphlets, books, periodical articles and novels, which revelled in all the sordid detail. The press made the most of the whole tawdry affair, and the case created acres of print long after the adultery trial was over as newspapers vied with each other to publish both serious commentary and satirical entertainment. There were also many column inches devoted to lengthy debates on the wider issues, like the implications of adultery and the public role of minor royals. Both HRH and Grosvenor were widely vilified for their profligate and dishonourable behaviour. The *Town and Country Magazine* ran an exclusive on Grosvenor's squalid sex life and addiction to prostitutes, nicknaming him 'the Cheshire Cornuto'.

The entire 512-page volume six of *Trials for Adultery* featured the case, allowing readers to share with witnesses in the vicarious thrill of watching adultery in action. Lady Camilla D'Onhoff described how she had caught the lovers at it when they visited her home in Cavendish Square, London:

> [I] saw Lady Grosvenor lying upon her back upon a couch in the drawing-room, with her petticoats up, and the Duke of Cumberland's breeches were unbuttoned, and he was laying upon the said Lady Grosvenor, and his body was in motion, and he and Lady Grosvenor were at such time in the very act of carnal copulation.[12]

There had been many other furtive couplings in snatched moments. The guilty pair were eventually entrapped during a stay at the White Hart inn, St Albans, by the servants attending them there, on a journey back to London. When the party arrived at the inn at half past five, the Grosvenor's butler, Matthew Stevens, found out that a man he suspected to be Cumberland was already there. He bored two holes in the door to Lady Grosvenor's bedchamber and stopped them up with paper. At around eleven o'clock, after serving supper and taking her a glass of negus (the hot sweetened wine and water she liked at bedtime), Stevens fetched one of the footman and his brother, who kept the nearby Woolpack. Together they broke open the bedchamber door with an iron poker and found the lovers inside. The duke was standing in the middle of the room buttoning his waistcoat, fully dressed in a darkish coat, a silk handkerchief about his neck, a dark wig, white breeches and stockings. He stood 'very much confused, like a statue, and could not speak', then tried to leave the room and began denying any wrongdoing.

Such embarrassing exposure of Cumberland's private sexual habits revealed to the public a very different side to the formal official persona he normally displayed. Thirty years later, in his maiden speech in the House of Lords during the 1800 Adultery Prevention Bill, he commented without apparent irony that few seducers wanted to marry their conquests, and he empathised with the plight of the outcast adulteress who was unable to remarry.[13] Obviously other peers present in Parliament were well aware of the unspoken subtext created by his own past conduct, and in fact, his personal experience probably gave the speech more substance for being founded in truth. As the prosecution counsel in the crim. con. action commented, 'He forgot what he owed to himself, to his birth, to the public … he forgot that and his own dignity' in debauching a peer's wife.[14]

Like the duke, the Right Hon. Richard Lord Grosvenor also appeared a ridiculous, unedifying figure in the guise of sexual predator, described by one witness as 'a tall, thin person, of a black complexion, marked with the smallpox, and has a longish nose'. Not exactly the stuff of romantic dreams. A series of witnesses called on behalf of his wife detailed his sleazy encounters with prostitutes in the back streets of London.

In an alley near Leicester-fields he met Elizabeth Roberts, asking, 'how do you do, my little wicked? Will you go and drink a glass of wine with me?', and he arranged to meet her in an upstairs room of a house known as the Hotel. There they drank 5s bowls of arrack punch and Grosvenor, spotting a picture of a naked woman over the fireplace, told the girl she would look as well naked as the woman in the print. He desired her to undress, but at first she objected to this unusual request. When he insisted, she did strip herself naked and lay down on the green bed. Following this he:

> … came to her, and was ready for action; but his breeches hurting the deponent's thighs, he got off again, and pulled off his breeches and shoes, and then came to her again, and r------d her; after which the deponent sat quite naked upon his Lordship's lap, for near a quarter of an hour, he being all that time without his breeches and shoes; and then Lord Grosvenor r------d her again.

Another prostitute, Mrs Molesworth, had also acted as his procuress and introduced other very young girls to him 'for his carnal use and knowledge' at her house in Arlington Street. The court judgement stated that ever since his marriage Grosvenor 'hath led, and doth continue to lead, a vicious, lewd, and debauched life … by visiting, corresponding with, and carnally knowing, divers strange women of loose character and prostitutes, at lodging-houses, and public places of resort.'[15] The actual details of this degrading behaviour by a nobleman, and its stark contrast with his public image, was both deeply shocking and tantalising for readers.

Despite the serious personal consequences of the trials, Lady Grosvenor herself emerged from the flood of printed material as a largely sympathetic figure who had been drawn into a misguided affair with the prince as a consequence of her disastrous marriage. In one of the novels written about the case, *Harriet: or, The Innocent Adultress*, she was portrayed as a charismatic heroine of 'superior beauty … gentleness and sweetness of disposition' who was a victim of her cruel husband.[16] The source of the plot in the real-life Grosvenor case was explicitly laid out in a lengthy preface which declared its intention of championing the cause of the injured sex. And, in the characteristic justification put forward by much literature of the period, the narrative was presented as interwoven strands of both fact and fiction. The author explained he had 'selected the material facts' but 'found it necessary to frame his characters – in a way the best to serve his present purpose – without regard to truth … [as] fancied persons', and concluded by hoping 'the whole will be, as in truth it is, received as fiction – excepting as to what appeared in evidence upon the trial'.

Separated but unable to divorce because of her husband's prior adultery, and permanently excluded from society, Henrietta spent the next few decades of her life living in retirement on the annual allowance of £1,200 granted by the court. She at last found happiness many years later when Lord Grosvenor died in 1802 and, at the age of 57, she was free to marry Lt-General George Porter, an MP many years her junior.

Only spicy sex scandals among the highest ranks attracted such extensive coverage in print as the Grosvenor case, but divorce lower down the social scale also drew some publicity if trials were especially titillating. One bizarre case of impotence, included in *Trials for Adultery: or, The History of Divorces* for its novelty value, was that of an Italian eunuch who ran off with a 14-year-old girl to whom he taught music. Ferdinando Tenducci was taken by his parents to be castrated when he was about 8 years old, sent to the Conservatorio at Naples for musical training, and later toured Europe as one of the celebrated castrati opera singers. He also gave private singing lessons, and while working in Dublin he took advantage of the naivety of one of his young pupils, Dorothea Maunsell, persuading her to go through an unlawful wedding ceremony.

In the later court action taken by Dorothea in 1775 to dissolve her marriage, no gruesome detail was spared of poor Tenducci's abnormal private parts. One witness, who had shared lodgings with him, 'often saw his privy parts' and said 'Tenducci's p---s was like a person's little finger, and his scrotum, or testicle-bag, was smooth and flat, without any swelling, as in the testicle-bags of entire men.' Another witness, a grocer who lodged with the singer at a house in Dublin, told the court that curiosity had made him question Tenducci about his castration: 'He thereupon unbuttoned his breeches and shewed the scar of the said operation … there were but very few hairs about Tenducci's private parts, and his scrotum, or testicle bag, at that time, appeared shrivelled, without anything contained in it to denote a testicle.' The grocer described how one day he saw Tenducci take a red velvet purse from his breeches pocket, and asked if it contained a religious relic. The eunuch replied, 'No; I have got my testicles preserved in this purse, and have had them here since my castration.' The judge ruled that the marriage was null and void.

An affair that caused another sensation was exposed at the crim. con. trial of Lady Seymour Dorothy Worsley. She was the wife of a baronet who had apparently encouraged her liaison with George Bisset, a fellow officer in the Hampshire Militia, and even arranged for him to spy on her stark naked in the bath. There was already gossip about Lady Worsley's dubious reputation, and the case sparked plenty of press coverage, including reports of the trial and an article in the risqué *Rambler's Magazine*. There were also many satirical prints for sale, most notably James Gillray's caricature titled *Sir Richard Worse-than-Sly, Exposing his Wifes Bottom; – O fye!* which graphically depicted a scene described during the trial, where Worsley held Bisset on his shoulders so he could look through the window at his wife stepping naked into the bath.

Another case involving a baronet's wife was the adultery of Lady Annabella Blake with George Boscawen, an officer in the Horse Grenadier Guards and MP for Truro. Lady Blake had accompanied her husband to the West Indies, living for several years on his sugar plantation on the island of St Christopher's, before sailing home to England alone in May 1775 to care for their five children at the family seat in Suffolk. She began an affair with Boscawen and the following summer the couple eloped to France. Witnesses at the crim. con. trial included the butler, the nursery maid and an Italian hairdresser called Vincienzo Moro, who was employed as Boscawen's valet and was able to describe their daily routine and sleeping arrangements in minute detail.

Although books of collected adultery trials included cases from various social classes, those involving the peerage naturally excited most public interest and were quickly seized on by the press. George Carpenter, the Earl of Tyrconnel, was just another titled name in the lists appearing in newspapers of fashionable figures attending society events until his divorce in 1777 brought a new and less welcome notoriety as a cuckold. Most of the leading daily papers carried regular reports on the progress of the Tyrconnel Divorce Bill, including the *St James Chronicle*, the *Morning Post* and the *Morning Chronicle*. And the full forty-page transcript of the court case at Doctors' Commons was printed in volume six of the bestseller *Trials for Adultery*, including an illustration of his wife and her lover 'amusing themselves on a sopha'. It was a very public humiliation.

He had been married to Lady Frances, the Marquis of Granby's daughter, for just four years when she started an affair with an army captain called Charles Loraine Smith. They arranged meetings in Hyde Park, rode out together on horseback and frequented public amusements like Ranelagh or Vauxhall Pleasure Gardens most evenings. The footman Samuel Merret noticed that the countess always gave Captain Smith a lift back to his lodgings in Portland Street in her coach, often travelling miles out of her way to ensure that other guests were dropped off first, leaving Smith alone with her for the last quarter of an hour.

When the family were in residence at Randall's, their country house in Surrey, Captain Smith breakfasted there on four mornings with the countess while her husband was away visiting his grandmother in Hampshire. Matters reached a crisis on Tuesday 13 July while Lord Tyrconnel was staying at Randall's. The countess was at their London home in Hanover Square, and while most of the household servants were out on errands she sent the porter Samuel Dickweed to fetch a chairman. When he returned, she had eloped with her lover.

On the Saturday night about ten o'clock, Captain Smith knocked on the door of a lodging-house in Rathbone Place, St Pancras, kept by Mrs Ann Hooper, and asked if they had lodgings for a single lady, just come out of the country. She showed him up to the first floor consisting of a dining room and bedchamber but insisted on seeing the lady first, saying she 'did not like to take a single lady as many of them were bad, and might get a bad name to the house'. Smith assured her the lady 'would see no company, and give very little trouble', so Mrs Hooper agreed to let the rooms for a guinea and an half a week. At the time she had no idea who the lady was, but, as she told the court later, she afterwards realised it was Lady Tyrconnel 'from what she read in the news-papers'.

Mary Mears, the lodging-house servant, observed how Captain Smith constantly visited the lady, sometimes coming to breakfast and staying till dinner or after midnight. Mary 'heard her singing to him, and laughing, and heard her tell him he took a great many liberties with her, and that he had the greatest assurance of any man she ever knew'. One evening, when the countess had been there for more than a week, Mary entered the dining room abruptly and saw the pair on a sofa together kissing, and then they both started up in great confusion. A few days later, the countess sent for an old woman who was a fortune-teller. Later, in the kitchen, the old woman asked if Mary knew who the lady was and told her she was the Marquis of Granby's daughter.

Desperate to avert a worse scandal, Lord Tyrconnel went to the lodgings and asked his wife to return home, promising to overlook what had happened. But by now the countess was pregnant with her lover's child and she refused, moving instead to a furnished house at Stanford Brook. A 53-year-old widow, Ann Pearce, went to live-in there as a servant and was able to tell the court all about Captain Smith's overnight visits. On several mornings she found that the bed made up for him was unused, while the countess's bed 'appeared very much tumbled' with the 'marks of two persons having lain therein'.

As final confirmation that the countess was carrying a bastard child, the Tyrconnel's former housemaid, Elizabeth White, gave evidence that the earl and countess had parted beds about the middle of March. While making the beds she had usually seen the shifts worn by the countess and noticed she 'was regularly out of order every month, as women generally are by nature, till the twenty-seventh of May last'. There could be no doubt about her guilt. The earl won the court case, and a few months later, in May 1777, the bill to dissolve the marriage was passed by Parliament. Yet another aristocratic marriage had ended, with all its embarrassing dirty linen washed in public. Whose would be next?

12

SECRET
ASSIGNATIONS

Published trial reports, with their mass of detail about daily life, showed how the peripatetic lifestyle of peers could give them the necessary freedom to indulge in illicit love affairs. Opportunities could be grasped by lovers brought together during the annual round of visits to country houses and fashionable spa towns, and the whirlwind sociability of the annual London Season. Participation in family, social or public activities, which often entailed lengthy journeys around the country, meant that married couples spent regular periods apart. Within this social framework infidelities often seemed to develop in a typical pattern: initial casual meetings in public places were followed by assignations at the marital home in London or the country, or secret visits to lodging houses, inns and rented houses, as the affair developed.

Court reports showed that adultery often took place during the husband's absence on estate, political or family duties. The Marchioness of Carmarthen invited her lover to her bedchamber while her husband was away for eight days in Bath visiting his sick father, the Duke of Leeds. The marquis returned home for a fortnight and then went alone to Yorkshire, while his wife spent two nights at their home in Sion Hill. Similarly, Lady Sarah Bunbury eloped with Lord William Gordon while her husband was away from home attending Parliament, and Lady Percy met her lover in the country while Baron Percy was abroad commanding his regiment in North America.

In these narratives charting the unfolding of adulterous love, recounted by witnesses in court, a large part of each trial was spent in establishing the opportunity to commit adultery through circumstantial evidence. Servants' accounts of what they saw and heard played an important part, so grooms, chairmen and coachmen often gave evidence of journeys made by the erring wife, while servants at inns or lodgings described clandestine visits. Unexpected disruption of the normal household routines could often provide clues to suspicious behaviour. Servants therefore outlined the usual daily activities and how these suddenly changed during visits by the wife's lover.

The attractions of fashionable town life were notoriously tempting for young women eager to join in the constant round of assemblies, balls and entertainments. But despite the moral dangers lurking beneath the surface of polite sociability, forbidding a wife to participate could easily provoke marital disharmony. As one writer warned, 'The husband sees his young wife giving into dissipation and public amusements: – hurries her into solitude and leaves her with the most dangerous of all companions, her own imagination. The stillness of the country … is unfit for the mind of a happy wife.'[17] The emerging commercialised leisure culture had created a host of new social venues for the moneyed classes, and with this came the chance to mix in a wide circle in public places which could be used as a cover for more clandestine arrangements.

Lady Elizabeth Howard was able to arrange frequent meetings with her lover, as her coachman testified, in Kensington Gardens, the opera-house, a ball at the Mansion-house, Ranelagh Gardens and during visits to watering places. Baroness Percy and her lover took trips out in a phaeton and were 'exceedingly indiscreet, observed by everybody … at all the public places of resort'. Lady Bolingbroke was able to meet Topham Beauclerk during a two-month stay at Tunbridge Wells.

Fashionable watering places, with their constantly fluctuating population of summer visitors, were a particularly convenient venue where lovers could adopt a new and transient identity during their stay. In the epistolary novel set in a spa town, *The Pupil of Pleasure*, the anti-hero Philip Sedley acted out the role of libertine that he copied from the true-life template in Lord Chesterfield's letters, declaring 'what our Garrick, is to Shakespeare, I am resolved to be to Chesterfield, – the living comment upon the dead text'.[18] The novel was so popular it was reprinted four times. It denounced the villains of Richardson's novels as poor imitations of the real arch-seducer Chesterfield and invoked his spirit to 'teach me to emulate thy genius'. The hero's imitation of Chesterfield's conduct, with its inherent contradiction between inner morality and outer appearances, highlighted the possibilities for duplicity in acting out codes of polite behaviour.

Many commentators voiced suspicions that politeness was merely a superficial urban code of manners used as a veneer to hide an underlying corruption, such as a cynical libertine's guide to seducing an heiress bluntly titled *The Polite Road to an Estate, or, Fornication One Great Source of Wealth and Pleasure*. The false politeness of public life seemed to prohibit frank conversation, but it could help to avoid hurting another's feelings. *A Dictionary of Love* suggested using the phrase 'I esteem you' because 'to tell you plainly that I hate you, would be too much against all the laws of politeness'. There was a clear difference between the false politeness displayed in the public social life of the city and genuine sincerity aligned to inner virtues.

These contrasting codes of behaviour underlined the distinction made between true nobility and members of the *ton* in 'fashionable society', a derogatory term used to denote those in a disreputable circle renowned for its loose morals. In her novel *The Sylph*, which exposed fashionable amorality, the Duchess of Devonshire repeatedly used the terms 'politeness', 'the polite world' and 'our world' to show how polite sociability could be used as a screen to hide bad behaviour. The novel contrasted corrupt London life ('this nursery of vice and folly') with innocent rural existence, and the heroine recalled 'the calm joys I left in the mountains' and longed 'to quit this destructive place, and retire into the peaceful country'.

The contrast between urban vice and country virtue often cropped up in the literature of the period and was best encapsulated in William Cowper's popular poem *The Task*, which described his rural retreat from worldly corruption. The town/country dichotomy and its moral symbolism had long been a stock idea in literature, originating in the pastoral poetry of ancient Greece with its beliefs that the natural setting for happy innocence was a rural Arcadia. The rapid urbanisation of the late eighteenth century created widespread rural nostalgia, and country virtues became the subject of so much literary output because the pleasures of city life attracted more and more people. The Georgian aristocracy was a class rooted in its country estates, with branches stretching out into a parallel city life of politics, business and sociability. This divided loyalty meant they were spending more time in London or resorts like Bath, in busy lives of constant mobility between different places.

Describing his country bolt-hole in a snug 'Surrey dell' at Pitt Place in Epsom, Thomas Lyttelton wrote, 'In what spot could a British peer find a more delightful retreat than mine, to solace himself in the interval of public duty?'[19] There was also the family seat at Hagley, which was 'certainly an Elysian scene'. George Lyttelton viewed his other house at Arley as 'agreeable to the idea of a rural retreat … to which we are to fly from the pride of Magnificence and the Bustle of Society, when our minds want repose'.[20] Arley was the perfect setting for a newly-married couple to enjoy wedded bliss together, and after his daughter Lucy's marriage to Arthur Annesley, he wrote, 'It is a true Arcadian villa and Lord Anglesey is at present a true Arcadian swain.' In similar vein, his poem *Monody* to his dead wife had celebrated the joys of pure married love in the rural idyll of Hagley. A letter from Lord Chatham after Thomas' marriage also used classical allusion, referring to Paphos as the birthplace of the Greek goddess of love: 'I cou'd not but smile to hear that Cupid knew his Hagley for true Paphian ground, and had taught his slow brother Hymen to mend his pace.'[21]

In spite of these traditional ideas, life in town or country was often a very different experience for men and women. For peers, country life offered a peaceful escape from the pressures of duty or politics in London, with the chance to cast off a formal public persona and relax into home comforts. For many aristocratic women, socialising in the city or spa towns was often much more fun than time spent in the dreary isolation of the countryside. But for other wives, like Anne, Baroness Percy, the seclusion of a country estate was the ideal place to enjoy the thrill of far more risky and exciting pastimes.

A heady romance with a 22-year-old student of Trinity College, Cambridge, made Anne throw caution to the wind and abandon her marriage. As the wife of Hugh Percy, heir to the wealthy Duke of Northumberland, she could have enjoyed a guaranteed lifetime of privilege at the pinnacle of society. But, apparently heedless of the consequences, she pursued a reckless affair, ignoring public gossip and family warnings about her shocking conduct.

Lady Anne Stuart, daughter of the 3rd Earl of Bute, was 17 when in 1764 she married Lord Percy in a private ceremony at her father's house in South Audley Street, London. Described as a thin, unattractive man with a large beaked nose, Lord Percy was also known to be honourable, generous and extremely eligible, as heir to an ancient family with vast estates, including Alnwick Castle in Northumberland and Syon Park near London, which had recently been lavishly redecorated with interiors designed by Robert Adam.

After thirteen years of marriage, the couple still had not produced any children and rumours were circulating about their sex life. The racy *Town and Country Magazine* had already alleged that Lord Percy was more or less impotent because of excessive masturbation as a schoolboy and frequent visits to brothels. It accused Anne of taking many lovers and described the couple as living 'in a state of married separation, her ladyship pursuing her innocent gallantries, while his lordship is enraptured by every new face in King's Place, Pall Mall'.[22]

In December 1776 Anne went to live at Ash Park, a country estate in Hampshire, with her married sister Lady Augusta Corbet. Built in the middle of a wood as a hunting lodge for the late Lord Craven, it was a quiet and secluded place, 2 miles from the nearest village of Overton. Lord Percy had been away fighting in North America for some time, as colonel with his Majesty's Fifth Regiment of Foot, and was hailed in the press as a war hero for his bravery.

In the summer of 1777 Anne and her sister's family went to stay in Southampton, where she first met William Bird, who had taken lodgings at a house next door in Bugle Street with his mother and sisters, also in town for the summer season. Now aged 30, Anne became infatuated with the student, who was eight years younger, and they spent the summer in an endless round of partying, excursions and wild nights together. Rumours of her indiscretions had quickly reached the London press, and in a mock advice column directed at notorious society figures, including the Duchess of Devonshire, the *Morning Post* warned Lady Percy to 'Return to the American hero; and while he fights to compel obedience in one quarter of the globe, do you endeavour to practise it in another.'

In Southampton, Anne seemed to be oblivious of the effect of her behaviour, which was noticed by everyone in town. The Rev. John Calder, who had first met the Percys a few years after their marriage during a grand dinner at Alnwick Castle, often saw her out on excursions with Bird:

> They were hardly ever seen asunder … her ladyship kept company more with the gentlemen than with the ladies. Lady Percy and Mr Bird seemed to be so particularly attentive to each other in public, that it was remarked by everybody; and the intimacy was in general looked upon as a criminal one.

At the end of September Bridget Fortune, the housekeeper at Ash Park, received a letter from her mistress saying she was bringing home company and directing her to have the beds well aired and get a good dinner. Anne arrived one afternoon in a phaeton with Bird, and for the next six months he was a regular visitor to the house, often staying for weeks at a time in the bedchamber adjoining hers. Becoming alarmed at the situation, Lady Augusta begged her sister to break off the connection, which was becoming the subject of gossip everywhere, but she stubbornly refused. Determined not to have her own reputation injured, Lady Augusta said she could no longer live under the same roof and on 15 November left Ash Park.

Anne moved to Bath for the winter season and then returned to Ash Park in the spring of 1778. Here she ordered her usual bedchamber to be freshly wallpapered and used the excuse to move into a spare room. William Bird made six or seven visits, which they arranged by letter. The footman Thomas Morris was often asked to take a parcel addressed to Bird for the Exeter coach and to collect a locked postbag of letters to which only Lady Percy and the postmaster had keys.

The estate gardener and gamekeeper William Froome, who took Bird out shooting, slept in a room directly over Lady Percy's. At night he some-times heard noises below as if someone was creeping about after dark, but he 'never looked to see what it was, for it was no business of his'. Froome noticed that Lady Percy's maid, Mrs Sarah Reeks, seemed very troubled, and on Thursday 12 March she told him that, 'she had seen such a sight that morning that she never saw in her life, and she did not think Lady Percy would ever see her anymore'. Though too discreet to give him all the details, Mrs Reeks had taken a shift up to Lady Percy's room and caught the lovers in bed, semi-naked. Bird had quickly jumped out of bed, snatched up his clothes and run out, in great confusion, across the passage to his own room.

In April 1778 Lady Percy moved to London, renting a furnished house in Brompton Row, near Knightsbridge, and continued to sleep with Bird. One morning the new housemaid, who was helping Mrs Reeks to make the bed, noticed stains on the sheets and remarked how much the bed was tumbled. Mrs Reeks laughed knowingly but said nothing.

The affair had been an open secret for far too long. Lord Percy was due to become the 2nd Duke of Northumberland, and what he needed was an heir, not a childless and troublesome wife. Later that year he sued Anne for adultery, and they were divorced in March 1779. The sixty-five-page account of the case published in *Trials for Adultery* included an illustration of the lovers being surprised in bed together by the maid. It reported that 'very indecent familiarities were seen and heard to pass between Mr Bird and Lady Percy, and Mr Bird kissed her with great ardour'. Lord Percy remar-ried two months later and went on to have three children, obviously not as incapable in the bedchamber as the malicious gossip had implied.

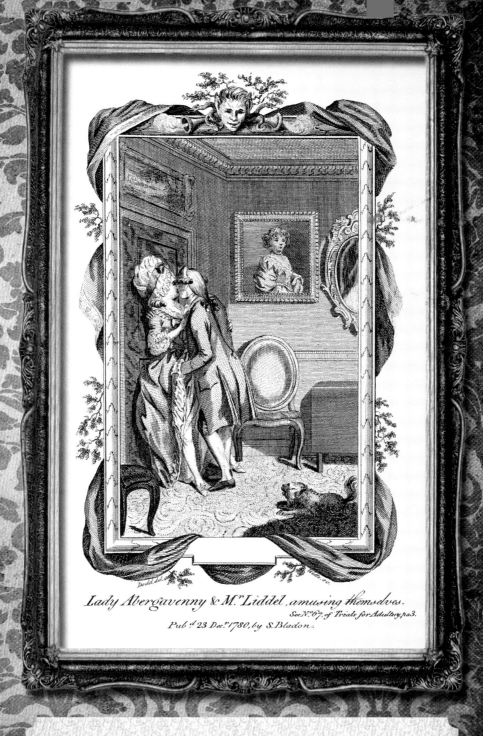

Lady Abergavenny & Mr Liddel, amusing themselves.

See Nº 67. of Trials for Adultery, pa 3.

Pubd 23 Decr 1780, by S. Bladon.

'Lady Abergavenny & Mr Liddel amusing themselves', in Volume 1 of the popular *Trials for Adultery*, gave readers a furtive glimpse of the passionate lovers. (© The British Library Board)

Above left: Augustus Henry Fitzroy, 3rd Duke of Grafton, painted by Pompeo Batoni in 1762. He was pilloried by the press for his scandalous affair with a courtesan. (© National Portrait Gallery, London)

Above right: Nancy Parsons in Turkish Dress, by George Willison *c*.1771, two years after her relationship with the Duke of Grafton ended. (© Yale Center for British Art, Paul Mellon Collection, USA/Bridgeman Images)

Right: Thomas Lyttelton, 2nd Baron Lyttelton, attributed to Richard Brompton, c. 1775. His youthful exploits and womanising earned him the nickname 'Wicked Lord Lyttelton'. (© National Portrait Gallery, London)

The Female Pilot.

A Prime Minister.

The Town and Country Magazine;

OR,

UNIVERSAL REPOSITORY

OF

Knowledge, Instruction, and Entertainment,

For MARCH, 1769.

HISTORIES of the Têtes-à-Têtes annexed. (N° 7, 8.) Palinurus and Annabella.

'The Female Pilot. A Prime Minister' in the *Town and Country Magazine*, March 1769, exposed the Duke of Grafton's adultery with Nancy Parsons. The magazine's 'Tête-à-Tête' series was one of the first celebrity gossip columns.
(© The British Library Board)

'Miss Roberts sitting naked in Ld Grosvenor's lap at the Hotel in Leicester Fields' in Volume 4 of *Trials for Adultery*, revealed Lord Grosvenor in a sleazy encounter with a prostitute. (© The British Library Board)

Henrietta Grosvenor (née Vernon), Countess Grosvenor, mezzotint published by Carrington Bowles in 1774. Trapped in an unhappy marriage, she had a disastrous liaison with HRH the Duke of Cumberland. (© National Portrait Gallery, London)

DERBY & JOAN,
or the Platonic Lovers,
A FARCE.

'Derby & Joan or the platonic lovers, a farce' (Elizabeth, Countess of Derby; Edward Smith Stanley, 12th Earl of Derby), etching by Robert Dighton, 1795. The middle-aged earl courted actress Elizabeth Farren for many years, before eventually marrying her. (© National Portrait Gallery, London)

George Spencer-Churchill, 5th Duke of Marlborough when Marquis of Blandford by William Whiston Barney, after Richard Cosway. Blandford's love affair with a married woman ended up in court when her husband sued him for 'criminal conversation'. (© National Portrait Gallery, London)

Right: John Parker and his sister Theresa, 1779, by Sir Joshua Reynolds. The young siblings' close friendship was later disrupted by John's long relationship with Lady Elizabeth Monck. (© National Trust Images/Rob Matheson)

Below: The west front of Saltram House, Devon. A hundred beds were made up for guests when the 16-year-old Lord Boringdon entertained the king and queen at his family home. (© National Trust Images/Rupert Truman)

Portrait of the Hon. Isabella Ingram, later Marchioness of Hertford, by John Hoppner. The press was convinced that Lady Hertford was the Prince Regent's mistress. (© Leeds Museums and Art Galleries (Temple Newsam House) UK/ Bridgeman Images)

Edward Law, 1st Earl of Ellenborough, by Frederick Richard Say, c. 1845. His scandalous divorce provoked a public outcry. (© National Portrait Gallery, London)

13

THE PURITY OF
NOBLE BLOOD

The vice of adultery had by 1779 apparently reached such a 'shameful height ... especially in the higher ranks of life', that serious concerns were being voiced about its insidious erosion of civil society.[23] Introducing a Bill for the More Effectual Discouragement of the Crime of Adultery, Shute Barrington, the Bishop of Llandaff, pointed out that there had been as many divorces in the present king's reign as during the whole history of England, partly because punishment for adultery was now less severe. He urged peers to support the bill to halt the progress of this fashionable evil, appealing to them as 'friends of their country' who wished to 'preserve the purity of their own noble blood, and to transmit their honours and estates to their own posterity; as the guardians of the liberties, civil and religious, of the people, both of which were invaded by this crime'. His argument neatly clarified the fundamental essence of nobility as power based on hereditary rank and property. And these Parliamentary debates about adultery went right to the heart of the aristocratic role, in which private interest and public duty were so inextricably linked.

The Bishop of Llandaff's Bill was the second of four attempts, of increasing seriousness, made to reduce the number of divorces by proposing legislation to stop women who committed adultery and then divorced from later marrying their lovers.[24] This time it passed through the House of Lords but received scant attention in the House of Commons, where Charles Fox 'treated the bill with great ridicule', joking that it was unfair to treat the ladies like the Americans by punishment without representation.[25] Lord Beauchamp and Lord Ongley voiced the main objection to the bill, namely its inequality in punishing only women and not the men who were most often to blame in adultery cases, either as seducers or neglectful husbands. It was rejected on second reading by fifty-one votes to forty, and the *London Magazine* reported, with evident disapproval, 'In short, the bill was not discussed in a serious deliberate manner, and the House was very thin when it was thrown out.' Despite its failure, the bill provoked wider public debate on the issues of adultery and divorce, which was to gather pace during the decade of moral panic and political uncertainty in the 1790s after the French Revolution had focused national consciousness on the dangers of social breakdown. Attitudes had substantially altered by the time the adultery prevention bill resurfaced in 1800, and this was reflected in the lengthy and serious consideration it was then given in both Houses.

In 1779 the argument focussed on how effective the bill was likely to be in actually discouraging adultery. The Earl of Effingham opposed it on the grounds that it was unlikely to do so, commenting that 'when immorality rose to such a height as to require political interference', great care was needed to ensure measures were sufficient. He proposed, with more than a hint of irony, that in fact compelling an adulteress to marry her lover immediately would be far more effective in curbing unlawful passion.

What was striking about the Parliamentary debates was the underlying assumption that the protection of peers' own personal property rights co-existed with their execution of public duty as guardians of the national interest. In an impassioned speech the Lord Chancellor, Edward Thurlow, denounced adultery as a crime mainly prevalent in the higher ranks, which 'has a tendency, by contaminating the blood of illustrious families, to affect the welfare of the nation'. He pointed out that the bill concerned all mankind, 'but it concerned their lordships more than any other order of people' because 'the purity of the blood of their descendants, was … an essential consideration in the breast of all the peers of the kingdom'. Speaking as a brand new peer himself, and a mere clergyman's son who had only been created a baron the year before, Lord Thurlow asserted the traditional ideal of hereditary aristocratic rule in which bloodline was paramount. With the clarity of vision available to a noted intellectual and relative outsider to the establishment, he knew exactly what was at stake, commenting that 'he saw the importance of the Bill to the peerage so clearly, that if he had the blood of forty generations of nobility flowing in his veins, he could not be more anxious to procure it'. Adultery was therefore not just an issue of morality, and legislation was necessary when infidelity had begun to openly disrupt social order.

The progress of the bill through both Houses was followed with interest by the press, with regular updates in all the leading newspapers. In a lengthy article on 31 March 1779 the *Morning Chronicle* reported the Lord Chancellor's 'truly masterly speech' which outlined the object of the bill 'to put a stop to the very alarming prevalence of a crime which struck at the root of domestic felicity, of private happiness, and of purity of blood in the descent of noble families, and which likewise tended toward the destruction of populations'. He said that although it had been argued it was absurd to enact laws against immorality, and it was not the business of the legislature, 'certainly when crimes against morality grew to such a number, and reached such a height as to become a matter of public notoriety, it was necessary to use legislative power to check the exercise of that depravity ... that their bad morals might not influence the morals of others and that the crime of adultery might not be sanctified by the number of examples of adulterous women.'

During the adultery debates, peers enacted their expected public roles as objective, fair-minded statesmen concerned with safeguarding social morality and stability, even when discussing a topic which had such strong personal resonances in their own lives. When appearing in Parliament, they used classical methods of rhetoric and logic to become independent orators free to criticise their own class and sex, debating issues and presenting other viewpoints in the national interest.

The House of Lords, with its physical layout having elements of both the contemporary courtroom and theatre, was like a national stage on which enthralling live performances took place. At one end of the chilly and poorly lit chamber in the medieval Palace of Westminster was the bar, where commoners stood to give evidence, and at the other end was the throne on a raised dais, with woolsacks in front for the Speaker of the House and judges. Members sat on benches of red cloth around three sides of the chamber and were expected to speak from their seats, while any commoners wanting to listen to debates had to stand outside by the door. Peers were both the actors and audience in this large echoing space, as they made speeches and interacted with each other during debates.

Such accomplished dramatic performances did not impress some more cynical observers. The satire *The Patricians* viewed the House of Lords merely as an arena for enacting meaningless rituals which masked the self-interest of men who had no genuine entitlement to a seat in it: '*Birth* alone has no pretence,/ To truth, or honour, dignity, or sense'.[26] The poem mocked behaviour in the House ('The question mov'd, regardless of debate,/ See how they silent sit, or idly prate!') and picked out various peers for ridicule, including the Earl of Sandwich, Lord Chatham, the Marquis of Rockingham and the 6th Earl of Denbigh, who was cruelly lampooned for his rustic manners and odd appearance.

The majority of speakers in the adultery debates spoke out strongly in favour of equal treatment for women, voicing a chivalric concern that their interests should be fairly represented and showing unexpected perception in their comments about the greater culpability of men in adultery cases. A clever satirical pamphlet entitled *The House of Peeresses: or, Female Oratory*, published anonymously by Dr Shute Barrington, addressed the main criticism of his own bill that it proposed punishment for women who were not allowed to speak on their own behalf in Parliament. In the pamphlet, gender roles were subverted as an imaginary gathering of peeresses was described debating the anti-adultery bill in the House of Lords, taking on the public role and free speech denied them in real life.

Notorious adulteresses, including the Duchess of Grafton, Lady Craven, Lady Grosvenor and the Countess of Jersey, were listed as principal speakers on the title page with their names only thinly disguised by a series of printed dashes. The fictionalised female Parliament was a hit with readers, and five editions of the pamphlet were printed that year. The ladies acted out their parts as members of the Lords, adopting the mannered and pompous language of debate with rhetorical devices, Latin quotations, literary allusions and typically male expressions such as 'Zounds', in a witty parody of boisterous Parliamentary behaviour. The debate was set out as a battle between the sexes, and they finally passed a motion to toss the Bishop of Landaff in a blanket, comparing him to the chivalrous hero of *Don Quixote* in a deft literary allusion which underlined the futility of fighting hopeless causes like the anti-adultery bill, which was declared ineffective.

The proposed legislation was widely seen as impractical, and even the editor of that popular handbook of vice *Trials for Adultery* acknowledged that it had been praiseworthy but badly framed:

It is indeed a difficult matter to deter those of an abandoned disposition, from the commission of crimes where the punishment is trivial: a separation is generally the worst consequence that can ensue in adulterous cases, and that is but too often what the offending parties devoutly wish.

A separation to safeguard the family bloodline was the object of a crim. con. action that took place during the same year Parliament debated the anti-adultery bill. The Right Hon. Francis Osborne, Marquis of Carmarthen, successfully won his case after his wife, Amelia, eloped with her lover. The couple had three children and had been married for less than five years when the marchioness began an affair. The household servants described how her lover, John Byron, an officer in the footguards, dined alone with her in the Blue Parlour at home in Grosvenor Square, London, and spent nights there while her husband was away visiting his sick father the Duke of Leeds. They reported seeing Byron go to her bedchamber, hearing the door bolted and bed curtains being drawn. The second housemaid, Jane Totty, undressed her ladyship in the powdering room and took up a candle to light her way into the bedchamber, but the marchioness said she would put herself to bed, went in and locked the door, something she had never done before. Next morning when Jane took up her ladyship's toast and water, she saw something in the bed and heard a man's snore. Later, when the second footman came up with her brown riding habit he saw a man's head peeping out from the room, and then he saw the man go downstairs, whistling.

Another day when Byron had been seen by several of the housemaids, the bed was tumbled, the sheets stained and a candlestick was found on the marquis' side of the bed. The marchioness called Jane in and said, 'You know of this affair, and if it is told to his lordship I shall be a ruined, undone woman.' She asked if the other servants knew and started crying, begging Jane to ask the others not to tell her husband and promising, 'I will take care it shall never happen again.' What the staff particularly resented was Byron's cock-sure behaviour, 'as if he had been master of the house'. When the marquis later found out what was going on, he was 'greatly affected' and called in the serv-ants to give an account of the matter. William Shadbolt, the under-butler, said he was sorry that the lady had put it in his power to hurt her and would not unless put on oath or forced. He had told Byron that, 'every servant will be bound to curse the day or hour when you first came into the house', and late one night he had refused to let him into the building, telling the marchioness he would not because 'it could end in a divorce'.[27]

As in all adultery trials, the servants played an important role as observers. They were called by the prosecution as honest upholders of morality, expressing loyalty to their master and alarm at the mistress's behaviour, which threatened the security of the household and their own employment. Many cases revealed the divided loyalties and complex relationships between servants and employers, and how the entire power balance of the normal social hierarchy was disrupted by adultery.

14

'A PRODIGIOUS SWARM OF TRASHY WRITERS'

By appearing on the stage of print, peers' lives became public property in a way that had not been possible before the advent of the commercial press. This new accessibility to a wider audience of readers accompanied a belief that the public had a right to know the truth about those in power, an opinion held by the controversial bookseller and political journalist John Almon, whose prolific output influenced public opinion for several decades from the 1760s: 'The nation has an interest in the characters of persons of high rank. If the idea may be permitted, they might be called the property of the public. They are born to the great offices of the state.'[28] By printing previously hidden details of their personal lives as entertaining morality tales, publishers adroitly manipulated the market appetite for nobility as a popular subject which guaranteed sales in all genres. This appealing combination of scandal and smug moral judgement was fully exploited in *The Prostitutes of Quality; or Adultery à-la-Mode. Being Authentic and Genuine Memoirs of Several Persons of the Highest Quality*, which promised readers it had 'unlock'd the Bosoms of the *guilty* Great' to show 'how much deceived those People are, who, blinded by a Glare of Grandeur, imagine Happiness consists in Wealth and Titles'.[29]

Regular snippets giving adultery updates kept readers of the *Morning Herald* amused, like the series of reports run in early 1783 on the unfolding case of Lady C. The first said, 'Lady C--- has recently made a sentimental faux pas with her own valet, and their intrigue has unfortunately been discovered: her noble Lord, it is said, convinced of this second and degrading species of infidelity, is determined no longer to wear his horns in his pocket!'

A month later the paper reported, 'A Lady of fashion who lately committed a faux-pas with a domestic, has come to a settlement with her Lord. She is to have fifteen hundred pounds a year while she resides on the Continent, but forfeits everything if she returns to Great Britain.' The next said:

> Lord C--- is said to have commenced a prosecution for Crim. Con. against a high and distinguished character in the Law ... The reason is now discerned why a certain Law Lord has been so great an enemy to divorces. He who is fond of indulging in crim. con. does not relish the punishment which attends it.

By April readers were told:

> Lady C--- has declared herself pregnant; and this offspring of her Ladyship's amorous sallies will, it is said, occasion a violent schism between the Law and the Gospel! A certain Prelate is expecting she will claim for it Archiepiscopal protection, at the same time that her noble Lord is resolved on making it a ward of Chancery!

No doubt the guessing game about who was involved only added to the fun for readers.

By the late eighteenth century the commercial press had become a powerful force in shaping public opinion on all the political and social issues of the day. This was made possible by the enormous growth of print culture after the Licensing Act lapsed in 1695, ending press censorship and the strict system of government control that had operated up until then. The subsequent loss of the Stationer's Company monopoly allowed, for the first time, provincial printers to produce printed material ranging from handbills to newspapers and, by the last quarter of the century, to publish books. Other print forms, including essays, pamphlets, plays, poetry, novels and satirical prints, all fuelled the expanding commercial marketplace. This new freedom created a surge in the number of newspaper titles both in London and the provinces, enabling the press to play a key part in national life by circulating new ideas, opinion and gossip. By mid-century most of the country had access to at least one local title and by 1785 there were forty-nine provincial newspapers being printed in thirty-four towns. The number of London daily papers also grew from nine in the 1770s, to fourteen by 1790.

Many new titles were only short-lived but others flourished, like *The Daily Universal Register*, first published as a two-pence halfpenny broadsheet in

1785, which three years later became *The Times* and went on to dominate the market, reaching a daily circulation of 40,000 by the 1840s.[30] The periodical press with its eclectic mix of news, gossip, essays, reviews and literary articles also grew to more than eighty titles by 1800. These ranged from the highly respectable *Spectator*, the *Tatler* and *Gentleman's Magazine* to *The Age*, the *Town and Country Magazine*, the racy *Bon Ton Magazine*, *Rambler's Magazine* (launched in 1783) and the semi-pornographic *Ranger's Magazine*.

By the end of the century all large towns had their own local newspaper, and the total sale of papers nationally was sixteen million a year. In addition to this proliferation of titles, the circulation figures for each were also growing as rising wages and literacy rates expanded the number of buyers, while coffee-houses and other public venues such as reading rooms provided greater access to a range of titles for their customers.[31] Readership of a weekly provincial paper could be up to ten times its actual sales of perhaps a few thousand copies, so its reach in a community was often substantial. Being able to dip into the London papers gave provincial readers a new egalitarian sense that they were part of the national political scene, and they could even participate by sending in letters to the editor for publication. One writer to *Lloyd's Evening Post* observed that 'Without newspapers … our Country Villager, the Curate, and the Black-smith, would lose the self-satisfaction of being as wise as our First Minister of State'.[32]

The dominant influence of newspapers in moulding public opinion was axiomatic to the eighteenth-century Englishman, and as Dr Johnson said, 'Knowledge is diffused among our people by the news-papers.'[33] To fill their pages London editors had to be resourceful, employing reporters to cover courts and Parliament, paying others to loiter in coffee-houses gathering gossip or to coax information from servants to the wealthy elite, and also exchanging news stories with provincial papers. There were plenty of contributions from unpaid correspondents keen to see their views in print, and thriving letters columns where all the hot topics were debated. Content typically included news reports on government, the court, foreign affairs, trade and shipping, crime, sport and leisure.

Newspaper columns contained an apparently random mix of factual reports on events, opinion, reported gossip and letters, often printed in successive paragraphs which used phrases such as 'we are informed' or 'it is said that' to signal potentially dubious claims of authenticity. In some cases the deliberate juxtaposition of items was used as a device to provide amusement or further information for canny readers, like a cryptic paragraph on the Continental travels of various courtesans in the *Morning Herald* on 5 May 1783 which was followed by the comment, 'If the sale of *Trials for Adultery*, with libidinous frontispieces, &c, was either stopped, or put under some proper regulation, society would be relieved from a most dangerous nuisance to its morals, and to the welfare of the rising generation!' Similarly, when the *Public Advertiser* printed a letter 'written by a great Man, immediately on his Divorce, to his Mistress', it was inserted directly beneath a paragraph reporting a social gathering hosted by the Duke of Grafton as a way of clearly identifying him as the unnamed letter writer.[34]

Although newspapers were an important source of information on public affairs, especially for those living outside London, they were also notoriously unreliable and well known for getting their facts wrong, as one exasperated reader commented in a letter to the Earl of Denbigh: 'Our unmerciful Newspapers have killed the Princess Dowager and the Duke of Gloucester, thank God! there is no truth in the report, on the contrary it is said that his R H is much better.' In a postscript, he added that more lies were being spread by an informer to the publisher of the *Whisperer*: 'I wish they were both hanged, and am sure a stop ought to be put to their present practice of defaming some of the most respectable Characters.'[35] Reporting of elite scandal, whether true or false, was a calculated method of boosting sales.

The resigned acceptance that publicity was the price of nobility, and the helpless frustration experienced by those who were defamed, was described by 'Wicked' Thomas Lyttelton who saw the popular press as a tool of Satan:

> I wish the *Morning Post*, and every other Post that scatters such malignant, false, and detestable histories, in the bottomless pit, with its writers, printers, editors, publishers, collectors, and purchasers. To be the subject of an occasional paragraph is not worth a frown. It is a tax which every-one in high station must pay, be he good, or be he bad, to that *Demon* of Calumny, who now has a temple prepared for his service at every breakfast-table in the metropolis. But, to be the sole theme of a scandalous chronicle, and to see it … raised into universal notice and reception, from its abusive histories of me, is a circumstance big with every pain and penalty of mortification. To add to my distress, no means of satisfaction or revenge are in my power.[36]

While it was hardly surprising that his bad behaviour attracted wide press coverage, it was clear that facts about him were being deliberately manipulated and distorted into fictions to amuse readers. Lyttelton was especially indignant at the humiliation of being an object of contempt, exposed to the comment of strangers including his social inferiors:

> I cannot enter an house where the page of my dishonour does not lie upon the table. Every man, who meets me in the street, tells me by his looks that he has read it. I have overheard my own servants observing upon it, and the very chairmen can repeat its tales. I expect, every day, that my horse, like Balaam's ass, will neigh scandal at me, not indeed from celestial, but hellish intervention.

The blurring of fact and fiction in newspapers was a traditional characteristic of the diverse range of print which had developed during the sixteenth and seventeenth centuries.[37] The Stamp Act of 1712 (which made printed news content taxable and other narratives such as history or fiction non-taxable) and the revised Act of 1724, marked the first attempts to define what constituted a factual or a fictional narrative. But despite the impact of this legislation in marking the legal boundary between potentially libellous journalism and non-libellous literature, it could not erase the long tradition of overlapping genres firmly embedded in English print culture.

The easy co-existence of fact and fiction was reflected in the columns of newspapers, and also in periodicals which contained an eclectic mix of contents, including biographical sketches, Parliamentary proceedings, foreign news and historical vignettes, alongside play scripts, extracts from classical literature and serialised fiction. Books, too, often combined the factual and the imaginary, with fiction masquerading as memoir, or true-life stories presented as *roman-à-clef* novels where real names were thinly disguised by hyphens. The popularity of circulating libraries, book clubs and reading societies meant that books now reached a wide public. Georgian readers were well practised in the mental agility of absorbing this tangle of different narrative forms merging into each other, and they felt comfortable within a fluid print landscape characterised by its very refusal to be imprisoned by definition.

The problematic issue of distinguishing fact from fiction (the blurring of boundaries between the two and the cunning ability of one to masquerade as the other) was a persistent feature across all genres of print culture. It provided a public stage on which writers could explore contemporary concerns and questions about the complex relationships between scientific truth and individual imagination, reason and religion, performance and reality. In print, the closely intertwined mix of narratives had a tendency to change, develop and blend together. Like quicksand, when readers stepped on what seemed at first sight to be a firm textual surface, they often found themselves falling through into another literary medium hidden below.

This relaxed combination of fact and fiction was reflected in the title of the *Convivial Magazine, and Polite Intelligencer; or, A Real Representation of the Characters and Sentiments of the Times*, a monthly periodical with a bizarre range of content, including 'portraits of … men of rank, conspicuous in the world', Parliamentary proceedings, foreign news and historical sketches, alongside play scripts, illustrations of characters from classical literature such as Circe and Dido, and the serialisation of stories like 'The Happy Divorce'. Publishers and readers saw no problem in using the phrase 'a real representation' to describe the contents and understood that a full insight into people and current thinking could best be provided by the whole diversity of literary genres. Both fiction and (what would today be labelled) cross-genre narratives of fact-based fiction played an important part by expressing some of the deeper moral truths revealed in their characters and stories.[38] A similarly eclectic miscellany of contents was to be found in other periodicals, such as the *London Magazine*, described by its publisher as 'a kind of historical dictionary', and in 'that delectable Hodge Podge of wit and humour called the *Gentleman's Magazine*'.[39]

The breadth of commercial literature was based on what would sell, and as its profit potential grew so did the opportunities for 'a prodigious swarm of insipid trashy writers' who were only too willing to cater for popular taste, as one commentator complained: 'Whatever author labours to accommodate himself to the taste of his age … will by degrees languish into obscurity in the next'.[40] Such writers may have been more concerned with cash than posterity, but they undoubtedly enjoyed an influential cultural position at the time as educators and opinion-formers. One publication that cashed in on the popular appeal of nobility was *A Satirical Peerage of England* published in 1784, mocking the family mottos of the titled. Of the Duke of Grafton it said, 'Peers get rewarded all their lives, / Can you say this – on both your wives?' And on the Earl of Derby's motto 'without changing' it commented: 'Constant indeed, let's hear no more, / You've chang'd your wife, and took a w----e.'

As well as newspapers and periodicals, many other literary genres flourished at this time, including novels, plays, pamphlets, sermons, essays, memoirs, historical or travel writing and poetry, which was a quick, cheap way to comment on topical issues. The majority of published authors were male, although they were being joined by an increasing number of women. This was partly attributable to the rise of the novel, which saw the number of new women authors grow by 50 per cent every decade from 1760, reaching a total of more than 200 living female novelists by 1830. There were also an estimated 400 female poets publishing during the period.

The diverse but overlapping forms of literary output together combined to create a powerful voice which both reflected and shaped public opinion. Georgian readers knew that printed texts had an active social function and, as the *Evangelical Magazine* pointed out, periodical publishing had in itself 'produced a surprising revolution in sentiments and manners.'[41] There was widespread acceptance that the texts created by a culture also had a real impact on that world. Texts were not merely passive reflections of reality but actually played a part in shaping thought, feeling and imagination, framing new possibilities or suggesting future options. The printed word could have a profound effect on society: 'Reading, all were sure, shaped the knowledge, the beliefs … the moral values, the sensibility, the memories, the dreams, and therefore, ultimately, the actions, of men, women, and children. Reading helped to shape mentalities and to determine the fate of the nation.'[42]

Within the aggressively commercial market of eighteenth-century print culture, literature in all its guises had a highly visceral impact on readers. Popular interest in elite lives and sexual scandal was deliberately manipulated by profit-hungry publishers, who had soon found that trials for adultery were guaranteed bestsellers. What really appealed was the amount of fascinating detail available for those eager to know the innermost secrets of their social superiors' lives. Through the circumstantial evidence of trial witnesses, readers were able to discover all the minutiae of their everyday personal lives – how they behaved in different places, their daily routines, even the layout and furnishings of their homes were laid bare as the formal public façade of nobility was torn aside. Far more humiliating were the revelations about their sex lives, which ordinary folk found enthralling.

A passing bricklayer saw Lady Ann Foley's amorous *al fresco* encounter in a shrubbery with the Earl of Peterborough, as he glanced through the fence railings of Stoke Park in Herefordshire. Ann was one of the Earl of Coventry's daughters, and her sister Lady Maria Bayntun had already gained notoriety two years earlier when her husband divorced her for adultery. During the Foley trial for crim. con. in 1785, witnesses described various places outdoors where the lovers had sex, and pamphlets publishing the full trial transcripts included illustrations of the couple embracing in a carriage, standing by an oak tree and lying behind a furze bush.[43] The brazen indecency of their conduct was shocking, and in court the defence counsel asked the jury, 'Can you believe, Gentlemen, that any woman could have prostituted herself in a shrubbery, liable to be exposed to the view of every passer-by, in the manner this woman has, if not lost to all sense of shame.' They were caught at it in the shrubbery when Ann cried out, 'Oh dear! You hurt me!' and the *Morning Post* of 6 May commented sardonically that it 'should be a warning to all young ladies who frequent shrubberies in an evening, not to cry out before their time – it seems the discovery had not happened, if the lady had not made some exclamations'. Dozens of other articles appeared during the trial in publications, including the *Hereford Journal, Daily Universal Register, Public Advertiser* and *Rambler's Magazine*.

Reading news reports like these was a way of crossing the strict social divide which normally upheld power relations between different classes. As more publications thrived on sensation, more readers could enjoy such tawdry personal revelations. But alongside the amusement was a growing sense of outrage about the shameful behaviour of the aristocracy, which was being flaunted so often in print. Those born to rule were now public property and it was clear that something had to change.

Part Four

Moral Reform and Scandals (1790s–1810)

'A virtuous nobility must be the greatest blessing to a nation, but a profligate nobility must be the greatest curse.'

The Evils of Adultery and Prostitution 1792

15

MORAL REFORM

'The higher ranks of society are to be considered as the fountain, whence the living manners of the time derive their origin: if, therefore, the fountain should happen to be corrupt, the smaller streams, which proceed from it, must of necessity, be tainted with the contagion.'[1] So said one pamphleteer, complaining about the disgusting vice of adultery among people of 'exalted rank … [who] have it in their power to stem the torrent of this prevailing corruption … they have rather promoted it, by their example, and upheld it by their arguments; so that they have contributed, in a remarkable degree, to the diffusion of this pernicious vice'.

Fears that widespread adultery would undermine national stability came to a head during the closing years of the eighteenth century, after the French Revolution and execution of King Louis XVI had sent shockwaves through English society and added to the existing mood of insecurity. In this tense climate of moral panic the purpose and social function of the aristocracy became the subject of heated discussion, hinging on its entitlement to rule and responsibility for moral leadership of the lower classes. The whole concept of noble identity was rooted in a hereditary entitlement to rule, where public authority was allied to exemplary personal behaviour. Aristocratic adultery called into question this 'natural' leadership during a period when public image was becoming ever more important and the commercial press was playing a key role in shaping public attitudes. The mass publication of intimate revelations from adultery trials had dragged the personal out of the bedchamber and into the harsh spotlight of the public gaze.

Successive waves of moral reform have been triggered throughout history at times of national insecurity, and in 1787 George III was persuaded to follow the example of several previous monarchs in issuing a proclamation against vice and immorality. Modelled partly on the earlier reform movement of the 1690s, the Proclamation Society had a broad agenda of improvement to 'repress the Progress of Vice wherever it appears', and it expected that 'the Force of Example … will be productive of many good Effects in the highest Ranks of Society'.[2] In fact, what distinguished it from other such movements in earlier and later eras was its notably aristocratic membership.[3] As figureheads for a worthy cause, peers could meet expectations of public leadership and personal virtue. Under the influence of William Wilberforce, members of the Proclamation Society deliberately set out to recruit a large section of the elite with the necessary prestige for attracting wider social support. This tactic also promoted the society's intention of reforming moral conduct within the highest ranks, not just in the lower orders whose behaviour had been targeted under previous reform initiatives. Other similar attempts to reform manners from the 1690s to early 1900s also focussed on the social consequences of immorality, but they did not have the distinctive elite element which was so prominent in the late 1700s.[4] A century earlier, reform movements, including the Society for the Reformation of Manners and the Society for Promoting Christian Knowledge, had also enlisted a volunteer network to clamp down on disorderly behaviour, profanity and non-observance of the Sabbath, using the threat of legal action to enforce its goals. But such activity was largely secular, receiving only half-hearted support from the Church in most parishes.

By the 1780s, increasing problems of social order created by urbanisation, crime and prostitution brought morality once again to public attention, stimulating a new zest for reform. The Proclamation Society was succeeded in 1802 by the Society for the Suppression of Vice, which concentrated its attention on the prosecution of obscene publications but also tackled Sabbath-breaking and other offences like keeping disorderly public houses, brothels and gaming houses.[5] Vice was therefore seen mainly as disruptive group behaviour, while the gratification of individual desires was only a subsidiary problem. Supporters of the Vice Society, as it was popularly known, were mainly from the middle-ranking professional and commercial classes and the clergy, together with titled former members of the old Proclamation Society, whose role was now much lower key. It continued campaigning until funds ran out in 1880. At the same time, a range of other specialist organisations sprang up and took over various strands of the broad reforming agenda pursued in the 1780s. These included the Guardian Society for the Preservation of Public Morals, which from 1812 tried to tackle the vast network of prostitution in London and ran a survey to uncover the extent of the problem, which revealed an astonishing 360 brothels in just three city parishes. Attempts to curb sexual vice recurred in each wave of reform, and they became particularly zealous in the later Victorian period with anti-prostitution initiatives such as the Contagious Diseases Acts of the 1860s, followed by the social purity movement which promoted chastity in both men and women.

The renewed sense of urgency driving late Georgian moral debates was created by political, economic and cultural factors, heightened by wartime anxieties and fuelled by the Evangelical religious revival. The Proclamation Society's aim was broad law reform 'to prevent and punish Vice, Profaneness and Immorality', from the suppression of indecent publications and upholding of the Sabbath to regulation of public houses and improvement of prisons.[6] The chance to be seen to promote such laudable ends proved highly appealing to men of the ruling classes, who were well aware that this public platform would display their own individual commitment to morality. As the clergyman and magistrate Samuel Glasse wrote, 'The reform, in short, must be *personal* ... and if his portion is among the Great, great will be the benefit derived from his conduct, to the community at large, from the effects of his influence and example'.[7]

Wilberforce enlisted the Duke of Montagu as president of the society, and by 1788 the membership of 149 included more than thirty peers and their sons, twenty bishops, well-connected commoners such as MPs and those in high public office and legal posts. Together they provided the respectability and influence needed to drive forward the campaign. Among its members were the newly-appointed Lord Chief Justice Lord Kenyon, the Bishop of Llandaff, the Earl of Radnor, the Evangelical Lord Dartmouth, the former prime minister, Lord North, and nine dukes, including the now pious reformed sinner the Duke of Grafton.[8] In the guise of crusading role models, they were highly visible on the national stage of the commercial press at a time when the public image of peers was becoming critical. What has been called 'the creation of a rhetoric of public service' in the closing decades of the century meant that, in contrast to the remote backstage influence of previous generations, the nobility now had to engage fully with its audience and give an appropriate public performance.[9] It was not so much the actual undertaking of public duty as being *seen* to do so which really mattered.

The new publicity afforded by a flourishing print culture was ably exploited by earnest Anglican religious reformers such as Wilberforce, Hannah More and the clergyman Thomas Gisborne, whose writings repeatedly stressed the need for the rich to shape the moral tone of society. Printed sermons and pamphlets denouncing adultery had proliferated since the 1770s. The Evangelical preoccupation with personal sin, divine judgement and the redemptive power of faith surfaced in a new wave of publications urging moral reform, which emerged in the 1790s and now put renewed emphasis on the responsibility of the higher ranks for exemplary leadership. Wilberforce's highly influential work *A Practical View of the Prevailing Religious System of Professed Christians, in the Higher and Middle Classes* argued that piety was needed to halt the country's moral decay. Citing the 'dreadful proofs' witnessed in France of the terrible consequences of 'manners corrupted, morals depraved ... above all, Religion discredited, and infidelity grown into repute and fashion', he called on 'men of authority and influence [to] promote the cause of good morals' not only 'by their personal conduct, though this mode will always be the most efficacious' but also by participation in public initiatives. 'Every effort should be used to raise the depressed tone of public morals. This is a duty particularly incumbent on all who are in the higher walks of life.'[10]

In similar vein the bluestocking writer and Evangelical activist Hannah More, who was a schoolmaster's daughter from the middling ranks, issued a patriotic rallying call for women of rank and fortune to help save their country, 'in this moment of alarm and peril' by using their influence to promote public morality and 'awaken the drowsy spirit of religious principle'.[11] In *Strictures on the Modern System of Female Education* she argued that women of higher classes held influence in society 'they can scarcely rate too highly' and on which could depend 'perhaps the very existence of that society'. She suggested various ways ladies should act as 'the guardians of public taste as well as public virtue', including taking a stand against the pernicious effects of novels in encouraging immoral behaviour. Using the evocative metaphor of literature as an invading army, More lamented that novels, these 'vehicles of vice and infidelity', were so popular with an impressionable readership very different to 'those readers, whose purer taste has been formed on the correct models of the old classic school'. So much so that 'the irruption of those swarms of publications ... like their ravaging predecessors of the darker ages, though with far other arms, are overrunning civilised society'.

More was convinced of literature's powerful impact on personal behaviour, denouncing the philosopher Jean Jacques Rousseau as 'the first popular dispenser of this complicated drug, in which the deleterious infusion was strong, thus corrupting the judgment and bewildering the understanding, as the most effectual way to inflame the imagination and deprave the heart'. By revealing the inner world of his characters' emotions and manipulating the reader's response, Rousseau peddled text like a mystical drug that seduced 'by falsehood those who love truth … allures the warm-hearted to vice … because he gives to vice so natural an air of virtue'. *Strictures* was a detailed guide to shaping ideal feminine behaviour, with sections addressing many of the current concerns such as female intellect, religious observance, the dangers of public amusements, dissipation in fashionable circles and the prevalence of adultery that 'always exhibits the most irrefragable proof of the dissoluteness of public manners'. Here, too, women of rank could exert influence in curbing the spread of infidelity, despite the impact of popular literary role models justifying adultery, like the heroines of Auguste von Kotzebue's tragedy *The Stranger* and Mary Wollstonecraft's novel *The Wrongs of Woman*, who were both adulteresses presented as figures of compassion. More's prolific literary output included two other attempts to remind the higher classes of their duty, both of which went through numerous editions. Her best-selling *Thoughts on the Importance of the Manners of the Great* argued that 'Reformation must begin with the GREAT, or it will never be effectual', and *An Estimate of the Religion of the Fashionable World* condemned the declining piety of 'those promiscuous myriads which compose the … gay world' who 'celebrate the orgies of dissipation'.[12]

Approval of More's writings, which 'exposed the dreadful consequences of prevailing irreligion and immorality among higher classes', was voiced in *Adultery Analysed*, one of a host of fervent publications with similar moral sentiments. Dedicated to 'a Married Couple of Fashionable Notoriety', it was a long and persuasive argument setting out the reasons for 'that dereliction of the moral principle which, so strikingly, marks the features of the present times' and included faults in female education, modern attitudes to marriage, the lack of punishment for offenders and the bad influence of popular drama and novels on behaviour. An entire section was devoted to a denunciation of Mary Wollstonecraft for being a champion of sexual licence. Its first chapter introduced the key point of the argument, which was reiterated in the conclusion:

The example set by the higher class of the community is of the very first importance in ameliorating public morals ... let, then, this class of society contribute their quota to the much desired reformation; and the influence of their conduct will, instantly, extend itself downwards.

The essay condemned 'female libertinism, especially of married women' as 'the crying sin of these eventful times' and blamed such corruption on 'the swarm of novels and high-wrought romances, which infest all our towns and villages through the medium of the circulating libraries'. Like More, the writer identified the insidious danger of novels as their ability to deceive readers with appealing but false scenes masquerading as the truth: they 'pretend to give a real picture of life and manners, and to hold out lessons of right conduct for the regulation of our behaviour; but instead ... give deceitful and seductive representations'.[13]

Such conviction about the impact of the printed word was not limited to professional writers, who not surprisingly believed in the power of the pen to change attitudes and behaviour. The author of *Adultery Analysed* was a clergyman and he too highlighted the alarming influence of novels, which 'confound the distinction between right and wrong, and in process of time drive morality and religion from the earth'. It was the discrepancy between fiction and reality that also lay at the heart of much criticism of the aristocracy, who were perceived to be acting a false role to disguise their true nature. Both the nobility and novels had the power to seduce and deceive audiences with an inauthentic performance. The writer highlighted this disparity between public display and private reality, complaining that 'our nobles, who ought to set an example of virtuous manners and sound morality, are the first to uphold the cause of vice ... the star which glitters on the breast of nobility will lose all its lustre when it is known that vice reigns beneath it'.

Another pamphlet typical of the new wave of reformist polemic was *The Evils of Adultery*, which also voiced popular opinion that the two main causes of adultery were elite immorality and publications 'that have such a powerful effect to corrupt the morals of the people'.[14] It cited the bad example of men of rank and fortune as 'the *first*, and a very powerful cause. It is from them that we are to expect the lead either in virtue or in vice', and argued that 'a general reformation of manners will never take place until great men take the lead. They have much power: a virtuous nobility must be the greatest blessing to a nation, but a profligate nobility must be the greatest curse.'

It labelled adulterers 'murderers of the peace of mankind' and deplored the popularity of scandal in those 'vehicles of vice' the daily papers and in novels that 'people of all ranks and ages do so greedily devour', which 'debauch the morals, and ... corrupt the taste'. Again, it was the insidious ability of novels to deceive readers and influence their lives which was so disturbing:

> Novels dress out vice in pleasing colours ... and thus insensibly instil the deadly poison into the thoughtless and unwary heart ... Full of the romantic ideas that they collect from such books, they long to copy the manners, and to share the fate of some of their favourite heroines.

The power of literature, this time in the guise of the periodical, was also described by the *Evangelical Magazine* in a preface to the first issue in 1793 giving the rationale for launching a publication to promote Christian thought. It explained that the periodical 'has produced a surprising revolution in sentiments and manners' because it reached a far larger readership than books and 'is therefore a powerful engine in the moral world, and may, by skilful management, be directed to the accomplishment of the most salutary or destructive purposes'. In a later issue, there was a full page diagram entitled 'The Spiritual Barometer' that listed a love of novels as one of the sins leading to perdition, only four grades less wicked than drunkenness and adultery.

The flood of printed matter urging moral reform emphasised the Church of England's belief in self-control to temper the passions, which needed to be 'placed under the controul of reason and religion'.[15] It was this religious doctrine, that human impulses should be feared and controlled by rigorous self-discipline, that contributed to the transformation of popular attitudes to sexuality. By the mid-eighteenth century earlier ideas that women had lustier sexual appetites than men were replaced by a new ideal of passive female sexuality under attack from predatory males.[16] Traditional positive views that natural sexual urges were healthy had changed to a conviction that sexual activity was dangerous though inevitable in men, but utterly deplorable in women. This sense of the alarming and destructive potential of unregulated sexuality was heightened in the 1790s as events unfolding in France were watched with growing horror and a foreboding that England too was on the verge of social chaos:

> If we but advance a very little farther in the path of vicious indulgence and moral depravity, we shall not be able to avoid the fate which has befallen our neighbours ...[we] probably shall ... by our vices, induce a revolution in this kingdom.[17]

The Earl of Denbigh summed up the nation's incredulity at the terrible behaviour of 'the French Monsters', writing, 'I look upon the French to be but little better than mad.'[18]

The corrupting influence of French immorality and widespread libertinism 'transplanted into this island', was blamed by many people for the rising number of crim. con. actions and a general decline in public manners which now threatened national security.[19] Popular notions of French sexual licence were not new, and had been graphically illustrated in Choderlos de Laclos' shocking 1782 novel *Les Liaisons Dangereuses*, which portrayed the cynical games of seduction played by a depraved aristocracy. The book's salacious content created a sensation and it was widely read in England, as Georgiana, Duchess of Devonshire admitted to her mother Countess Spencer: 'As to the Liaisons it was the noise the book made, that tempted me to read it – I plead guilty.'[20] Written in a series of letters, the novel illustrated the conflict between reason and emotion in the two main protagonists, French aristocrats who disguised their more vulnerable emotions by deliberately acting as callous seducers. The process of manipulating others was explained by the scheming Marquise de Merteuil: 'It amused me to assume different disguises, and … I began to display upon the great stage the talents I had acquired', 'my principles … are the fruit of profound reflection. I have created them: I might say that I have created myself.' Distrust of the nobility itself was often framed as a fear of this cunning ability to create a fictitious public persona.

These concerns fed into the increasingly heated political debates on the role of the aristocracy, which were fuelled by Edmund Burke's *Reflections on the Revolution in France* and radical responses like Thomas Paine's *Rights of Man* which advocated the abolition of the aristocracy.[21] Against this backdrop, fears of an imminent French invasion and the subsequent threat to social order were naturally sending shivers of apprehension through the English nobility. Repeated references to the impending danger cropped up in their correspondence from the 1790s right through into the early 1800s. Writing about a recent society gathering, the Earl of Morley's sister Theresa noted that 'Lady Mt Edgecumbe thinks and talks of nothing but the French, and the dangerous Consequences that she thinks the Revolution in France likely to produce in England.'[22] In another letter written from the country, she said, 'They are making such Preparations in London I should like to know what is going on, for we who are so quiet here do not quite comprehend what the Dangers are that they seem to be so afraid of in the Newspapers.'[23] Four years later the threat still loomed, as the wife of the Ambassador to Spain, the Marchioness of Bute, confirmed: 'They say the French are to invade us in Harvest Time.'[24] In summer 1801 the king cancelled his planned visit to Saltram, Morley's Devon estate, due to the threat of invasion, and Theresa wrote to a relative, 'What do you think of an Invasion? It seems quite to be believ'd in London, and indeed I can't see what shd prevent it.'[25] Two years later she was even more worried: 'I really live in dread of the Invasion from morng till night and I even dream of it.'[26]

As the sense of anxiety deepened in the aftermath of the Revolution, beliefs that a corrupt French aristocracy had brought about the collapse of society increased concerns about elite immorality in England and the likely consequences: 'Alas! look to the most exalted ranks, and see in them the most disgraceful depredations on the customs and decencies of moral life, and … thence downward … trace the melancholy effects of high example.'[27] Mary Wollstonecraft's response to Burke, entitled *A Vindication of the Rights of Men*, denigrated decadent French aristocracy and condemned the example of the English nobility, whose 'numberless vices, forced in the hot-bed of wealth, assume a sightly form to dazzle the senses' of the lower ranks. She added, 'And we express surprise that adulteries are so common!'[28]

Similar views were outlined in the 1799 pamphlet *Thoughts on Marriage, and Criminal Conversation* written by 'a Friend to Social Order', who said recent changes apparent in the human mind were as astonishing as revolutionary changes witnessed in the same period and criticised 'the frequent custom among such as fill the great and opulent ranks, of trampling on those matrimonial obligations which … they pretend to support, perhaps as legislators to guard'. The aristocratic role was to be falsely hypocritical, with a veneer of public authority hiding an entirely different reality underneath. The pamphlet printed a front-page dedication to Lord Kenyon, praising his patriotic intentions in imposing 'severe and exemplary punishments' against 'the deformers of society' but arguing that prison sentences for adulterers would be more effective as punishment: 'Pecuniary fines, almost exceeding the means of the offender, have been imposed … without abolishing, and almost without diminishing, the prevalence of this heinous vice'.[29]

Influenced by his strong religious faith, Lord Kenyon believed that 'the morals of the people are in some manner entrusted to our care'. He had led what amounted to a personal anti-adultery crusade since becoming Lord Chief Justice in 1788, by promoting the award of huge damages in crim. con. trials which were meant to act as a deterrent to other prospective adulterers. The number of cases where fines exceeding £2,000 were awarded quadrupled during his fourteen years in office and later reached their maximum of around twenty-two legal actions in 1810–19.[30] Summing up in the Marquis of Blandford's trial, Kenyon expressed his hopes for the reforming power of the law:

> Cases of this sort, I am sorry to say, multiply beyond measure. Whether … by holding the parties up to contempt and infamy, and by putting one's hands deep into the purses of defendants, they may be at last suppressed, is more than I will venture to promise.[31]

Addressing the jury in the cause brought by the Earl of Mountnorris, who was awarded £2,000 damages (roughly £120,000 now) against his wife's lover, Kenyon criticised 'the depravity of the age' which produced so much adultery and said juries in past cases had co-operated with him by imposing punitive damages, 'endeavouring to administer Justice to the party injured, not only to repair the injury, but to see if we could not repress the licentiousness of the times. Hitherto the history of the day shews it has not been done'.[32] In fact, such large potential damages were actually having the opposite effect and were one reason behind the rising number of crim. con. trials, together with the requirement for this lawsuit in all cases before a Parliamentary divorce could be granted.

As the number of crim. con. actions peaked at forty-one in the decade of the 1790s, a moral reaction set in against monetary damages which evidently were not proving an effective deterrent anyway. The diarist Mrs Thrale noted, 'Never were there so many Adultery Causes brought forward in the Ecclesiastical Courts as this Year 1794. One follows another so rapidly – 'tis shocking; nor do the enormous Damages awarded seem in any wise to lessen their Number.'[33] The highest ever number of divorce petitions presented to Parliament in one year was twelve during 1799. Not only was there widespread disapproval of the idea that a wife's fidelity could have a price, but it had become clear that the plaintiff's motive in most cases was not to win payment from the defendant for the injury, but to enable himself and his wife to divorce and remarry by deliberate collusion between all parties in setting up the case.

The sizeable fines awarded in some well-publicised trials involving the nobility began to provoke adverse public comment, and one pamphlet satirising the Bible's ten commandments joked that 'adultery is certainly one of the most lucrative trades', with wise couples deliberately plotting to ensnare a rich lover, demand damages and 'enjoy themselves in private over the booty'.[34] In a sweeping attack on the poor moral example of those in high life, it noted, 'The chief thing in which fine breeding and manners consist, is the passing off the counterfeit with a good air, and defending the deceit at the risk of life itself.' Here again elite performance was seen through and denounced as fake, with genuinely respected personal qualities being assumed like stage costumes as a disguise for personal immorality. Women were making only a pretence of modesty and men a pretence of honour. Not only was adultery a betrayal of true nobility but the crime was then compounded by the charade of collusive crim. con. trials where all parties conspired in a deception by acting false roles.

The need for a hasty remarriage was the motive in the case of Lady Elizabeth Howard, who was heavily pregnant by her lover when her adultery trial took place in 1794. At nineteen she had been the victim of a forced marriage by her ambitious parents, the Earl and Countess of Fauconberg, who wanted a duke for their daughter and not the mere earl's son she was already in love with. Their preferred suitor was Bernard Howard, heir to the Duke of Norfolk and the spectacular family seat of Arundel Castle in West Sussex. He proposed at a grand ball hosted by the Duchess of Devonshire and they were married in April 1789, going on to have one son. But the marriage was unhappy from the start because Elizabeth was still in love with her sweetheart Richard Bingham, heir to the 2nd Earl of Lucan.

One of the many newspaper reports of the crim. con. trial appeared in the *Morning Post* on 25 February 1794. It printed all the evidence given by witnesses, including Elizabeth's maid Mrs Bishop, who said that after the wedding ceremony the young bride 'wept, appeared very distressed and trembled exceedingly'. The couple spent a three-week honeymoon in the country and then returned to London where Elizabeth was formally presented at court. 'She often cried, threw herself into a chair, often went to sleep in it and with difficulty was prevailed on to go to bed', said Mrs Bishop. Mark Singleton, Esquire, a neighbour of Howard's in the country, said they did not appear to be a happy couple and did not cohabit like people attached to each other. At this point in the report the *Morning Post* inserted the note, 'Here the witness shewed strong symptoms of embarrassment in being obliged to disclose the private secrets of his friend.' Singleton went on to say that Howard told him shortly after the marriage that 'he had not the affection of Lady Elizabeth and his wife would not allow him to have any connexion with her for two months'.

Bingham left London soon after the wedding, retiring to the country to try and overcome his feelings, but within a year the young lovers were meeting secretly again. When Howard found out he reasoned with his wife, suggesting she went to stay with her family to try and forget about the affair. On one occasion she pretended to visit her father but instead went to Bingham's house in Park Lane. At the adultery trial held in Westminster Hall before Lord Kenyon, prosecuting counsel Mr Mingay stressed the importance of the case, which involved the family of Norfolk, 'a name of the first celebrity' and the heir to Lord Lucan, who were 'two persons of high rank and station in the country'. He said the whole house of Howard had a right to complain because the illegitimate child might inherit the title if the present duke died without issue.[35] 'We live in an age where newspapers decide before the courts, and the dailies have said Mr Howard knew she loved Bingham before their marriage.' In fact, as the defence lawyer Thomas Erskine said, 'they cordially hated one another'. Elizabeth refused Howard the privileges of a husband and often slept on a couch in tears. When she did go to bed with him, she would throw desponding arms round the neck of her maid and 'wept as a criminal preparing for execution'. The rejected husband told a relative, 'Elizabeth never loved me.' Even the old Duke of Norfolk was sympathetic to his heir's errant wife, saying in a letter he felt commiseration for an unhappy lady, who was the object of the sincerest pity.

Summing up in Bingham's defence, Erskine took care to emphasise that money was not the motive in this case of 'an inauspicious marriage which should never have existed' and said Bingham had acted honourably. The judge agreed, commenting that it was a very unfortunate case in which he felt extremely for both parties, and little blame could be attributed to Bingham who had tried to end his affections for the lady: 'Alas, it has appeared that the plaintiff never had the affection of this woman; her love was engaged, and though the object absented himself for a time, yet when they met, the unextinguished flame lighted again.' Because of the unusual nature of the case Lord Kenyon awarded damages of £1,000 (roughly £60,000 today) intended to be 'not nominal but not large, to show the morality of the defendant'. He said, 'This cause has a character different from all I have ever witnessed. The plaintiff acted with the honour belonging to an illustrious house, but her affection was engaged from the beginning to another person.'

The court case and Howard Divorce Bill hearing received extensive coverage in the press, including the *Sun*, the *Morning Advertiser* and the *Whitehall Evening Post*. The divorce was granted in May and the same month

Elizabeth married Bingham, but wedded bliss did not last and the couple separated ten years later. Howard eventually succeeded to the title as twelfth Duke of Norfolk in 1815, but after such a bad experience first time round he never remarried.

Several pamphlets printing a full report of the trial went on sale, one a seventy-seven-page verbatim transcript of the court proceedings 'taken in short-hand by a student of the Inner Temple' and priced at two shillings. Another forty-six-page trial report was 'embellished with a striking likeness of the lady' in a sketch showing Elizabeth with one naked breast exposed, the typical pose denoting a woman of easy virtue at the time, and wearing a headdress topped with a fashionable long feather to imply membership of the morally dubious *bon ton*.

During the court hearing, Erskine seized the chance to make a political point with a stark warning:

> Let the aristocracy of England, which trembles so much for itself, take heed to its own security. Let the nobles of England, if they mean to preserve that superiority which in some shape or other must exist in every social community, take care to support it. Instead of matching themselves to supply wealth, idly squandered in debauchery and excesses, or to round the quarters of a family shield … let them live as their fathers of old lived – marry as affection and prudence lead the way, and in the ardours of mutual affection and the simplicity of rural life, lay the foundations of a vigorous race of men.

He concluded with an ominous reference to the terrifying example of the French Revolution: 'Let them do this and instead of dangerous divisions between different ranks of life, and jealousies of the multitude, big with destruction, we should see our country living as one large and harmonious family, which will never take place amid vice and corruption.'

16

Scandalous Entertainment

As morality became a key issue in public arenas a natural counter-reaction set in, so that scandalous behaviour and sexual indiscretions in elite circles became both more shocking and more titillating. At the same time as religious groups were making use of the press to spread messages of moral reform, profit-conscious publishers were finding new ways to feed readers' apparently insatiable appetite for scandal. The best means of catering to popular taste was the clever manipulation in print of the lives and characters of the great, creating a range of appealing aristocratic figures that would meet the market demand for entertainment.

The latest wave of moral reform had heightened public awareness of the dissolute conduct of the elite and hardened attitudes towards adultery, which seemed to be worrying evidence of a corrupt nobility no longer fit to lead society. Peers were now having to accept their new visibility to the broad national audience of the reading public, but this high profile brought with it greater exposure to public criticism. Since the 1770s satirical publications surveying the aristocracy had become popular, such as Coleman's *A Satirical Peerage*, *The Patricians*, and *Miniature Pictures* which tellingly presented peers as theatrical figures. Many other new publications arrived in the crowded literary marketplace aiming to satisfy the public obsession with elite lives.

Among these titles was *Bon Ton Magazine*, launched in 1791 specifically to cash in on this fad. It appeared monthly and had the eclectic mix of factual and fictional articles so characteristic of late eighteenth-century periodicals. In addition to straightforward 'Tales, Anecdotes and Adventures' it offered a titillating read with the assistance of some witty if gentle innuendo and illustrations which succinctly made their point, such as one example featuring a lecherous old man grasping a large walking stick. Each issue included amusing snippets on fashionable life, popular songs, serialised fiction, an adultery trial, theatrical gossip, poetry, historical or mythical tales, satirical articles and eccentric pieces like the evidently popular series on eunuchs which ran for six months from August 1793.

Typical in its focus on elite sexual scandal was the series called 'Dictionary of the Bon Ton', which ran for several months from March 1791, listing under the letter A, 'Adultery – a very fashionable amusement for married ladies, and never so greatly in vogue, particularly in high life, as at present.' In an amusing reference to the endearment often used in love letters reported at crim. con. trials, 'A Modern Glossary' defined Angel as 'the name of a woman, commonly of a very bad one.'[36] An item in the news column for July 1791 reported, 'The late rise in the prices of crim. con. has induced several of the honest Gentlemen, who have handsome wives, to send them to the Watering Places so that they may be out of harm's way.' And in another topical reference to current concerns, an article 'On Divorces' argued it was unfair that only the rich were 'permitted to get rid of their frail and roving spouses whenever they please'.[37]

The preface to the first issue set out the magazine's intention of 'exhibiting the *great* world in epitome', a phrase that was particularly significant as it described precisely its method of presenting the elite in a series of caricatures supposedly emblematic of the group as a whole. This aim was also emphasised in the magazine's subtitle *Microscope of Fashion and Folly*, which signalled clearly to readers that inside they could expect to find a range of entertaining aristocratic stock characters like the libertine, the 'Bacchanalian Peer', the adulteress who 'has actually seduced an athletic young man of 22 who performed at Astleys', the frivolous lady of fashion 'who bought a dress and paid for it in farthings', or the laughable old lord 'who has lately written an elaborate treatise on *rice pudding*'.[38]

Audiences in the Georgian playhouse expected to play an active part in dramatic productions and were highly influential in shaping performances via comment and interaction with the cast. Audiences of readers and writers had similar power and took on the same active role in relation to performances by public figures. Publishers created profitable texts by feeding readers' appetite for aristocratic scandal, and readers then interacted with these publications to interpret the performances on the page.

The *Bon Ton* presented its own version of an immoral and ridiculous aristocracy whose various disguises were no longer believable. Through the clever selection and manipulation of reported behaviour by real peers, together with extra imaginary touches of artistic licence, the magazine created a cast of archetypal roles for a discredited nobility guaranteed to satisfy reader expectations. It fulfilled the seller's part of the commercial transaction by providing the entertainment readers had paid for. And as paying consumers with clear expectations, *Bon Ton* readers became complicit in perpetuating these pseudo-fictitious aristocratic roles they wanted to believe existed.

The magazine folded in 1796 when its method of holding up the aristocracy to ridicule could well have been viewed as politically dangerous due to the subversive way it undermined their public image and authority. Publishers had become understandably more nervous in the uneasy atmosphere of the 1790s, after the introduction of new measures to limit the freedom of the press. Stamp duties, licensing requirements and other new regulations led to vast increases in taxes on printed matter, while legislation such as the 1792 Libel Act boosted the number of prosecutions of booksellers and publishers for seditious, obscene and blasphemous libel. However, *Bon Ton*'s explicit purpose of providing entertainment by exposing vice in high places was reaffirmed when it emerged again under different publishers as *New Bon Ton Magazine* in 1818.

A distinctive feature of the *Bon Ton*'s method of manipulating elite figures like puppets was its repeated use of the idea of aristocracy as entertainers parading for the delight of readers. In some articles real aristocrats were presented as fictional characters in a story, portrayed for example as 'the heroine of our present narrative', or 'our heroine'.[39] In others they became synonymous with actors putting on a show, notably in the back pages of each issue which were given over to a regular column of news and anecdotes entitled 'Bon Ton &c' in which aristocracy and theatre merged. Reports of leading actors and stage news were interspersed at random with the everyday activities of lords and ladies, and this deliberate juxtaposition became increasingly prominent in later issues when the column was expanded and headed 'Bon Ton Intelligence'.

A typical example from August 1795 included rumours that Lord Mountnorris would 'act the part of Noodle to Lady Buckingham's Tom Thumb', a report that the Duke of Hamilton and the actress Mrs Esten were to visit Southampton where she was performing, news of repairs at Covent Garden Theatre, the Duke of Clarence's debts and the debut of a player at the Haymarket Theatre. Similarly, the October 1795 issue reported on the Duke of Bedford's cropped hair, the new green room at Drury Lane, an overture composed by the Duchess of Leeds and confusion over two peeress's invitation cards. The January 1796 column included news of the Duchess of Gordon's daughter, Mrs Esten the actress, Lady Campbell's dress, the Duke of Rutland's auburn hair, Lady Wallace's stay at Margate, the actor Mr Kemble, a pantomime at Drury Lane, Lord Carlisle's baby, an actress's benefit night, the Countess of Buckinghamshire's appearance in private theatricals and Lord Bridport's visit to Bath. This intermingling of gossip about high life and the theatrical world was both highly effective and cleverly calculated to achieve *Bon Ton*'s mission of presenting the nobility 'in epitome' to amuse its readers.

Real life was reworked as fiction in an article for the August 1791 issue 'Tête-à-tête of the Amorous Margrave and the Titled Wanderer', a satirical tale about the infidelities and European exile of the notorious adulteress Elizabeth Craven, wife of the 6th Baron Craven whose estates included Benham near Newbury in Berkshire and Combe Abbey in Warwickshire. In the story Lady Craven starred as 'our heroine' and her second husband, the Margrave of Brandenburg-Anspach, as 'the hero of our present narrative'. The narrator criticised Lady Craven's own published travel writings for giving a heavily edited version of reality: 'In the publication, we find blanks, which in private correspondence, were no doubt filled with the most glowing representations.' She was cast as an alluring Cleopatra figure who persuaded her lover 'like a second Antony' to give up his public role in Prussia to become 'a private individual … in this character, it is thought, he will remain for the remainder of his existence'. Readers were drawn into the illusion that the nobility were cunning masters of disguise who could assume and discard glamorous roles as they pleased. Reputedly beautiful and captivating, Lady Craven had first created a scandal years earlier, as a socialite in her twenties, by having an affair with the French Ambassador, which was reported in *Town and Country Magazine*. After many more indiscreet liaisons Lord Craven insisted on a separation but never divorced her, and was content to live happily with his long-term mistress. Lady Craven moved to France where she met the margrave and became a prolific writer of travel memoirs and plays. On her return to England as the Margravine of Anspach after the death of Lord Craven in 1791, she indulged her theatrical pretensions by hosting and acting in performances at the private theatre of their new home Brandenburg House in London.[40]

Private theatricals like this had by now become a popular pastime in elite circles and several stately homes (notably Richmond House, home of the Duke of Richmond) had their own theatres where family members and their friends staged plays, sometimes with the help of professional actors. Fans included the Earl of Morley, who while a student at Oxford University attended the theatre at his friend Lord Spencer's home Blenheim Palace, reporting:

> The actors were Lt C Spencer, his son John Spencer (who performed very well indeed) … Lord Blandford (who has a most violent impediment off stage but much better when acting) … I went each night with Spencer, so I got very good places and staying till everybody was gone, Ld Blandford shewd me the dressing rooms &c. The Theatre at Blenheim is uncommonly pretty.[41]

However, Morley harboured no thespian aspirations for himself, as he admitted to his guardian: 'You may be well assured that nothing in the world would induce me to act, nor do I think that anything cd make me an actor, nor indeed do I wish it would.'[42] Despite his rejection of acting in the literal sense, he later became adept in various different roles at court, in the Lords and in his private life.

Theatre and everyday life did sometimes merge completely as in the case of Elizabeth Farren, an actress famous for her convincing stage performances of ladies of quality, who later successfully transferred her signature role into real life when she married Edward Smith Stanley, the 12th Earl of Derby. Best-known as founder of the horse-race called 'the Derby' at Epsom, he was a regular performer in private theatricals put on by his aristocratic friends, and it was probably due to his influence that Miss Farren was asked to supervise productions at Richmond House which were attended by royalty and fashionable society.[43] The earl had been separated from his wife, Elizabeth, since her ill-fated affair in 1779 with her girlhood sweetheart John Sackville, 3rd Duke of Dorset, whom she had been prevented from marrying by her socially ambitious mother. Dorset, whose estate was Knole Park near Sevenoaks in Kent, was a habitual womaniser whose other mistresses included the courtesan Nancy Parsons and Georgiana, Duchess of Devonshire. He soon split up with Elizabeth and moved on to his next conquest, leaving her to an uncertain future. A poem, *The Rocks of Meillerie*, published about the affair described her predicament:

When the deluded Mob of Fashion's crew
Reflected phantoms from my memory drew,
E'en then, let dire Remorse the truth impart,
I gave to D-r-y, what was D-r-t's heart,

But where's my Lover? Is my D-r-t fled
The dear Deserter of my injur'd bed?
Can he be false the Author of my fall?
Can he betray, for whom I've ruin'd all?

Ye Lauras and Horatias of the hour,
Warned by my fate, behold my fall'n power!

Despite the scandal, Derby took the ultimate revenge by refusing to take legal action or divorce her, so Elizabeth spent the next eighteen years as a social outcast unable to remarry, while he enjoyed a long courtship with Miss Farren, who apparently refused to become his mistress. The couple eventually married in 1797 six weeks after Elizabeth's death, when the new Countess of Derby retired from the theatre and officially adopted the role she had been rehearsing on stage for years, rising 'from the shade of obscurity ... to the enviable distinctions of opulence and rank'. [44]

The idea that a stage role had actually been transposed into real life must have been particularly satisfying to theatre-loving contemporaries. The fact that it seemed to confirm popular notions that aristocracy was basically a calculated performance only gave it an added resonance. In *The Testimony of Truth to Exalted Merit ... in Refutation of a False and Scandalous Libel*, Miss Farren's story was framed as a classic tale of female virtue under siege which is rewarded by marriage and social elevation, 'she ... preserved her reputation unsullied, and moved forward to honour with a steadiness of virtue almost unparalleled!' Both personal qualities and acting skills had contributed to her successful transition from performer to peeress: 'If she was happy at being a favourite with the town at large in her professional capacity, she was still more so in the elevated connections, to which the excellence of her moral character, and her elegant manners and accomplishments, served as the only introduction.'

The pamphlet was printed in reply to a satirical attack on Miss Farren entitled *Memoirs of the Present Countess of Derby*, which rapidly sold out and was reprinted five times. It presented her as a scheming social climber who used her professional skills to train herself in the art of personifying a fine lady, describing how she 'began now to behold, in fancy, the golden circle of Nobility … and she applied with such indefatigable pains to improvement, as within a few years to be justly considered a finished pattern of Female Fashion and Elegance'.[45] When her disguise was complete, she 'had the good fortune to be transferred from the mimic grandeur of the Stage to the real splendors [sic] of a Court'. Referring to her introduction at court, the writer commented that 'here her triumph was complete', but added sarcastically that 'here her ladyship's conversation … smelt of the Shop'. Nobility was again confirmed as a role which could be assumed, and which comprised a believable performance masking the fake hidden beneath. Miss Farren was not the only actress to marry into the peerage, and other marriages included Harriot Mellon to the 9th Duke of Beauclerk and Louisa Brunton to the 1st Earl of Craven.

Persistent ideas of the theatricality of aristocracy were reaffirmed in many published forms. Especially popular with female readers were novels featuring the love lives of aristocratic ladies or poor girls who married into the aristocracy, and masses of similar titles such as *True Delicacy; or, the History of Lady Frances Tilney* and *Twas Wrong to Marry Him; or the History of Lady Dursley* were churned out by publishers determined to cash in on this market. Despite their dubious literary qualities, these romances often topped the lending lists of circulating libraries. As a critic of *The Way to Lose Him* pointed out disparagingly in the *London Magazine*: 'Written solely for the use of the Circulating Library, and very proper to debauch all young women who are still undebauched.'

Publishers cleverly framed their offer to consumers as useful stories of moral instruction and entertainment, assuring readers that they published 'only such Novels as have for their objects … amusement, instruction, decency and morality'. In *The Way to Please Him, or, The History of Lady Sedley*, the long-suffering heroine neglected by her adulterous husband was 'an exemplary wife, and may serve as a pattern to married ladies in similar circumstances'. Here again aristocratic stereotypes were created and manipulated in text to give readers what they wanted, which was privileged access to the imagined personal lives of the titled. Novels were the ideal format in which to explore individual morality and roles in society by creating vivid images to engage the reader's imagination. They could evoke the inner emotions and motivations of characters, offering insights into situations which readers themselves could never hope to experience. This creation of a believable fantasy world was what worried critics, who thought the corrupting power of literature, and especially the novel, was its ability to enchant readers by distorting reality so they believed fiction as truth.

17

COURTESANS,
LORDS AND LADIES

The Duke of Ancaster picked up a high-class prostitute in a shop by buying her a pineapple for one guinea. She was so impressed with this extravagant gesture that she soon agreed to become his mistress. Attracting a wealthy and titled man was the ambition of every young girl, but if a wedding ring was not on offer there were plenty of other luxuries to be enjoyed in return for sexual favours.

Rich and powerful men never had a problem finding women more than keen to become their mistresses, whether for a brief lusty fling or a long-term arrangement. The unconventional domestic life of the 3rd Earl of Egremont was the subject of endless gossip, spawning exaggerated tales of his vast mansion filled with unruly mistresses and bastards. During a stay at his country estate Petworth House in Sussex, Lady Bessborough reported the rumours described by a friend:

> Nothing will persuade her that Ld Egremont has not forty three Children who all live in the House with him and their respective Mothers ... when any quarrels arise, which few days pass without, each mother takes part with her Progeny, bursts into the drawing room, fight with each other, Ld E, his Children, and I believe the Company, and make scenes worthy of Billinsgate or a Mad House.

Other peers preferred to keep that part of their life separate, like the 5th Duke of Bedford who lived peacefully with his wife at Woburn Abbey in

Bedfordshire, while enjoying extra-marital comforts elsewhere. He later left annuities in his will to three women in Marylebone and a large sum of money to Mrs Palmer of Curzon Street for the education of his two illegitimate children.[46]

Women who were 'taken into keeping' by a rich protector worked in an elite form of prostitution, far removed from the hazardous existence of grubby streetwalkers who could be bought for a few pennies in the Strand or whores at brothels concentrated in the sleazy Covent Garden and Southwark districts of London. It was a short-lived and precarious occupation, and once past their early twenties it was hard for girls to make a living, especially in the capital, which by the 1790s had more than 50,000 prostitutes competing for work. At the very top of the career ladder were the most beautiful and highly paid courtesans known as demi-reps, who possessed the beauty, sexual charm, intelligence, wit and cunning to attract aristocratic clients. They were not merely casual mistresses to be enjoyed and thrown aside but chose their own patrons and cultivated long-term relationships that effectively gave them the status of a common-law wife. These women of the *demi-monde* led a glamorous existence, living with their keepers or at their own establishments in elegantly furnished houses in St James' Square and Pall Mall, with their own servants and often the ultimate luxury of their own carriage. They dressed in the latest fashions and wore the lavish jewels gifted by besotted admirers. The lucky ones like Nancy Parsons managed to hang on to each lover for many years, and when the affair finally ended they were often passed on to other peers in the same small circle, perhaps gratefully pensioned off with a small income or left a bequest in a will. Only a rare few actually went on to marry a client, like Elizabeth Armistead whose wealthy keepers included the 2nd Viscount Bolingbroke, the Earl of Derby and Duke of Dorset before she began a long relationship with the politician Charles Fox and eventually married him in 1795.

Another way of earning financial security from a career as a successful courtesan was for girls to publish a kiss-and-tell memoir revealing the secret private lives of their many titled lovers. These juicy tales of the *demi-monde* cleverly blended fact and imagination in highly fictionalised accounts masquerading as biography. Some were published as a form of blackmail by which to extort money from clients in exchange for anonymity, while others were actually written by canny anonymous male authors merely pretending to be women of easy virtue. They created a beguiling fantasy world of depravity and intrigue in these 'memoirs' which relied on stereotypes, like the cunning rake and the virtuous fallen woman, in predictable story lines which would have been familiar to novel readers. Rich in anecdotes of sexual liaisons with wealthy men, the memoirs gave a fascinating new perspective on public figures with tantalising glimpses of their personal behaviour. In the role of sexual predator, clients were presented in an unappealing light as laughable figures unable to control their base appetites, or ageing libertines who carelessly exploited young women forced by economic necessity to sell themselves to the highest bidder.

It was well known that some actresses subsidised a stage career with better-paid work as a courtesan. One best-selling biography framed as a touching morality tale was *The Memoirs of Mrs Sophia Baddeley, late of Drury-Lane Theatre*, published by her friend and companion Elizabeth Steele.[47] A stunning beauty who collected crowds of ardent admirers, Sophia was, according to the *Town and Country Magazine*, originally encouraged by her husband to make the most of her talents: 'Not satisfied with the emoluments of his wife's acting, he resolved to turn her to every possible advantage, and profit by the first opportunity that offered to dispose of her charms.' On stage she was best known for roles of innocent femininity in genteel comedy, while off-stage she took the part of mistress to a series of rich old men, including 1st Viscount Melbourne and the 4th Duke of Ancaster, who had told her, 'You are such a wonder of nature that no man can gaze on you unwounded.' He was immediately smitten when he met her in a shop, and after buying the exotic fruit as a gift to impress he later sent round an unsigned note hinting at his intentions:

> The unexpected pleasure of seeing Mrs B this morning gave no time for imparting a matter of some consequence to her. The pineapple will inform who writes this, and this evening he will call at nine to communicate what it is to Mrs B.

It was this sort of thrilling anecdote that readers enjoyed so much, and the 'memoir' reported Sophia's encounters with peers in detail, portraying her clients as both exploiters and exploited, tiresome lechers who lusted after her body but were tolerated as a useful means of paying off her debts. It showed an ambivalent attitude to the titled, as a class to be both admired and scorned. Describing their attendance at a subscription ball for the nobility, Mrs Steele commented that, 'the attention universally shewn us by men of the first rank … was exceedingly flattering, but absolutely trouble-some'. Next day three eager dukes and a handful of lords all came round to call.[48] The book recounted at length Sophia's brief but dazzling time as a celebrity at the pinnacle of fashionable life, when she was Lord Melbourne's mistress. But the descriptions of extravagant society goings-on were inter-spersed with sarcastic comments which subtly undermined his superior status:'Lord Melbourne was not the brightest man of the age, as his letters sent to Mrs Baddeley at times, will shew, and he … was acquainted neither with good grammar or orthography.'[49]

The nobility were again depicted as pathetic, easily manipulated figures in the memoirs of actress and courtesan George Anne Bellamy, who was actually the illegitimate daughter of Lord Tyrawley. Told in a series of letters, *An Apology for the Life of George Anne Bellamy, late of Covent-Garden Theatre. Written by Herself* was actually penned by journalist Alexander Bicknell, who was obviously well aware of the market for scandal. In the preface he criticised those writers 'who wantonly rob others of their good name' and commented on, with amusing hypocrisy:

> … the indecent lengths to which personal reflections are carried in some publications … a character is often mangled, and the fair fame of the devoted prey blasted, upon hearsay assertions, and the most groundless and improb-able conjectures, merely to make a paragraph. I am sorry to say, that the writers know that scandal is almost universally acceptable; and so they can, by dealing out a sufficient quantity of it, enhance the value of their publica-tions, and encrease their emoluments. [50]

A series of anecdotes about Miss Bellamy's involvement with various lords and ladies portrayed them as superior beings whose patronage was an honour, and at the same time as predictable characters who she manip-ulated – the men by her sexual charms and the women by her enviable knowledge of fashion. In a smug tone that was alternately boastful and moralising, Miss Bellamy stressed her own self-importance by recounting the notice paid to her by members of high society, their presents of money and requests for advice. This strange blend of homage and belittlement encapsulated the appeal of many publications which traded in aristocracy as a lucrative commodity. Clever writers like Bicknell identified readers' ambivalent attitude to social superiors, and then crafted their work to satisfy these mixed feelings of curiosity, reluctant admiration and envy.

The coupling of scandal with morality consistently proved to be a successful sales device. Miss Bellamy's life story, published in five volumes, was presented as an educational tale of corrupted innocence and was so popular it was serialised in newspapers and reprinted in pirate editions by rival publishers.[51] A review in the *Universal Magazine* noted, 'These Memoirs ... are uncommonly instructive. Vice appears not here in attractive colours', while the *European Magazine* commented that they would 'serve to warn the young, the giddy, and the gay, of the softer sex from the syren shore of vanity, dissipation, and illicit pleasures'.[52] Competition was so fierce that a legal battle ensued and *The Morning Chronicle* reported that the High Court had granted an injunction prohibiting sales of a cheaper pirated version of the *Memoirs* which were 'a Grub-street Mutilation' of the original books printed by J. Bell of the Strand for 15s. The rival publisher J. Walker of Paternoster-row appealed and the following month the court dissolved the injunction, ruling that their book written by 'a gentleman of Covent Garden Theatre' was 'a fair and correct abridgement'. It went back on sale at 2s 6d, successfully undercutting J. Bell's original.

The autobiography of another well-known actress and courtesan, Mary Robinson, was published in 1801 after her death, and the four-volume *Memoirs of the Late Mrs Robinson, Written by Herself* included some of her poetry. She had had a brief stage career before becoming mistress to the young Prince George, among others, and achieving fame as an author. A later memoir that also caused a sensation was published by Harriette Wilson, the most sought-after courtesan of her day, who made money from the book's huge sales and also by blackmailing some of her rich former clients who were prepared to pay hush money to keep their names and sexual proclivities out of print. When the fourth volume appeared later than expected, one of the many newspapers printing extracts from it reported that the delay in publication had, 'arisen from the policy of omitting an exposure of a certain distinguished family ... A negociation [sic] was opened, and we understand the offensive matter was withdrawn'. The article explained how a noble duke had agreed to settle a £200 annuity on Harriette for life, but the paper cautiously added, 'We give this as the *on dit* of the day – it is the topic of general conversation among the lovers of scandal, and may or may not have foundation.' There was no doubt about the authenticity of the *Memoirs*, and everyone had heard of Harriette's conquests in the highest ranks, including Lord Craven, Sir Arthur Wellesley the future Duke of Wellington, and the diplomat Lord Ponsonby, so each volume was eagerly anticipated:

Few publications in modern times have excited such curiosity, or produced more extraordinary sensations in fashionable life. It finds its way into all circles, and the grave and the gay, the starched puritan and the professed libertine, are equally sedulous in perusing its pages … It seems that many characters in higher circles, are yet to be *shewn up*, and as strong testimony has been borne to the truth of the statements, the forthcoming numbers are expected with the greatest impatience.

An element of scandal like this inevitably attracted readers, but there was also a market for more conservative memoirs presenting the respectable public face of aristocracy. In addition to book-length autobiographical accounts of individual lives, brief potted biographies of lords and ladies, also entitled 'memoirs', appeared as regular features in periodicals such as the *London Magazine* and the *Ladies' Monthly Museum,* which showcased the most admirable individuals as masculine and feminine role models. Selected details of real lives were edited and shaped into familiar stock figures of virtue, in the same way that more scandalous lives were served up to the reading public as templates of vice. Life and literature were merged to create a new and different reality for purely commercial purposes.

The qualities admired in the model peer were summed up in a memoir of Earl Bathurst, which began, 'This nobleman, who has eminently distinguished himself by the integrity of his conduct in publick stations, and by his many virtues in private life, is descended from a very ancient family.' A memoir of the Lord Privy Seal, the Earl of Dartmouth, praised his devotion to serious study and pious domestic life: 'His attachment to letters, and to the endearments of domestic life, together with a pious turn of mind have secluded him from the bustle of public life.' It commended the 'immaculate integrity' of his character and held him up as a model speaker in the House of Peers, who needed 'little or no aid from the flowers of oratory'. In the case of the Lord Chief Justice, Lord Camden, he was lauded for success as a judge and his personal qualities as 'a sincere, honest man', but censured for not attending Parliament as regularly as expected, which was 'a very conspicuous blemish in his public conduct'.

Attention to public duty and the possession of a virtuous private character were prerequisites for the archetypal peer who should be a 'great and good man' who could be judged against the ideal role models of classical antiquity. This idea of exemplary leadership was summed up neatly in one article entitled 'On grandeur or strength of mind in publick characters', which eulogised

Roman senators as 'that great unparalleled … body of sages and heroes' and contrasted it unfavourably with their modern counterparts who were preoccupied merely with the shallow public display of power:

> Their majesty and consequence did not consist in circumstances, but in sentiment,
> shone not in a splendid equipage, but in magnanimous actions … Their lives
> were not idle and effeminate, dissipated in scenes of gaiety and places of publick
> resort; but hardy and laborious … and solely devoted to the public good.[53]

Manly leadership required physical and mental superiority demonstrated by action in government or war, complemented by personal virtues such as humility and serious-mindedness.

The perfect lady was portrayed as a wife and mother endowed with personal charms, fashionable accomplishments and a placid enjoyment of peaceful domesticity. Lady Augusta Campbell was described as 'a model for imitation in these degenerate times', who was 'distinguished from that herd of gay, dissipated women of fashion, whose whole time is devoted to a round of intoxicating public amusements'. Instead she devoted herself to useful learning and polite accomplishments 'to adorn the marriage state, and render it a scene of permanent domestic bliss'.[54] Similarly, the Duchess of Roxburgh was 'held up as a model well worthy the imitation of many of our modern quality', who enjoyed reading and music in the country in preference to 'the noisy and tumultuous scenes which constitute what is called high life'. And the Duchess of Gordon was praised for her 'affability of manners', intelligent conversation, aversion to gambling, and devotion to 'the duties of a parent'.[55]

Ladies who behaved like courtesans were the most intriguing figures of all. Shocking but fascinating in their apparently carefree promiscuity, they were part of society but flagrantly breaking all its rules. One of the most notorious adulteresses of the time was Frances Villiers, Countess of Jersey, who had a string of affairs before reaching the pinnacle of infidelity as long-term mistress of George, the future Prince Regent.[56] At seventeen she married the courtier George Bussy Villiers, 4th Earl of Jersey, but a quiet life of wifely duty at Middleton Park in Oxfordshire was not for her, and she was soon drawn into the racy Devonshire House circle and an endless round of fashionable dissipation. Tall, thin and elegant, with flamboyantly styled dark hair, Lady Jersey had a seductive charm that men found enthralling. But this glossy exterior concealed a malicious and calculating personality who enjoyed tormenting her rivals with a quick, biting wit that was satirised by Richard Sheridan as the unpleasant character Lady Sneerwell in his hit play *The School for Scandal*. Her lovers included Frederick Howard, the 5th Earl of Carlisle, and Georgiana's husband, the Duke of Devonshire, but it was not until she embarked on a long liaison with the Prince in 1793 that she became a figure of public hatred. Despite his wife's repeated infidelities there was never any question of divorce, and Lord Jersey seemed content to benefit from her royal influence by accepting a comfortable sinecure as Master of the Horse.

She was a grandmother in her forties when the royal affair began, but she soon exerted such influence over the infatuated prince that she encouraged him to marry his wealthy but fat, coarse and unattractive German cousin Princess Caroline of Brunswick in 1795. Ostensibly a way of paying off his debts, it was a cunning scheme of Lady Jersey's designed to rid him of Maria Fitzherbert, the Catholic widow he had 'married' in an invalid ceremony, and to secure her own position at court by contriving her appointment as a Lady of the Bedchamber. So unappealing, filthy and foul-smelling was the bride, that the prince apparently had to get drunk on brandy before he could face his wedding night duty and fell into the fireplace before managing valiantly to consummate the marriage.

After their daughter's birth the couple lived separately, but there was widespread public sympathy for Princess Caroline; dozens of satirical prints appeared condemning the prince's relationship with Lady Jersey, portraying her as a scrawny old hag who was being pimped by her pathetic husband. In one sketch by James Gillray titled *Fashionable-Jockeyship* the corpulent prince was pictured at his mistress' bedside, riding on the back of a diminutive Lord Jersey. And in Isaac Cruikshank's *Future Prospects, or Symptoms of Love in High Life* the prince shouted abuse at Caroline while through an open door Lord Jersey, wearing cuckold's horns, pointed towards his wife sprawled topless on a sofa.[57] The prince's behaviour was criticised by the press, including *The Times* which said:

> When high personages, placed in the most exalted ranks of society, discard all the respect they owe to themselves; when they stoop to the most disgraceful connexions, and above all when their vices, disorders and impudence raise just apprehensions for the welfare of the State ... it is then that the liberty of the Press ought to resume its dignity and denounce and point out to the public opinion him whom public justice cannot attaint.

Respectable society was careful to keep its distance from the poisonous royal mistress, as the Marchioness of Bute explained in a letter to the Earl of Denbigh: 'Lady Jersey gave a Concert and Supper last Monday – the Table was laid for forty People – only one lady staid – She a Mrs Campbell well known in the fashionable world.'[58] Despite her powerful position at court she became increasingly unpopular, and Lady Palmerston wrote:

> I thought Lady Jersey was as cunning as a serpent … Her worst enemy cannot wish her to pursue a line of conduct so destructive to the stability of her empire. She must feel like her cousin Robespierre (for I am sure they are related) and that ere long she may not be murdered but she will be driven from society.

She was hissed at in the streets of London and slogans saying 'no Lady Jersey' were daubed on walls around the city. When stories began to circulate that she had stolen sensitive letters written by Princess Caroline and passed them on to the queen, she was vilified throughout the press. The *Sun* newspaper commented:

> There are few crimes, which in the eye of morality, are more atrocious; few, which in the eye of the law, are more seriously deserving of punishment, than the CONCEALMENT AND OPENING OF PRIVATE LETTERS … the crime, which is the violation of virtue, of decency, and of honour, so gross, so scandalous, so offensive, as to excite the most marked and general indignation, and to effect the exclusion of the culprit from all societies in which vice is detested and virtue cherished.

Such was the level of public feeling that her effigy was burnt in the street, and she was forced to leave her house in Pall Mall after it was attacked by a furious mob. Eventually she resigned her court post and vacated the house near the prince's official residence of Carlton House, where he had installed her. Her influence was waning, and in 1798 she was discarded by the prince for other women and possibly bribed to go abroad to allow the furore to die down. But she was not granted the annuity that might have been expected for a cast-off mistress, her husband lost his cushy post in the royal household and their debts grew so bad that Lord Jersey was at one point threatened with debtors' prison. It was a humiliating end to all her ambitious scheming.

18

'A Sin of the Deepest Dye'

At the turn of the century the moral state of the nation was clearly a source of great unhappiness for many people, and it was against this troubled backdrop that two new attempts were made to curb adultery through Parliamentary legislation in 1800 and 1809. The first was similar to its predecessor in 1779 but amended to propose that adultery was made a criminal offence punishable by fines and a prison sentence. It also addressed concerns about the collusion evident in many crim. con. actions by prohibiting later marriage between an adulterous wife and her lover.[59] Although both bills were eventually defeated, these new proposals were discussed at length with a seriousness and urgency in marked contrast to the scant attention paid to earlier bills in the 1770s. The debates were reported widely in the press and provoked strong reactions, such as the comments appearing in the *Anti-Jacobin Review* protesting at the bill's rejection by Parliament 'as a public calamity, as a fatal wound to the religious and moral character of the nation'.[60] It questioned why adultery, 'a sin of the deepest dye', which 'shakes the whole fabric of civil society' was not considered a crime when the petty theft of a rabbit or a fish incurred the death penalty.

Introducing the 1800 bill, Lord Auckland said that adultery had 'become a dangerous and scandalous evil', and he cited the moral decay witnessed in France as a warning of the dire consequences for the nation if the crime went unchecked: 'Great Britain has preserved her existence amidst the paroxysms … and downfalls of nations, by the effect of our being a little less irreligious and less immoral than others.' The Bishop of Rochester was convinced that the frequency of divorce 'was the source of all the evil that sapped the morality and manners of the people', noting that in France the profanation of marriage was the first step taken 'to break down the fences of law, religion, and morality, and to introduce that violence ... and anarchy, that had over-run so many states'.[61] And he condemned the motive of collusion so often seen in cases involving the characters of 'the indifferent husband, the gay wife, the amorous seducer'. Lord Eldon argued that nine out of ten cases of crim. con. 'were founded in the most infamous collusion, and that as the law stood, it was a farce and mockery, most of the cases being previously settled in some room in the City, and juries are called to give exemplary damages, which are never paid to, nor expected by, the injured husband'.[62]

The issue of collusion and the likelihood of punishment deterring others were among the main points debated. The notion of divorce for all (which would finally become law in the Divorce Reform Act of 1857) also emerged, and many shared the views of Lord Auckland who acknowledged the 'privileges and distinctions which belonged to rank and property' but argued that the higher classes should not enjoy the exclusive right to divorce merely because of the expense incurred. He criticised the system of Parliamentary divorce as 'a code of adultery for a privileged caste'. The deciding point which led to the defeat of the 1800 bill in the House of Commons at its second reading was its unfairness to women. Viscount Wentworth gave a proxy vote in favour of the bill on behalf of his friend the Earl of Denbigh but wrote to him afterwards:

> If I had voted it would have been against it. It was however, completely scouted in the House of Commons. Lord Kenyon burnt his fingers by advocating Lord Carlisle's speech ... but we let him off very gently. The Chancellor made one of the poorest speeches in his behalf ever heard.[63]

Many speakers addressed the issue of male honour and the need to safeguard female virtue and, as in the debates of the 1770s, it was notable how many of them made a point of arguing forcibly on behalf of women's rights. The female role in the adultery scenario was perceived to be that of a passive victim acting on impulse who deserved to be pitied, while a man took active responsibility for his own behaviour either as neglectful husband, honourable seducer or heartless rake. The majority of the bill's opponents took the view that most male seducers were nonetheless honourable men who wished to marry the object of their passion, and preventing this union would be unfair to both parties but especially the adulteress. Lord Mulgrave argued the bill was 'opposed to justice and humanity' as it would deny women the chance of moral rehabilitation and of rejoining respectable society, instead driving them 'to prostitution or desperation' while encouraging the seducer. Lord Eldon believed the House should take on the task of protecting virtue: 'One way to do so was to enable females to be on their guard … against the attacks of these same "men of honour," who … ought to be consigned to public infamy'. The Duke of Clarence also opposed the bill on the grounds that it did not provide for 'the poor unfortunate female who should fall a victim to her own vanity, or weakness', and he urged peers to 'consider the case as their own. Let them ask themselves, whether they thought their own ladies, if by any misfortune it should be their fate to be parties complained of in divorce bills, ought to be turned over from their exalted situations, to all the misery and wretchedness' that this legislation would expose them to.

A prominent adultery case that hit the headlines at this time seemed to illustrate the behaviour of the worst sort of predatory seducer that women had to beware of. The Duke of Marlborough's heir, George Spencer-Churchill, Marquis of Blandford, was involved in an affair with a married woman, and when she gave birth to an illegitimate child her husband sued for damages. Lady Mary Anne Sturt, daughter of the Earl of Shaftesbury, was a captivating blonde with bright blue eyes he had fallen for over ten years earlier when she was already married to Charles Sturt, the MP for Bridport. He tried to overcome his feelings by marrying Lady Susan Stewart, but when one of his sisters married Lady Mary's brother, the old romance was re-kindled. He later wrote to her:

> You know that my love for you is not a sudden thought; you know that it is grounded on near eleven years intimacy; you know that I married to get the better of it, and that that failed; you know that I tried an absence from you for four years, and that failed also. I know you love me … no two mortals ever loved each other more.

During the trial for crim. con. at the Court of King's Bench, Westminster, in May 1801, the judge Lord Kenyon said, 'Cases of this sort, I am sorry to say, multiply beyond measure. Whether by holding the parties up to contempt and infamy, and by putting one's hands deep into the purses of defendants, they may be at last suppressed, is more than I will venture to presume.' He pointed out that during the trial 'different kinds of characters have been exhibited', some exciting indignation, some deserving admiration and others pity. Sir Edward Law, the Attorney General, acting in Blandford's defence, argued that Charles Sturt had been 'the accessary in producing the destruction and misery of two noble houses, by his shameful negligence ... the prime cause of her ruin and misery'.[64] The case hinged on evidence that Sturt had neglected his wife and for years kept a celebrated harp player called Madame Krumpholtz as his mistress, by whom he had several children.

Thomas Erskine, prosecuting, read out Blandford's passionate love letters as evidence of his depraved nature and commented:

> Such is the manner in which Lord Blandford addresses this guilty woman, and drives her on to destruction. After having invaded the bed of her husband, ... having accomplished the ruin of the soul and body of this wretched wife ... [he] makes use of Religion and Providence as a stalking-horse.

As heir to a dukedom and a married man himself, Blandford had not behaved honourably: 'There is an awful duty imposed on persons in high stations ... the Noble Marquis has not conducted himself with discretion, either as regards his family or himself.' In his summing-up, Lord Kenyon told the jury that husbands had a duty to be kind and affectionate, not deserting their wife's bed to become the 'debauched paramours of worthless women'. He added that 'no man can have a bill of divorce, whose conduct has not been irreproachable ... Religion and morality would be deeply wounded by a contrary practice.' The jury took only half a minute to reach its verdict and awarded token damages of £100 because of Sturt's own adultery, but despite this provocation Lady Mary was nonetheless found guilty for taking a lover herself.

Immediately after the trial Charles Sturt published a 150-page pamphlet giving his side of the story and refuting accusations that he had connived at his wife's adultery in order to win payment of damages. It included an annotated trial report with detailed comments on certain contentious points raised in court. He admitted in the preface that although he was himself partly to blame, it was no justification of his wife's immoral conduct or Blandford's treachery. He argued that Lady Mary had been 'persuaded by the vile, unmanly arts' of Blandford, who had sent love letters hidden inside parcels with gifts, including parmesan cheese, a roasting pig, novels and gowns, and he condemned 'the vicious tendency of his letters; for surely such a mass of wickedness, of designing art … never was written by any man above the level of a lacquey'.

There was no doubt that Blandford was genuinely in love with Lady Mary at the time, and his long emotional letters to her poured out all his passion and anguish. When they were separated while she awaited child-birth, he wrote:

> I am more wretched, more in torture now; than I ever was in my life, and that I cannot long bear it … was I to live a thousand years, I could not tell you half what I have felt for you. Curse the childish tears that are now falling on the paper, but I cannot help them, my heart is ready to break.

And after their daughter was born he exclaimed:

> Oh, my wife! My dear, my adored wife! The blessed mother of my child, what a poor conveyance language is to express the feelings of a heart already overcome with affection and love! I love you ten million times more than I ever did. Love my poor Georgiana for the sake of your George, your Blandford, your *husband*, your devoted half! Oh! Could I now press my child and its dear mother to my arms … write as if you acknowledged me as your husband, for so I am by every *divine law*. Most religiously and unalterably yours.

It was the language of Blandford's love letters like this that infuriated the public and drew criticism of his deplorable hypocrisy from the press. In an angry editorial comment printed alongside the adultery trial report, *The Morning Post and Gazetteer* said:

> Never was anything more calculated to expose the blasphemous canting now in such general use. In law, in politics, in every trade and profession, little hypocrites abound, who would mix religion with the vilest vices, and make it subservient to the basest purposes. The correspondence adds to this amiable catalogue a religious adulterer; for in that light the following letters of the Marquis to Lady Mary Anne Sturt represent him.

The paper then printed some of his letters, including a sentimental thank you note headed simply, 11.30pm Tuesday Night:

The plant you sent me I keep in my room, and put it out at the window every day, and take it in in the evening: I value it more, ten millions of times, than my whole collection, and shall let no one have the care of it while I am here, but water it and foster it myself. You tied it up with pink cotton; I have taken off the cotton, and keep it in my box, with everything else which you ever gave me; I would not lose it for worlds. Good night my love; I hope I shall dream of you; indeed I do. I am so glad you have not had the heart-burn and that you take magnesia for it.

Blandford's trial was covered at length during the summer of 1801 by many other local and national newspapers, including the *Morning Chronicle*, the *Bury and Norwich Post*, and *Caledonian Mercury*. There were also lots of satirical references to the case, and a paragraph appeared in the *Morning Post* in a witty column full of cryptic allusions titled 'The Fashionable World', which mocked Blandford's gift of cheese to Lady Mary: 'A *Parmezan* body-guard was sent to meet the new King of Etruria. This corps must commit great havoc among the Maids of Honour, according to the Marquis of Blandford's tactics.'

After the adultery was discovered Blandford had initially hoped to settle damages privately with Sturt to avoid the bruising publicity of a trial. But Sturt was determined to press his case, and Blandford begged Lady Mary to go abroad to Switzerland with him:

> Can you renounce the world for my sake? Let us, my adored Mary Anne … grasp at the happiness now within our reach … I know it will always be a sincere regret to you, that we did not first meet when we were both single. Can you doubt for a moment that we were born for each other?

He assured her he had made arrangements to provide for his wife and children, settling on them half of the £2,000 annual income he received from his father, plus profits from the estate:

> I know that everything will go on better when I am gone. Do not imagine that this plan is formed in consequence of irritation, passion or hurry; no, it is on mature reflection and sober reasoning … I am quite aware of all I give up and all I obtain: I know that I give my enemies subject for their malevolence but I despise them all.

It seems that Lady Mary for some reason could not be persuaded, and the plan came to nothing. He considered leaving England in despair, telling her,

'I feel I can never be of use to society again in any way; losing your affection has totally overset me … I have no hope, and yet I adore you.' In another note he said, 'I appear to some people in a situation to be envied; God knows how much the worse it is in reality.'

A sensitive and highly intelligent man, Blandford devoted much of his life to his twin passions of books and horticulture, amassing a vast library and creating ambitious gardens at his estate White Knights near Reading and later Blenheim Palace. But the doomed love affair had made him a laughing stock. He had failed dismally to preserve a dignified public front and uphold the tradition of honourable conduct expected from the nobility.

The Parliamentary debates on adultery showed peers in their best light, acting as champions of manly honour and feminine virtue, as defenders of family life and national welfare. Despite the fact that legislation to crimi-nalise adultery would personally affect many men in the Upper Chamber, speakers tried to present an objective viewpoint on this highly contentious issue. But inevitably personal and public interest were linked in discussions of this contentious topic. Lord Eldon argued that the bill was needed 'for the preservation of the morals of private families, and consequently the aggregate family of the state'.[65] In a long, impassioned speech support-ing the bill, the Bishop of Rochester appealed to peers as compassionate fathers, 'My lords, I too call upon you as fathers … But … I address you not as fathers individually: I say, that the innocence of daughters is a matter in which fathers ought to make a common cause'. In a cleverly evocative metaphor, he asked for justice and mercy for 'conjugal fidelity, domestic happiness, public manners, the virtue of the sex! These, my lords, are the suppliants now kneeling before you'.

Rochester's speech, like many others, was a well-crafted and eloquent example of persuasive oratory using traditional rhetoric to make its point forcefully, drawing on classical and contemporary preconceptions of strong masculine leadership. Many lords invoked classical authority as a form of shorthand to clarify or add weight to their argument. The Earl of Carlisle emphasised the difficulty of moral reform with a reference to cleaning the Augean stables, one of the labours of Hercules. Lord Auckland enlisted the full panoply of literary heavyweights to bolster his speech, quoting from Juvenal's *Satires* on the corrupting example of vice, from Tacitus on Roman punishment of adultery and reciting a passage from William Cowper's poem *The Task* on the threat of infidelity to domestic peace. Such overkill may have been counterproductive, though, as Lord Mulgrave was scathing about the 'long string of verses' used to mislead the House, instead of speech 'in the plain shape of a prose paragraph'.

As described in the earlier satire *The House of Peeresses*, Parliament was a public arena of combat where opponents used speech as weapons to fight for their cause. And as in battle, the best performing orators defeated the enemy and carried the day. Membership of the peerage was most visibly demonstrated through public performances like this in their symbolic home of Parliament. Outlining the duties of peers, Thomas Gisborne stressed the importance of diligently employing their personal abilities as members of the House of Lords. A nobleman who did this 'would find his pains rewarded by a greater addition of reputation, of consequence, of power to do good, of advantages of every kind'.[66] In order to fulfil this public duty he should not 'overlook an attainment indispensably requisite ... the talent of public speaking'. To acquire 'that manly copiousness of expression' needed for effective parliamentary speaking, Gisborne advised 'frequent and contemplative perusal of the works of the ancient masters of oratory'. Studying the speeches of classical orators should include attention to 'their mode of arrangement, to their choice of arguments and illustrations, and to their skill in adapting the style as well as the matter of the discourse to the subject on which they spoke, and the persons whom they addressed'. The classics provided guidance on how a peer could 'tread in the steps of his illustrious predecessors' and be a worthy statesman 'endeavouring to promote the true happiness of this Nation'.

19

THE EARL OF MORLEY AND
'A CERTAIN LIAISON'

Peers could present themselves as worthy public men on the stage of the House of Lords, displaying the requisite qualities of honourable manhood and leadership. But this ritual performance ended at the door of the Upper Chamber and once outside the private man was free to be himself, as long as the press never picked up any hint of scandal.

John Parker, the 1st Earl of Morley, managed successfully to lead a secret double life for years, hiding his long-standing affair with a married woman behind a façade of model respectability as an active politician and responsible landowner. It was only when his young wife eloped with another man and he was forced to divorce her, that his turbulent domestic life was revealed.

Born into a wealthy gentry family which had risen up the social scale through expedient marriages to titled women, his father had married a baron's daughter. With this social cachet and ownership of the Saltram estate near Plymouth, he had the right credentials to be created 1st Baron Boringdon.[67] As the largest house in Devon and situated near an important naval base, Saltram played an integral part in the family's social progression, welcoming a constant stream of prominent visitors from military, government and society circles. When John was only three, his mother died shortly after giving birth to his younger sister, Theresa, and the two children were brought up by their aunt Anne Robinson, Lord Grantham's sister. The siblings enjoyed a close and affectionate relationship, staying involved in each other's lives and writing regularly to keep in touch when they were apart.

Morley had to grow up suddenly when his father died, and at only sixteen he inherited the title, later becoming 1st Earl of Morley in 1815. He was now responsible for his extended family and a large estate, and was expected to uphold the family's prominent social position with lavish hospitality. A few months after he succeeded as Lord Boringdon, a hundred beds were made up for guests when he entertained the king and queen at Saltram. While Theresa spent her adolescent years at home with her aunt, her brother, like all young peers, was sent away to school, followed by Oxford University and travel in Europe on the Grand Tour. He was given a classical education in preparation for his public role in life, while her girlhood was devoted to learning polite accomplishments which would lead to a good marriage. Concerns about the shortcomings of this very limited kind of female education were summed up by one exasperated commentator:

> Women, in the present system of education, are treated as the playthings and amusements of the other sex, as without usefulness and without a character. Music, dancing, drawing, &c. all elegant accomplishments, are the parts of education to which the greatest attention is paid ... but of little service to her when called upon to direct a house and to preside in a family.[68]

Worse still, girls then wasted their time attending balls and assemblies, reading novels and thinking about dresses: 'Every thing is contrived, as if on purpose, to sement [sic] every evil passion, and to encourage dissipation and debauchery. All is gay and entertaining; nothing useful and serious.' Girls and boys from aristocratic families were given completely different kinds of upbringing, and girls underwent a sudden transition from the sheltered world of the schoolroom into the public world of social engagements.

As her brother was enjoying his freedom on the Grand Tour amid the cultural and social delights of sunny Europe, Theresa lived a dull and confined life at home in rainy Devon, where occasional visitors enlivened the tedium of the household routine. A major preoccupation was the progress of her needlework or featherwork, which at the time was a popular handicraft for women. Aged 18, she wrote to her aunt, 'Nothing particular has happen'd since you left us but that I have ... finished another breadth of my Petticoat and drawn a new Pattern'.[69] Her frustration was evident in another letter:

I am glad you liked the feathers. Wet weather has prevented our picking any up lately … I am afraid you will think my Letters stupid, but you will not be so much surprised when I tell you that since Lady Chatham left us, the only person we have seen is Mr - - at church; and you know that one day is so exactly like another that there is not much to write about.[70]

The same month, Morley wrote to his aunt from St Petersburg with news about Russian social circles, entertainments and a society dinner he had attended.[71] Theresa's focus was on much smaller matters: 'I have just done a little Box with Feathers. How do you make your feathers stick? I did mine with Gum which I think alters the shape of the feathers too much.'[72] Despite the restricted daily round of her own life, she had a lively interest in wider issues and in one letter chatted about her brother's plans to visit Dresden, his improved French, the social engagements of various peers and their wives, local news of Exeter races and the unrest in Paris: 'What a dreadful piece of work they are making at Paris. I am so afraid that they will kill the poor King and Queen.'[73]

Although alike in their forthright opinions on people and events, Theresa's perspective was that of a detached onlooker, while Morley was experiencing an exciting kaleidoscope of new scenes and sociability. Travelling through war-torn Europe he witnessed events at first hand which were later to fuel his political beliefs, and mixed in refined Continental social circles which gave him the necessary polish for a man of his rank. He became fluent in French and Italian and developed an educated taste for the fine arts. Writing from Vienna, he criticised the partition of Poland as 'so ill-timed, so profligate, so disgusting an exercise of power the history of the world has never afforded.'[74] And from Brussels he wrote, 'The Town is filled with French, wch I am very glad of, as after my own country-people I think they are much the pleasantest society – particularly the women'.[75]

In contrast to her brother's busy and varied existence, Theresa's life was, until her marriage, limited to local social circles, family and friends, enlivened only by occasional visits to neighbouring estates or a ball. In 1798 she married George Villiers, son of the 1st Earl of Clarendon, heralding a new phase in her life when she could at last escape the confines of Saltram and enjoy new experiences in wider society. Fashionable social gatherings, however, sometimes turned out to be surprisingly tedious. After a stay at Hatfield House one summer, hosted by the Marquis of Salisbury, she described to her aunt meeting the formidable judge and scourge of adulterers Lord Kenyon:

It was with some difficulty I <u>kept alive</u> at Hatfield the first day, it was so terrible dull and formal – tho' to be sure I had some amusement in seeing Lord Kenyon make the agreeable to Lady Salisbury and Lady Melbourne, as one cd not help thinking what <u>fine sport</u> he might have with them, if he got them within his own dominions. I was rather disturb'd at Ld Kenyon's having a <u>red nose</u>, a dirty coat, and a worn out wig, as the respectability of his appearance was <u>somewhat</u> diminished thereby; I got into good humour at Hatfield the second day by seeing the Place wch is most uncommonly beautiful and magnificent, and <u>Place seeing</u> was always as you know one of my great delights.

Brother and sister kept up their regular correspondence with each other and with their aunt back home at Saltram. Theresa's entertaining letters were full of outspoken comments, showing her lively intelligence and a keen interest in national affairs. Writing about one of her brother's speeches in the Lords that argued for a negotiated peace with France, Theresa said:

> I was very happy to hear that my Brother had spoke so well on Tuesday. He was so good as to send me a Parliamentary Journal which he said gave a pretty good account of his speech and I think it seems to be excellent. I think he is quite right in being so moderate.[76]

Many of her letters written from home were naturally preoccupied with the domestic concerns of children, health, homely activities like gardening or needlework and social gossip. Others were written from royal residences while she and her husband, who held various sinecures, were engaged on court duties. Writing from Kew Palace, where she reported that 'the king is certainly much better for being here', she highlighted the often invisible female influence on a husband's public position:

> I am sure you would give me great credit if you knew how instrumental I have been to our remaining here for Mr V has been very near resigning several times, and I have prevail'd upon him to go on a little longer ... I see that he is literally the only person who does any good here, and he certainly does a great deal – and I think he wd be vex'd with himself if he was to go away in <u>dudgeon</u>.[77]

When living away from home she missed her children, telling her aunt, 'My two little ones will really quite forget me and it frets me very much to be so much away from them.' But she wittily described life in Queen Charlotte's household:

> You know full well how little this sort of life suits me … I get <u>seven</u> hours amusement every day, as I dine at the Queen's table, drive out with some of them (sometimes have the <u>happiness</u> of a four hours tete-a-tete with the Queen) drink tea and sup there!! … The Duchess of Cumberland and Cambridge are generally there, wch takes off some of the <u>dullness</u>, but tell on the other hand such Jokes such Stories as I shd have thought never wd have got higher than the Servants Hall, and what perhaps will astonish you the Q is the greatest promoter of them.

Morley could not be so frank about his own life, since he had met Lady Elizabeth Monck towards the end of 1793 during a stay in Rome on his Grand Tour, when he was 21. She was the Earl of Arran's daughter and a sophisticated married woman of 28, with two children. Writing home from Italy he said, 'I own I am in no sort of hurry, as I am most extremely pleased at this place – we have so much to see and do every morning'.[78] He commented on pleasant evening gatherings with English and European families, which would have included the Moncks. He continued his travels round Italy but was irresistibly drawn back to see Elizabeth again, and an apparently casual note written from Milan six weeks later said, 'I shall probably return to Rome (where I have yet much to see) in a short time.'[79] It was the start of a long and highly irregular liaison. On his return to England, Morley divided his time between Parliament, his regiment the North Devon militia, estate duties and social engagements all over the country, such as Lord Morpeth's lavish coming-of-age celebrations at Castle Howard when 14,000 people were given dinner in the park. He was an active Tory member of the House of Lords, supporting progressive measures, including Catholic emancipation, smallpox vaccination and Parliamentary reform.

The holiday romance with Elizabeth developed into a close relationship which lasted more than ten years and produced three illegitimate sons. With the apparent acquiescence of her husband, she spent long periods living at Saltram and her constant presence began to strain family relations. Other guests at the lively house-parties seemed to appreciate her charms, as General Dyott recorded in his journal: 'In August, September and October I passed a good deal of time at Saltram, Lord Boringdon's and generally a house full of people. A very pleasant and one of the prettiest women in England there most of the summer Lady Elizabeth Monck.' Despite their earlier closeness Morley began to distance himself from his sister and aunt to avoid their disapproval, and Theresa was upset at the rift which Elizabeth had caused, admitting that, 'tis foolish to fret about it, as I hope all will come right <u>in time</u>, but it is not very pleasant *in attendant*.'[80]

A year later the situation remained fraught and Theresa confided to her aunt:

> I am now much more than ever convinc'd that I am right in my conjectures about her being the cause of coolness in another Quarter … I despair of much amendment in that respect at least at present for I think it grows worse and worse, and all I can do is to think of it as little as I can, for it is a most painful reflection … the more so from being perfectly unexpected. This is of course entirely *entre nous*, for indeed you are the only person I have ever nam'd it to.[81]

Theresa held strong moral views which surfaced in her letters as forthright comments on society scandals, including the divorce of their neighbour the Marquis of Abercorn and the Prince of Wales's liaison with Lady Jersey, to whom she was related by marriage. Writing with news that the prince had tired of Lady Jersey and taken up with the manager of Brighton Theatre's daughter, a former mistress of Lord Egremont, she exclaimed:

> 'Tis dreadful to think of the open profligacy of that Monster, and it shows how immediately we must all go to the dogs shd he ever unfortunately come to the throne. Some people say this fancy is only temporary, and that he will return to Ldy Jersey, but I hope not, for … one cannot help feeling a degree of satisfaction at that vile woman's Suffering a little of the Misery she has for so many years inflicted on others, and of course if she is unprotected by the Prince the little Notice that has been taken of her by the World of late years will totally cease, and as for … her Husband I suppose he will be kicked into his <u>proper place</u> the <u>Kennel</u>.[82]

The heir to the throne was demanding the return of all his letters by his cast-off mistress, and Theresa commented:

> … the Prince's character cannot appear in more odious colours than it has already done, and as he cannot be more abhor'd and detested than he is by everybody, there seems no reason why he shd want his letters and papers from her, for was she to publish them he is <u>past</u> being hurt by them.

She was equally scathing about Lord Jersey, 'such a little fawning cringing <u>Beast</u>', and determined not to visit the unpopular couple, who had recently taken a house nearby.

Her brother's adulterous relationship was highly embarrassing for the family, putting Theresa and her husband (Mr V) in an awkward position at court, as she noted in a letter recounting her brother's trip to France with Elizabeth: 'The King told Mr V he was glad he was gone as he thought it indicated that a certain liaison was at an end – Mr V cd not bring himself to undeceive him but I dare say he will find it out.'[83] Eventually, however, the situation was resolved when Elizabeth apparently refused to marry Morley to spare her husband and daughters from the scandal of a divorce. He was now 32 and to fulfil his family duty needed a wife, so in 1804 he married the 10th Earl of Westmorland's daughter Lady Augusta Fane, who, as a naïve young bride of 18, was unaware of her husband's continuing attachment. She had experienced a similarly restricted girlhood to Theresa, who foresaw that Augusta was completely unprepared for the realities of marriage to a man of the world with a mistress and three illegitimate children:

She is most <u>beautiful</u> ... I do most fervently hope that my brother will take my advice and never lose sight of her being 18 & only 18 & really a Child just out of the Nursery – Thinking of Marriage as I do, I have many anxious moments about these people.[84]

Theresa approved of the new bride but with typical candour expressed her concern that the liaison with Elizabeth was bound to undermine the match:

Both Mr V and I are delighted with her, and think her both amiable and sensible beyond what I cd have expected either from her age or education. I am decidedly of the opinion that it will not be *her* fault if she is not an excellent wife.[85]

Her loyalty to her brother and relief he had at last married was clear:

I think the World has been very unfair towards her, and indeed so many people misrepresented her to me ... that I will own to you I was not prejudiced in her favour, and as I wd not acknowledge that, I of course said nothing but now that I can speak the truth with satisfaction I am anxious to tell it to everybody. I do wish she wd follow my example in the <u>multiplying way</u>, she is in such robust health that I cannot understand her not being in that way.

The couple did have one son in May 1806, but the marriage was not happy for either of them. Morley was continuing to see Elizabeth and also had another illegitimate child born to a ballet dancer from Bristol. Stung by her husband's indifference, Augusta had begun a flirtation with Sir Arthur Paget, the second son of Lord Uxbridge and a former ambassador to the court of Vienna, and in May 1808 they eloped. Public sympathy was all on her side: 'Lord Boringdon is now greatly blamed, he had kept up an intimacy, formed before his marriage, with Lady Elizabeth Monck, and the knowledge of it caused a great deal of uneasiness to Lady Boringdon.'[86]

The press made the most of the scandal and action for crim. con. that followed on 19 July 1808 at the Court of King's Bench. Reports of the trial in 2s pamphlets and dozens of newspapers, including *The Times*, the *Examiner* and the *Morning Post*, told the story of the adultery as a drama of high life which would have enthralled readers. The nursemaid gave evidence that she had accompanied Augusta when she went out in the carriage on daily visits to Kensington Gardens, where she met Sir Arthur at the Bayswater Gate. The lovers walked in one direction, while the nurse took the child off another way. Prosecuting counsel cast Morley as an affectionate husband whose wife had enjoyed clandestine meetings with Paget while he was attending the House of Lords. He emphasised Morley's public reputation as a man devoted to duty, telling the jury he had been 'as you must know if you read the newspapers, very attentive to his duty in parliament' but urging them to ignore derogatory personal gossip (presumably referring to his own extramarital affairs) which had appeared in the press since the scandal.

Mr Garrow, defence counsel, argued Paget had not been responsible for the 'libellous paragraphs' in the newspapers and he denigrated the press's appetite for scandal: 'Where is there a domestic misfortune in life that is not daily held forth to public view by the Newspapers?' It was widely known that Paget was a ladies' man who had previously eloped with the Duke of Bedford's cook, but Garrow portrayed him as an honourable figure who 'was the ambassador of nothing and of nobody but love; all powerful and allmighty love; he was the slave of Lady Boringdon'. Garrow said the case called for compassion and he blamed the conventions of fashionable life for what had happened, including the scanty education of girls, arranged matches and the conduct of married life where couples spent very little time together.

In a long report on the trial covering half of page two, *The Times* of Wednesday 20 July summarised Garrow's speech:

He considered that the real cause of these things in fashionable life proceeded in a great measure from the course of education which young ladies of rank receive, and from the manner they are introduced into life ... After marriage, Fashion (which he feared was often the bitterest enemy of our happiness) made them see but little of each other. Fashion might drive a Nobleman to attend his Parliamentary duty, and might drive his Lady to some other mode of passing her time ... Fashion had made separate beds necessary among married people in high life, and it made the pursuits of the husband and wife different.

The judge directed the jury to match the compensation to the means of the parties and, in contrast to Lord Kenyon's stance that juries had a duty to uphold morality, told them, 'You will take care that your verdict does not operate as a vindictive verdict; you are not the censors of the public morals.'[87] The case was clearly one of collusion between both sides and Morley won the huge sum of £10,000 damages (around £600,000 today) against Paget. Rival publishers competed for sales of their pamphlets printing the whole proceedings, and the *Morning Chronicle* of 18 August insisted:

> We have authority to say that the letters of Lady Boringdon, as given in Plomer's Trial of Sir Arthur Paget, are the only correct manuscripts of her ladyship's correspondence, and that the paragraphs asserting to the contrary, are intended only as puffs to Gurney's very inferior edition.

The divorce was granted the following year and reported in half a column on the front page of *The Times* of 7 February 1809. Augusta married Paget and Morley wed his second wife, Frances Talbot, a surgeon's daughter. For Morley, this second marriage marked a new, more conventional chapter in his life and the earlier troubled romances became a forgotten part of his past. He was able to assume the role of the respectable family and public man with the approval of the local community. A Saltram neighbour, Lord Mount Edgcumbe, was later asked if he saw anything of the couple and replied, 'Oh yes we do now! But during the Augustan age, and the Monckish era, we did not.'

In keeping with attitudes being expressed in the House of Lords debates on adultery at the time, Augusta emerged as a sympathetic figure, an innocent young wife who had escaped a cold arranged marriage by falling in love with a dashing suitor. This romanticised portrait of injured femininity emerged in the courtroom narrative, press reports and in private correspondence about the case. As a fascinating illustration of some of society's major preoccupations, Augusta's love story also inspired the plot of Jane Austen's novel *Mansfield Park*, which was begun in 1811 and published three years later. Austen's brother was chaplain to the Parker family, and the novel dramatised contemporary concerns about mercenary marriage, girls' education and its consequences. Augusta's scandal was rewritten as the story of Maria Bertram, an ambitious baronet's daughter, educated in all the polite accomplishments, who married for money but later eloped with the charming Henry Crawford. The controversial play performed in the novel, Kotzebue's *Lovers' Vows*, celebrated the joys of sexual freedom and feeling over the restrictions of conventional arranged marriage.

In contrast to the sympathy that Augusta's plight attracted, Elizabeth Monck was later cast in the archetypal role of the sinful adulteress by her own son, Augustus Stapleton. He pitied his mother as someone emblematic of an amoral aristocracy in a bygone age. All the complexities and emotional dilemmas of what had been a serious love affair were simplified into a standard morality tale in the family memoir he wrote in 1854. Later published as *Heirs Without Title*, it was inevitably haunted by the bitter regrets of a man denied his true aristocratic position in life. Morley had made their three illegitimate sons a financial settlement, and Stapleton went on to a successful career, becoming private secretary to Lord Canning. But although they suspected the truth, the boys had never been told who their natural parents were, and it was not until the age of 76 that Elizabeth confessed the real situation to Stapleton:

> From my earliest recollection she had always been like a mother to us …
> But there had never been any avowal on her side of the fact, nor on the other
> hand had I or my brothers asked her questions on the subject … she avowed
> to me the fact, expressed the deepest penitence for her guilty conduct and
> implored me not to despise her for it during the little time she had to live …
> I of course assured her of my unalterable love, affection and gratitude.

Looking back from the safe moral high ground of Victorian England, Stapleton approved of his mother's penitence for her sins. In a confidential note left for his children to read after his death, he said sanctimoniously:

> It is a great satisfaction to think that she lived to ask pardon of a merciful God
> and Saviour for her sad misconduct at that period of her life. She unhappily
> lived in an age when amongst the highest nobles in the land, chastity was a
> virtue, which too few preserved and that a tone of morals prevailed, which of
> late years has been much improved.'

Part Five

Changing Roles
(1810–1830s)

'The character of the public discontent
has entirely changed within the last
forty years: the people now regard the
Aristocracy, not as their friends, but
their enemies … the influence of the
Aristocracy [is] gliding away from
beneath their feet in consequence of
their own thoughtlessness and folly.'

Hints to the Aristocracy, 1834

20

Public Roles and
Private Lives

In the reflective post-war decades of the early nineteenth century, a general dissatisfaction about the position of the ruling elite began to harden into focussed opposition. The aristocracy now seemed to many people an out-dated relic of the past, abusing its privileges while abandoning its hereditary duties: 'Times have changed and the spirit of Aristocracy has changed with them … It is now a spirit of paltry compromise and petty peddling cabal – a spirit of lying hypocrisy, and fraud.'[1] Other commentators voiced similar criticism of the peerage, which they claimed had radically altered in recent times: 'The character of the public discontent has entirely changed within the last forty years: the people now regard the Aristocracy, not as their friends, but their enemies, not their protectors, but oppressors.'[2] Aristocratic influence was 'gliding away from beneath their feet in consequence of their own thoughtlessness and folly'.

Debates about the behaviour of the ruling class had gradually intensified in the climate of moral panic during the preceding decades, culminating in a fundamental reassessment of the social function of hereditary rule. The specific moral concerns of previous years were now partly subsumed into more general discussion of aristocratic power, as a new sense of propriety emerged. Traditionally both public duty and personal honour had underpinned the foundations of nobility, an ideology based on beliefs that social order reflected a natural moral order. Those of highest rank were expected to possess honour as an inherited quality combining superior birth, private virtue and appropriate public display. This acceptance of rank co-existing with honour had been steadily eroded and now the whole meaning and purpose of the aristocracy, as government by those of superior birth, was called into question.

Such widespread disenchantment was summed up by a letter printed in the satirical *Rambler's Magazine* headed 'Remark on the Degeneracy of the Nobility', which said, 'Indeed, nobility at this period, is but a degenerated race of men, whom education hath only informed of new vices … [they] debauch themselves and their inferiors – ruin their own honour, and the kingdom's.' It declared that honour and virtue were now confined to the middling classes, and instead of being 'superior to the rest of mankind' peers were actually 'below the level of the people over whom they arrogantly and impudently assume a superiority'.[3] The writer expressed the new sense of propriety surfacing during this transitional period in public attitudes, as the easy-going libertinism of the Georgian and Regency periods began to fade away into what would eventually become Victorian prudery. Aristocratic adultery continued to attract prurient interest and condemnation, as such cases were seized on to provide further evidence of a corrupt class which was out of step with the times and no longer deserved its privileged status.

Adultery was still a topical entertainment for the reading public and there was no sign of it petering out yet; as *La Belle Assemblee* magazine noted, 'The frequency of this crime in Great Britain being a proof of national depravity … and on examination it will be found to have increased considerably'. Notions persisted that lax morals were particularly apparent among the higher classes, and a writer in the *Satirist; or, the Censor of the Times* complained, 'adultery is the privilege of the aristocracy: it has been attached to "the order" from time immemorial'.[4] Printed court reports of adultery trials in pamphlets, newspapers and periodicals remained popular, though they were now declining in number after the craze of the 1790s. Even in the late 1830s, the bluntly named *Crim Con Gazette* was circulating all the salacious details of recent scandals and rehashing cases that had happened decades before.

Liaisons involving the nobility were of course the most widely read, such as Lady Rosebery's affair with her dead sister's husband, which was described by a lawyer in court as a case 'differing so much from everything he had ever seen, read, or heard of before, in the extraordinary atrocity by which it was peculiarly distinguished'. Shortly after the death of his wife, Sir Henry Mildmay had sought consolation from her relatives and fallen in love with her sister Harriet, who was married to the Earl of Rosebery. Not only had he seduced a married woman and 'violated all the ties of friendship … but added to those crimes was the additional one of multiplied incest … Sir Henry debauched the wife of his friend, the sister of his deceased wife, and the sister of the wife of his own brother.' So shocking was the case that on Monday 12 December 1814 *The Times* devoted two columns on page two to a long report of the action for crim. con. brought by the Earl of Rosebery. Because of the seriousness of the case, Rosebery was initially seeking the staggering sum of £30,000 (roughly £1.8 million today) in damages from Sir Henry but was eventually awarded the still considerable payment of £15,000 (equivalent to around £900,000 now).

At the hearing held in the Sheriff of Middlesex' Office in Bedford Street, London, the jury was told that in 1808 Archibald John Primrose, 4th Earl of Rosebery, had married Harriet, who was the 18-year-old daughter of the Hon. Bartholomew Bouverie (later Earl of Radnor). One of her sisters married the wealthy baronet Sir Henry Mildmay and another sister wedded Sir Henry's brother. It was a highly complicated web of family relations, which was torn apart when Sir Henry's wife died and he found solace in Harriet's company. The couple grew closer, and when in March 1814 the earl had to go back to the family seat in Scotland where his father was dying, Harriet also left London for their Norfolk country estate, where Sir Henry made frequent visits. Prosecuting counsel said that Sir Henry 'availed himself of opportunities to ingratiate himself with this lady, to alienate her affections, to seduce her mind, and debauch her person – for it certainly appeared, that recently after her return from Norfolk … there was a visible difference in her behaviour' towards her husband, who remonstrated with Sir Henry about his 'too marked attentions' to Harriet. But by now the illicit affair was unstoppable and Sir Henry was writing passionate letters to Harriet 'in terms which any man of honour should be ashamed of; begging her to elope, and telling her that he would roam the world with her; pressing her at once to leave her husband and family, and to take him as a partner for life.'

When Harriet and her husband went to stay at the medieval family seat of Barnbougle Castle near Edinburgh, Sir Henry travelled up to Scotland under the assumed name of Colonel De Grey of the footguards and took a room at a nearby inn. Desperate to see his lover again, he concocted a ludicrous plan, letting his beard grow and enlisting the help of a waterman to disguise himself as a sailor. Each evening the Rosebery family dined at six o'clock and the ladies retired to the drawing room an hour later, leaving the men together till nine. On several occasions Harriet left the dinner table and went directly to her bedchamber. There had been reports of a stranger in the locality and, suspecting something was afoot, Lord Rosebery's brother Mr Primrose went upstairs one evening to find her bedchamber door locked and tried to break it open. The game was clearly up now, so Harriet reluctantly opened the door. Standing in the room with her was Sir Henry disguised as a common sailor, armed with a brace of loaded pistols. Harriet was wearing a coloured silk gown 'not cut quite so low in the bosom as the fashion sanctified', but one corner of the bodice was unpinned and she was not wearing the neckerchief she had been seen in at dinner. The centre of the bed was indented and the carpet rumpled and dirty by the window. Realising instantly that the discovery would mean separation from her three children, Harriet cried out, 'I will see my children, nobody shall prevent me!' But despite her distress she was detained in the bedchamber and told she could never see them again, unless their father gave permission. Mr Primrose ordered Sir Henry to leave the house the same way he had come, through the window. The next day Harriet was told to return to her father's house but instead she met Sir Henry and eloped with him to the Continent.

In court, Mr Brougham, defending Sir Henry, said, 'I feel my situation to be peculiarly painful, intimate as I am with every branch of these noble families.' But he told the jury that this was not the story of a cold seducer: 'You have before you the melancholy story of a mutual, sincere, ardent, devouring passion, overwhelming with misery two young and unfortunate persons.' Sir Henry had told Harriet he intended to make her husband call him out to a duel with pistols, not to shoot him but to give his lordship honourable satisfaction. He was so besotted he had even taken to wearing Harriet's yellow garters as an intimate keepsake, because they had 'been twined round, and encircled his dear Harriet's limbs – bliss unspeakable!' One of his ardent love letters, which began, 'Dearest of earthly beings' declared that he thought he had been in love before but he had never felt love's all-conquering power until now. In another letter he addressed her as 'Dearest, Darling Woman' and implored her 'by every happy moment they had passed in each other's arms, by every burning kiss he had imprinted on her heavenly lips', to avert her departure for Scotland so he could see her. Prosecuting counsel decried the letters, exclaiming, 'Hypocrisy, base and detestable! This man to be talking of love in terms that would disgrace the obscene books exposed for sale at the Palais Royal.' It was no wonder the case caused a sensation throughout the country when it was reported in the newspapers, including the *Morning Chronicle, Morning Post, Ipswich Journal, Bury & Norwich Post* and *Hampshire Telegraph*.

In April the following year *The Times* reported on page three the Rosebery divorce proceedings held at the Consistory Court, Doctors' Commons. Soon after the marriage was dissolved Harriet married Sir Henry, but to avoid his arrest for non-payment of the damages awarded in the case, they had to spend the rest of their lives in exile abroad. Lord Rosebery took Anne Anson (the Earl of Lichfield's daughter) as his second wife. He later moved the family seat to Dalmeny House near Edinburgh and was a popular figure in the Forth valley, respected as a public-spirited landowner. He played an active role in Parliament, where he was a strong supporter of the Reform Bill, and his grandson the 5th Earl of Rosebery eventually became prime minister.

Another scandal in high life erupted later that year in December 1815 with the trial of the Duke of Wellington's niece Lady Anne Abdy for crim. con. with Lord Charles Bentinck, younger brother of the Duke of Portland. Soon after Bentinck's wife died, he became friendly with Sir William Abdy and often dined at his London home in Berkeley Square. When the Abdys travelled to Paris, Bentinck turned up and took lodgings in the same street, and when that summer they visited Worthing and Brighton, he followed them there too. When Sir William was invited to spend the shooting season at a relative's house in Cambridgeshire, Anne excused herself and stayed in London. A few days later she eloped with Bentinck. His passionate love letters were read out in court and, as defence counsel remarked:

> ... when a man is in love, he writes *nonsense*! ... What does the trash contained in these letters tell you? Why, truly, that Lord Charles Bentinck was desperately in love. And, as the wisest of men have acted foolishly, when that passion, I was going to call it *disease* of the mind, predominated so he, being subdued by its influence, made use of, what you Gentlemen, in the exercise of your sober senses, will perhaps denominate absurd and extravagant language.[5]

The trial transcript was printed as a thirty-four-page pamphlet that highlighted on its front page with two bold exclamation marks the huge sum of £7,000 damages (over £400,000 today) awarded against Bentinck, which forced him to flee to Paris as he could not afford to pay.

Such sexual scandals in fashionable society confirmed public suspicions of an entrenched moral corruption and hardened anti-elite feeling among a disaffected population, unhappy about class inequalities perpetuated by taxation and the Parliamentary system. The expectation of propriety, which demanded a rightness or correctness of behaviour, had become an important aspect of social life due to the growing influence of the moral middle classes. The concept of propriety emerged originally to articulate the acceptable limits of female sexuality and social knowledge, by enforcing modest behaviour in a woman to convey her personal integrity. Public conduct was interpreted as an expression of true inner character, so conforming to ideals of virtuous self-restraint ensured respectability and social acceptance. A broader notion of propriety as a desirable code of conduct for both men and women was firmly entrenched in the national consciousness by the 1820s, a decade which has been described as a 'watershed in the history of manners'.[6] But these changing attitudes to behaviour were viewed by many not as evidence of growing morality but of growing hypocrisy and a cunning duplicity in public display. The requirement to put on a performance which would meet audience expectations was especially relevant for peers, as the *Morning Chronicle* observed:

> Our men of rank may occasionally *assume* a virtue which they have not, they may sometimes be greater hypocrites than their forefathers were, but hypocrisy is, at all events, a homage offered to public opinion, and supposes the existence of a fear of the people.[7]

It was not only good behaviour but the outward appearance of virtue that mattered, so for an aristocracy under siege from a hostile public, the right image was crucial. As the prime minister, the 2nd Earl Grey, observed, 'The respect that the people of this country are always willing to pay to rank is doubled ... when accompanied by good conduct'.[8] In his Parliamentary speech introducing the second reading of the Reform Bill, Earl Grey cleverly exploited the power of image by sketching an idealised portrait of an indispensable peerage devoted to a life of public service:

> The nobility of this country are mixed and blended with the people. They share all their burthens ... they unite in the discharge of all their duties, they are landed proprietors, they live on their estates, they perform their duty as Magistrates, they are known as neighbours; in all these ways, and many others, they acquire esteem and confidence, which are given not so much on account of rank, as in consideration of their good conduct, and the kind offices they bestow.

Many peers undoubtedly did try and conform to these expectations of conscientious public duty, operating within a small interlinking circle of

Parliamentary, social and family relationships. But it was exactly this exclusive, closed world of influence and patronage which was now coming under fire as unfair and outdated. The monthly magazine the *Moral Reformer, and Protestor Against the Vices, Abuses, and Corruptions of the Age* noted how 'general has become the feeling against all men in power'.[9] It accused the Lords of self-interest, being 'selfish, arbitrary, and opposed to the people' and legislating 'for themselves alone'. Such animosity against the House of Lords as a collective body now surfaced regularly in print. An article in the *Satirist* voiced complaints that it 'is a mere useless ornament; it is a guardian of no rights but its own', while a piece in *The Age* questioned its whole future, saying, 'The Lords may now be fairly said to belong to history, as a legislative body ... People will soon begin to inquire what is the use of such a House at all.'[10]

These debates showed the House of Lords as an anachronistic private members' club which was intent on preserving its own interests at all costs. Writers raised specific points about the function and purpose of peers, examining their public remit, criticising their neglect of duty and questioning the existence of pensions and lucrative sinecures which did not give the public value for money. *A Peep at the Peers,* a twenty-five-page pamphlet sold for 6d, gave an alphabetical listing of all peers and their various political, military and church appointments. It calculated that the 365 peers sitting in the Upper Chamber, and their families, took salaries and emoluments totalling almost £3 million (roughly £180 million today). Another 209 Scotch and Irish peers who did not sit in the Lords enjoyed nearly £1 million (£60 million now) in privileged benefits.

These revelations of an endemic corruption were presented as evidence that the whole system of government needed a thorough reform. That was the thrust of John Wade's bestseller *The Black Book; or Corruption Unmasked!,* which was published in 1820 and reprinted six times over the next fifteen years. It gave more than 900 pages of publicly funded establishment positions in the Church, government, the law and the army. The book listed members of the aristocracy, their appointments, pensions and family connections, claiming that 'at no former period of history was the power of the Aristocracy so absolute'.[11] It had 'swallowed up' the rights of the people, the prerogatives of the Crown and Church immunities, and 'having obtained the power, the Aristocracy has exercised it as uncontrolled power usually is exercised, namely, solely for their own advantage', discarding traditional duties while monopolizing honours and emoluments.

21

FACTS OR
FICTIONS?

Despite, or perhaps because of, the momentous social changes taking place, there was a tangible sense of nostalgia for the aristocracy of olden days. And contemporaries often laughed at the way the nobility continued to fascinate the middling ranks:

> One convincing proof of the amazing extent of this passion may be found in the multitude and success of the novels purporting to portray the manners of the great which have recently issued from the press; and the eagerness with which they are devoured.[12]

The public was still in thrall to the compelling legacy of England's feudal past, romanticised in Shakespeare's plays and Sir Walter Scott's novels, which would 'throw over the mind of youth unseen chains, more powerful than all the stings of envy, or all the allurements of ambition in after life'.

The many different literary portraits of the aristocracy were not created merely to satisfy the random whims of individual authors but were produced specifically to satisfy readers' tastes, by commercial publishers who had by now become adept at packaging and selling nobility to make a profit. The continuing public appetite for peers in print was illustrated by one page of advertisements for books in *The Age* magazine, which included *Debrett's Peerage, Burke's Dictionary of the Peerage* and *The Heraldry of Crests*, and the novels *Tales of our Counties, The Exclusives* and *The Lost Heir*.[13] This keen interest in nobility, especially their private lives and loves, was reflected in the contents of novels and periodicals, which were the most widely read forms of literature at the time. The popular *Rambler's Magazine* covered an eclectic mix of topics, including arts, politics, theatre, adultery trials, humour and 'The Gay Variety of Supreme Bon Ton'. The preface to the January 1822 issue showed a canny market awareness by declaring, 'we have made LOVE our principal theme', and its first article entitled 'On Love' argued that as love was the strongest human passion the magazine was 'subscribing to the religion of NATURE'.

A similar variety of topical items could be found in the *New Bon Ton Magazine, or Telescope of the Times*, which was published from 1818–21, its purpose that of 'displaying *vice* in its most revolting form, and, by lashing it in the highest circles, shew in how little the estimation of *nobility* is held without the support of *virtue*'.[14] It claimed more depravity existed in exalted circles than in the middle ranks and noted that 'we scarce ever take up a daily print, but it has some fulsome account of *noble vices* recorded in its columns'. Like its predecessor *Bon Ton Magazine* twenty years earlier, it promised a close scrutiny of fashionable society for the amusement of readers and claimed the same moral mission of exposing vice to public scorn: 'The virtue of society it is our object to maintain … to guard the *poor* against the vices, follies, and crimes, which, in our times, have made the terms of *rich* and *contemptible* synonimous.' It vowed an 'unremitting zeal in the *public cause*, by a constant exposure of corruption and petty tyranny in every shape and form'. Its content, 'a mingled nature, some-thing of satire, a little of scandal, and much of truth', included poems, short topical comment pieces like 'On the Expediency of Divorces', amusing features, letters from anonymous contributors, theatrical coverage and news items.[15] Articles were noticeably shorter, sometimes only a few paragraphs long, and designed for casual readers to browse through intermittently. The extensive back page gossip columns titled 'Bon Ton &c', which were a popular feature of the old magazine, were not revived in this new version.

Although the magazine had a lighter tone than the old *Bon Ton*, it still used the effective method of presenting aristocrats as striking caricatures intended to be emblematic of the whole discredited class. This was made explicit in an article in the September 1818 issue, 'The Stamford Dandy or Modern Peeping Tom', that satirised a young peer described as 'the object of our present Caricature'. It exposed his behaviour as a typical case of elite degeneracy and recommended that such titled dandies read classical authors like Virgil and Horace to 'find lessons of ancient elegance worthy of modern example'. The article declared:

When men of rank and family descend to make themselves obnoxious to the public, they cannot be surprised at being made the objects of public animadversion. The public have a voice, and a most powerful one; they have also a press ... which will vindicate their rights ... against the oppression of arbitrary power in every shape; or the assuming arrogance of wealth and title.

This notion of the press as the people's champion, holding up the guilty to be judged, soon became a recurring theme: 'We will persist in making *high life* amenable to the tribunal of public opinion.'

The *New Bon Ton* continued to focus on establishment figures, including aristocrats, and deliberately positioned itself as straddling the fact/fiction boundary. It included many funny anecdotes about the lives of real people whose identities were thinly disguised with printed dashes. A typical example from December 1818 mocked the useless life of a lecherous old peer who had previously been the defendant in an adultery trial. The article titled 'Lord M-- and Crim. Con.' declared that, 'He has never distinguished himself in any honourable walk of public life' but though of 'rather repulsive' appearance, 'he certainly strove, by every means in his power, to encrease our population'.

Another article, written as a letter to the editor, satirised the personal and public life of Lord D--y, highlighting the disparity between surface appearances and underlying substance. It described him as 'a good father, as far as good fathers go amongst noblemen; that is, he likes to see his children once a month, enquires the name of each of them ... and tells them to be good children.' His public duty was limited to superficial token gestures of 'that kind of neutralised good which neither advances or recedes' causes, and although commending his charitable subscriptions to Sunday Schools and Bible Societies, the writer wished, 'he would set an example, outwardly at least, of moral deportment and decent zeal in the interests of religion'. Other similar pieces of amusing caricature included 'The Great Duke and the Opera Girl', 'The Driving Countess' and 'The Fat Marchioness', which referred to the Prince Regent's friend the Marchioness of Hertford.[16] Every month the magazine also featured brief snippets of 'news' that ridiculed the behaviour of peers, such as the anecdote entitled 'Patrician Taste', which described how: 'A certain nobleman, who is in the habit of making a beast of himself ... was discovered by the patrole asleep on a *dunghill* the other night, dead drunk'.[17]

Periodical articles like these used wit and ridicule to play on the fact that members of the nobility were part of a privileged species very different from ordinary folk but also fallible human beings just like everyone else. As captives on the printed page, the aristocracy was for once powerless to defend itself. And writers were free to do as they wanted, indiscriminately mixing elements of fact and fiction until the truth was obscured. This was what happened in the case of Isabella, Lady Hertford, a plump woman in her fifties who the press was convinced was the Prince Regent's mistress. Both overweight and middle aged, they made an unlikely romantic couple but provided irresistible material for lampooning in hundreds of articles and satirical prints.

Isabella was the second wife of Francis Seymour-Conway, the 2nd Marquis of Hertford, seventeen years her senior and an ambitious political player who had inherited a vast fortune along with the magnificent Palladian family seat Ragley Hall near Alcester in Warwickshire. Intelligent, witty and still attractive, with a buxom, maternal appeal, in middle age she was a prominent society hostess with the blowsy, overblown charm of a rose past its best. Her long relationship with the Prince Regent began in 1807 when he turned to her for emotional support during an illness, and she soon became his closest confidante. The exact nature of their relationship was a source of endless speculation, but it was obvious to everyone that Lady Hertford had become the major influence in his life, advising him on his health, his choice of friends and even in political matters.

When the Hertfords were in London at their palatial home Manchester House, the prince drove over from Carlton House in his canary-yellow carriage to visit every day and often dined alone with the couple. He was also a regular guest at their country estates and was especially fond of Ragley Hall, admiring its tranquil setting and enjoying the reassuring company of his 'dear nurse'. During these leisurely family house parties the prince took a particular liking to the Hertfords' son Lord Yarmouth. Nicknamed Red Herrings due to his ginger hair, he was a highly intelligent and cultured man known as an art connoisseur but also such a notorious womaniser that the novelist William Thackeray used him as the model for the debauched Marquess of Steyne in *Vanity Fair*.

By 1812, Lady Hertford and the prince were widely known to be intimate friends. That year she had managed to secure the posts of Lord Chamberlain of the Household for her husband and Vice-Chamberlain for her son, and regular attacks on her undue influence at court were appearing in print. Like the prince's earlier mistress, Lady Jersey, who was mocked as a skinny old hag, Lady Hertford's age and size also provided ammunition for a hostile press. The prince was already highly unpopular with the public and the pair became objects of cruel satire, which was particularly vicious in the brilliant cartoon drawings of George Cruikshank sold at print shops. His print *Merry Making on the Regents Birth Day, 1812* depicted a grossly fat Lady Hertford, with balloon-like stomach and breasts, dancing with a red-faced drunken prince, while outside the ragged poor looked on in disgust. In the background, satyrs played a pair of French horns over the willing cuckold Lord Hertford's head. A later print titled *Royal Hobby's, or The Hertfordshire Cock-Horse!* showed an even more obese Lady Hertford riding on the back of a bloated Prince, brandishing a whip and saying, 'G up! G O! Oh dear!! This is a delightful way of Riding!!' A signpost by the roadside pointed the way to the Horns Inn, Hertford.[18] Some prints even hinted at the prince's unusual personal sexual tastes and could be far more daring than written attacks in the press.

The malicious gossip turned to real vitriol as the prince, who had been made regent in 1811 when his father became seriously ill, changed his political allegiance from the Whig party to the Tories and supported the new Tory prime minister, Lord Liverpool. Lady Hertford was blamed for persuading him to desert the Whigs and accused by Lord Grey, in a House of Lords speech, of being a 'cursed and baleful' influence that 'lurked behind the throne'. Political opponents seized on the prince's dissolute private life to undermine him, and dozens of angry articles appeared in the press, including one in the radical weekly newspaper the *Examiner* on 22 March 1812 denouncing him as, 'a violator of his word, a libertine over head and ears in debt and disgrace, a despiser of domestic ties, the companion of gamblers and demi-reps, a man who has just closed half a century without one single claim to the gratitude of his country or the respect of posterity'. This was the last straw for the beleaguered prince, and he successfully prosecuted the publishers Leigh Hunt and his brother John for libel. They received a two-year sentence and £500 fine each but defiantly carried on producing the paper from prison.

Lady Hertford's close friendship with the prince continued throughout the decade, and her celebrity status and lavish parties meant she often appeared in the press. One essay defending her against scandalous gossip appeared in the *Ladies' Monthly Museum* on 1 August 1816, but its tone was so obsequious it appeared to be sarcastic:

It is pleasing to record, after a matrimonial union of *forty* years, that the domestic felicity of Lord and Lady Hertford continues unimpaired … May they long continue to enjoy their worldly happiness, not only for their own comfort and satisfaction, but also for the comfort and advantages which indigent merit, and the suffering poor, continually derive from their patronage and bounty. Their extensive charities, particularly in their own immediate neighbourhoods of Ragley in Warwickshire and Sudbourn Hall in Suffolk, are such as to endear them to all classes of society. The Marchioness is in her person, although tending to the *embonpoint*, at once graceful and elegant, her manners are uncommonly fascinating, and notwithstanding she has passed, what is usually called the meridian of life, being now in the *fifty-eighth* year of her age, it must be confessed, that her ladyship still possesses the charms of attraction very superior to many of greater juvenility. Yet, 'Envy will merit, as its shade, pursue.' And 'Nothing is so swift in its progress as calumny; nothing is more readily received, and nothing can be more widely spread abroad.' Or, as our poet has it, 'On eagles' wings immortal scandals fly'.

Lady Hertford's charms did eventually pall for the Prince Regent, and by the time he finally became king in January 1820, he had lost interest in her and moved on to his next mistress. Whether or not the pair actually did have a sexual relationship remains in doubt.

The issue of immorality in high life and the rightful leadership of society came to a head that same year, when as King George IV he put Queen Caroline on trial for adultery. It provoked even greater public hostility against the new sovereign, who had for many years openly consorted with a string of mistresses but accused his estranged wife of adultery so he could divorce her and stop her being crowned queen.[19] The Bill of Pains and Penalties, which would have enabled the royal divorce to go ahead, caused such widespread protest that it was rapidly abandoned by the government in order to defuse the situation. But during the trial in the House of Lords, the fitness of morally dubious peers to judge the queen came under fire.

The case was hotly debated in the press, and the main issues were highlighted in a popular pamphlet *Fair Play: or, Who are the Adulterers, Slanderers and Demoralizers?* which was printed in response to questions raised by *The News* as to how many of the Queen's judges had themselves committed adultery. The pamphlet explicitly linked political corruption with personal vice, listing peers who held public sinecures together with details of family scandals and exclaiming, 'These are the men that live upon the fat of the land, and look down with scorn on the swinish multitude!'[20] A similar stance was taken in a 1s pamphlet, *A Volley at the Peers*, which protested that the queen's fate was 'in the hands of rank adulterers, gross libertines, or men of prejudiced minds … so much is the habit of vice in the higher orders openly practised, as if indeed they gloried in it. Half our nobility are recorded adulterers, or victims of adultery.'[21] It went on to list their names, asking, 'Can it be expected that such men will form a correct judgment upon the conduct of others, who have proved themselves incapable of directing their own? Where is their sense of honour, as men, or their dignity as Peers?'

22

'The Spell is Broken'

The contentious question of what exactly England's aristocracy was there *for* evoked heated debate during the late Georgian period. The perennial conflict between tradition and change seemed to be embodied in the fundamental meaning of hereditary aristocracy as a link in the chain between past and future generations. One commentator observed nostalgically, 'The bones and sinews of Old England, her ornaments in peace and her leaders in war, are still to be found in her Aristocratic families', but 'times are gone by, when they can expect to receive respect, and command influence, independently of personal conduct and exertion'.[22] The function and purpose of the nobility was now no longer accepted without question by a vocal and rapidly growing middle class, who felt they were entitled to an equal share of power and privilege:

> Men of fortune, talent, and information, in the class of gentlemen, feel the injustice of that invidious line, which the exclusive system has drawn between them and their superiors in rank, but their equals in birth, and their inferiors, possibly, in every elegant or useful requirement.

Of course, this was not the first time the nobility had borne the brunt of popular antagonism, and during the upheaval of the Civil War the House of Lords itself had been abolished as 'useless and dangerous', only to be reinstated in 1660 as an ancient bulwark of the constitution.[23] By the early nineteenth century it was no longer perceived as dangerous, but more as the symbol of an outdated and corrupt system that unfairly privileged bloodline over individual merit. This growing resentment against the ruling class was fed by a burgeoning print culture, which ensured that aristocratic lives became more visible to the nation than ever before on the public stage of print. Noble conduct in public and private life came increasingly under fire from critics, although Georgian aristocrats were not markedly less virtuous or dutiful than their forebears had been. What had changed, however, were public attitudes towards them, and at precisely the moment when the commercial press realised its full potential as a powerful agent of social transformation.

Aristocracy was inevitably a public role, and publicity about adultery in the upper ranks highlighted the enormous gulf between the acceptable public face of authority and the unpalatable facts of their private lives. If aristocracy itself was merely a superficial performance with no substance underneath, then why should real gentlemen of honour, wealth and duty not aspire to leadership of the nation? Such questioning of the whole basis of aristocratic rule overturned the traditional rationale that it was guaranteed to protect the country's interests. In 1830 this principle prompted the prime minister, Earl Grey, to select the most aristocratic cabinet of the century, including only two commoners, one of them a baronet:

> ... to show that in these times of democracy and Jacobinism it is possible to find real capacity in the high Aristocracy – not that I wish to exclude merit if I should meet with it in the commonalty, but, given an equal merit, I admit that I should select the aristocrat, for that class is a guarantee for the safety of the state and of the throne.[24]

But this was by now a minority viewpoint as economic changes had consolidated the influence of the middle classes, who were demanding wholesale reform of government.

Reform had originally been discussed back in the 1760s, and from 1792 the idea of cautious change was adopted as political policy by the Whigs, to protect the legitimate rights of rank and landownership by eradicating rotten boroughs, extending the middle-class voting franchise and safeguarding the position of Parliament. Growing calls for change in the austere post-war years after 1815 eventually resulted in the First Reform Bill being introduced in March 1831, and arguments used in the 1790s radical attacks on aristocracy were now revived in support of reform.[25] The amended bill, passed in June 1832, gave the vote to all male adults occupying property with an annual rent valuation of £10 or more. It abolished sixty small constituencies, axed one of the two MPs returned in forty-seven boroughs and granted extra members to thirty-two towns.

Opposition to the changes in the House of Lords and their rejection of the second Reform Bill led to riots throughout the country. After threats of a mass creation of new titles to force it through the Upper House, the bill was passed, although many peers abstained. Others shared Earl Grey's view that the bill did not prejudice aristocratic interests. As one political insider, Sir George Francis Seymour, commented, 'The Reform Bill had rather given power to the middle classes than deprived the men of property of influence.'[26] In fact, boundary changes and more county seats actually strengthened the landowning interest, leaving the social make-up of Parliament very similar to before. And reform at this point may well have helped to ensure the long-term survival of the Upper House.[27] Sir George, Lord Hertford's grandson, inhabited the inner circles of the royal household and held various official posts, including Master of the Robes to William IV, who had taken the throne in 1830. He was well placed to witness behind-the-scenes manoeuvring as contentious proposals were modified, and he noted that many peers feared the wholesale creation of new titles 'would destroy the House of Lords'.[28] He saw a letter to the king in which the Duke of Wellington wrote that 'if the House is to be swamped by a Coup d'Etat', he could name twenty peers who would leave immediately. Sir George recorded the active role played in the process by the king, who 'without disputing the necessity of a wise Reform … laboured assiduously to induce his Gvt to moderate its provisions and thereby lessen … the opposition felt against the Bill by many of the most sagacious men in the country'.

Opponents of the bill, like the Earl of Dudley, were horrified at 'the stupendous magnitude' of proposals that would alter the constitution and jeopardise aristocratic privilege, bowing to 'the clamour of a people incapable of judging what was best for their advantage'.[29] Supporters of Reform felt more confidence in the strength of their hereditary position, as Viscount Goderich argued:

> There would be no necessity, as some noble Lords who opposed the measure seemed to think, for the Aristocracy to court mob popularity. Why should they? The sons of peers … had something better to rely upon. They had their own talents – they had their own characters – they had a thousand individual ties to bind the people of the country to them.

The enormous power of the press in shaping popular opinion was acknowledged by the Lord Chancellor, who said:

The Press is now the only organ of public opinion. This title it assumes; but …
it is rendered legitimate by defects of the Parliamentary Constitution …
The periodical Press is the rival of the House of Commons; and it is, and it will
be, the successful rival as long as that House does not represent the people.[30]

The debates on the Reform Bill in the House of Lords put peers in an extraordinarily difficult position. They had to argue as personal men safeguarding what they naturally viewed as their rightful inherited position, while at the same time trying to give a rational viewpoint on the principles of changing a system which upheld their political power. By performing the traditional aristocratic role of holding family land and title in trust as life tenants, they had always formed a solid link between past and future. Now they faced the prospect of betraying the position entrusted to them by generations of ancestors. By speaking publicly on an issue so fundamental to their own future, peers had to consider the profound implications of their words and actions. As the Archbishop of Canterbury pointed out, although he believed the aristocracy held 'the sacred charge of upholding the rights of Crown and people', he knew his vote would be 'one in which my character, as … a Peer of England, is deeply implicated'. Many speakers were mindful of the impression they made on the public, as Lord Lyndhurst commented, 'If they think we have not done our duty, but have deserted it from base, personal, or selfish motives, they would turn from the contemplation of our conduct with disgust.'

The passing of the Great Reform Act was a pivotal moment with profound implications for the whole nation, altering the way society saw itself in terms of its social hierarchies. In one way the Act marked the culmination of a long process of change, by enshrining in legislation the major shifts in social composition and attitudes that had been evolving for over half a century. In another way, it marked a threshold into the future which enabled more wide-reaching political and social change to take place in the following century. The 1832 Act had many effects, but most importantly it signalled an imaginative refocusing of society, a subtle metamorphosis in the political unconscious that opened up previously unthinkable possibilities for the middle class. The Reform Act has been described as a key moment in the making of national identity, that changed ideas about 'who were the imagined insiders' and redefined citizenship as 'the rule of difference' by male property owners.[31] It was certainly a catalyst for social change and effectively brought the middle class into existence, as a recognised group now fully entitled to challenge traditional aristocratic privilege.

The Reform Bill debates allowed a range of views to be aired about the rightful leadership of society. But far more than the mechanics of the voting franchise were being discussed, as one periodical stressed: 'It is not the nation, but the Peers, who are brought to the bar – whose fate depends on the verdict.'[32] Many people feared the consequences of such radical changes, which they believed would ultimately lead to a republic; the 5th Marquis of Hertford later commented, 'My father is quite low and desponding about it and cannot convince himself that the Reform Bill has not quite destroyed all chance of preserving the institutions of the Country ... in short he is quite Chief Mourner to the Constitution'.[33] The future looked highly uncertain and peers themselves were on trial, fighting for survival by proving their worth in a changing world. Attitudes to the aristocracy were shifting to reflect these changes and there was a growing sense of nostalgia for an idealised past.

Writers repeatedly referred to the superior quality of earlier generations deemed worthy of admiration, who were respected figures with an integral part to play in national life:

> Dignity of life and character is only to be achieved ... by virtue, sense and courage; by these virtues our ancient nobles gained their titles and reputations ... Read of the heroes and statesmen of former days, and compare their names and virtues with the pigmy things of this hour, and then see what nobility was, and what it is. It was honour, sense, and courage: now it is idleness, insignificance, mockery, and disease.[34]

Similar views were put forward in an article in Blackwood's *Edinburgh Magazine* for January 1834 entitled 'Hints to the Aristocracy. A Retrospect of Forty Years', which observed: 'It is impossible to conceal that the influence of the higher classes of the landholders, and of the Aristocracy, has signally declined within the last fifteen years, and it is as impossible to deny that it has declined very much in consequence of their own conduct.' In the past, a 'mysterious compound of gratitude, admiration, and flattered ambition' secured the position of great families who were fully involved in their estates and county life. But now all that had changed:

> The secluded and exclusive Aristocratic families frequently lead a luxurious, indolent life, associating solely with each other ... and knowing as little of the people, whose support is necessary to preserve their own estates or honours from the clutches of the Radicals, as they do of the Kalmucs or Hindoos ...

as if no danger threatened them and their country; as if no Reform Bill had transferred to impassioned millions ... the influence which should be centred in those whose measures are steadied by the possession of property.

The aristocracy was often portrayed in this way, as the pathetic remnants of a once powerful body that had not only outlived its usefulness but was wilfully perpetuating a grossly unfair system. In *A Letter to the Earl of Wilton* the writer, who described himself as being from a middle-ranking family with commercial interests, calculated that classes were taxed in inverse ratio to their means. So the aristocracy paid only one-twelfth of their income in tax, while the working class paid a third. 'Can you wonder, my Lord, that ... the multitude show no great love to those who apparently legislate not for the great body of their countrymen ... but for themselves?' Hereditary privilege alone was no longer enough to justify respect: 'I should prefer conceding it rather to the nobleness of their conduct, than to the nobil- ity of their descent.' More radical writers condemned the whole principle on which the peerage was based as an absurd anachronism that should be abolished: 'Primogeniture, observed in its effects and references to the state, presents then, no other result but a surplus of vice over virtue, the ascend- ancy of disaffection, and the depression of patriotism among citizens.'

A satirical pamphlet *The People or the Peerage?* ridiculed the entire ruling class, declaring, 'we bear no ill-will to individual Peers, any more than we do to individual pickpockets, or any other of those peculiar classes that form the public nuisances of the time.' It described a peerage so estranged from the nation that they were 'a people dwelling at the antipodes ... *have they* A RIGHT *to govern us? That* is the question. ... The HEREDITARY ARISTOCRACY of England, and the PEOPLE of England, have become two distinct catego- ries; and each must henceforth stand alone, if it stand at all.' The pamphlet, whose anonymous author signed himself 'one of the people', listed recent fashionable sexual scandals, including a peer who 'exchanges wives with his friend' and 'palms his cast off mistresses upon the public purse'. It said peers had made the fatal mistake of ignoring the need to behave with propriety: 'They scorn to "assume a virtue" which they have not. There is no vice under heaven ... that they do not commit as habitually and openly as they take their food.' It portrayed 'that gilded abstraction' the aristocracy, as 'mis- erable mummers' who had up to now managed to hoodwink the nation by convincing performances of superiority. But they had stupidly removed the disguise which had kept them in power for so long:

The English Aristocracy formerly had the wit to wear a mask, – at least when they condescended to come into the company of their inferiors [but now they] have lately been struck with the insane passion of (not disguising themselves as heretofore, but) setting themselves forth in their true aspect and colours, for the mingled amusement and instruction of the world beneath them!

Now the mask had been removed they had lost their power because the public had seen through the illusion of the sham performance and felt only disgust and contempt: 'The spell is broken – the mystery is dissipated, and the whole thing is changed into a vulgar Bartholomew-fair mockery.' In one sense the spell *had* been broken and real-life roles were irrevocably changing for the aristocracy. But paradoxically, as its political influence waned, it began to exert an increasing hold on the nation's imagination from the pages of novels.

Pages 'Dried with Diamond Dust'

While the aristocracy braced itself against the onslaught, the newly popular 'silver fork novel' flourished as readers indulged their nostalgia for an exotic species facing extinction. By dramatising the personal lives of the nobility, such romantic fictions allowed the public to satisfy mixed feelings of envy, curiosity, admiration and contempt. Many of these books adroitly combined scandalous real-life memoir with fiction, both glamorising and criticising high society.

The introduction to the 1833 edition of *Burke's Peerage* was keen to stress the new equality of peers and people, saying, 'The aristocracy of the British Empire, like its other inimitable institutions, exists but as a link in the great chain which connects the community at large, – a link, more polished, perhaps, than any of the other – hardly more powerful.'[35] The conflict between this ideal of a superior aristocracy and scandalous gossip about their personal lives was what made peers so topical and therefore profitable for the commercial press. It was no coincidence that Henry Colburn, 'the prince of publishers', began producing *Burke's Peerage* in 1826, using the back pages of each volume to advertise titles of the many silver fork novels he also published.

Silver fork novels were aimed at a largely female middle-class readership, who enjoyed tantalising glimpses inside the glamorous world of fashionable society to which they aspired. The whole attraction of these books lay in their promise to reveal hidden secrets of life among the *bon ton* by deliberate mixing elements of fact and fiction. The real identity of both authors and their fictional characters was the topic of endless speculation, while the veracity of the imaginary episodes described could be discussed at length by readers. This appeal was accurately summed up by a reviewer of the novel *Tales of Ton*, who was 'happy to see the follies and vices of the age so completely exposed' and commented that 'most of the scenes can be brought home to real life, which doubtless increases the interest, and sanctifies the whole with the charm of truth.'[36]

Originally referred to simply as 'fashionable novels', after 1831 silver fork novels became more commonly known by this new generic term derived from a derogatory phrase of William Hazlitt, who in an essay for the *Examiner* mocking a popular author of the 'Dandy School' said, 'Provided a few select persons eat fish with silver forks, he considers it a circumstance of no consequence if a whole country starves.'[37] One of the main innovators of the silver fork genre was the publisher Henry Colburn, who was seeking new ways of securing his business in the difficult financial climate of the mid-1820s at a time when two-thirds of publishing houses went bankrupt. He astutely exploited the social aspirations of the wealthy middle class, who had the leisure time to read, by publishing exposés of high society, written by writers who were either titled or rumoured to be of aristocratic birth. While other publishers struggled, Colburn expanded his list, which was predominantly fiction but also included journals like the *New Monthly Magazine* and *Literary Gazette*, which he used assiduously to puff his own titles. By 1829 around half of all new novels appearing that year were published by Colburn, most of them expensive three-volume sets.

The silver fork craze lasted for around two decades from the mid-1820s and finally died out completely in the 1850s. It has been described as the cultural expression of the conflict between the middle and upper classes which reached a peak at this time, giving an outlet for readers' contradictory impulses of emulation and challenge.[38] Readers of silver fork novels could experience the excitement of peeping through the keyhole at other people's lives, to relish the details of a luxurious existence so very different from their own. As fascinated voyeurs and disapproving moral judges, readers could inhabit the fashionable world of their imagination, while at the same time scorning the excesses of aristocratic lifestyles. Such novels described the minutiae of fashionable etiquette, behaviour and conversation, acting as handbooks of information about the homes, possessions, clothes and leisure pursuits of high society.

As authenticity was essential, genuine or implied authorship by a member of the nobility was considered to be an important selling-point, and the *Belle Assemblee* of February 1830 exclaimed excitedly, 'High Life is now threatened with serious exposures. There was a time when Commoners of very low degree used to sketch what they called the upper circles ... But now the very Lords of the Creation turn king's evidence.' Titled authors purporting to give an insider's view included Lady Charlotte Bury (a duke's daughter and former lady-in-waiting to Queen Caroline), the Countess of Blessington and Lady Caroline Lamb, whose 1816 *roman-à-clef* called *Glenarvon* detailed her brief liaison with Lord Byron. One of the genre's most prolific writers was Catherine Gore, who had privileged access to high society during three years living with her mother's cousin Lady Wentworth. Male silver fork authors included Edward Bulwer Lytton (later created a baron), whose 1828 novel *Pelham* became one of the best-known examples of the genre, and Lord Normanby, who wrote during his posting as a diplomat in Italy. Robert Plumer Ward, a former secretary of state, was best known for his first work *Tremaine*, while Benjamin Disraeli, who later became prime minister and 2nd Earl of Beaconsfield, also achieved great success as a popular novelist. Some books were deliberately published anonymously and puffed by the circulation of rumours about the possible identity of their high society authors. *The Age* of 13 May 1827 said, 'We have reason to think that the writer of *English Fashionables Abroad* is, in reality, a lady of rank, who has for some time resided in Rome.' This tactic of enticing readers was used by Colburn when he published Disraeli's *Vivian Grey* anonymously as a *roman-à-clef* by a distinguished author, although at the time he was still an unknown youth working in legal practice.

Periodicals regularly played on the appeal of insider secrets by reporting gossip on the possible identity of fictional characters. An article in the Colburn-owned satirical *John Bull* magazine on Mrs Gore's first novel (also published by Colburn) noted that, 'The character of Lady Isabella V--- in the new novel of *The Manners of the Day*, is said to be sketched from a certain elegante well known in Parisian society'.[39] This kind of guessing game was part of the fun for readers, and publishers tried to pique curiosity by promoting speculation in the press even before publication. A brief item in *The Age* exclaimed, 'A work entitled *Tales of our Counties*, is shortly to appear, which it is said anatomises above one hundred distinguished characters!'[40] The formula for a silver fork bestseller was satirised by a character in Lord Normanby's second novel *Yes and No: A Tale of the Day*, who joked that it must be written by 'a gentlemanly man' and stuffed full of titles, then the writer should:

> … open the Peerage at random, pick a suppositious author out of one page of it, and fix the imaginary characters upon some of the rest; mix it all up with a *quantum suff* of puff, and the book is in the second edition before ninety-nine readers out of a hundred have found out that the one is as little likely to have written, as the others to have done, what is attributed to them.

This element of real or assumed *roman-à-clef* was exploited by the publication of 'Keys', which unlocked a novel's hidden meaning by revealing the identity of its characters. A review in *The Age* in April 1828 of *Key to 'Almack's Revisited'* by Charles White noted it was 'in great request among the higher circles: it certainly adds materially to the pleasure of the perusal of these saucy volumes'. Hints that the book attracted an elite readership added to its appeal for the aspiring middle classes, as did its title reference to Almack's, the exclusive social club in Pall Mall presided over by a select committee of aristocratic patronesses. The notoriety of the venue was also exploited in *Almack's, a Novel*, by Marianne Hudson. A critique of the novel in the *Monthly Review* in January 1827 opened with speculation that its author was actually Lady Westmoreland and said the accuracy with which it portrayed the manners, conversation and daily activities of fashionable society proved it must be the work of a lady:

> It is impossible not to perceive, that the author has painted all her various and striking portraits from the life ... and though her characters are all masqued under heterogeneous names, yet we feel that they have all of them figured ... in the very scenes where she employs them.

The reviewer praised the work as a valuable exposé of 'the puerile and inconsequential usages, the numerous follies and mean intrigues' of high life which might help to reform the nobility, and should console middle-class readers 'that their condition is ... really the most enviable'. To this end, *Almack's* portrayed a range of morally reprehensible characters, including a stereotypical cameo of the Norbury family. This comprised the cold and manipulative Lord Norbury ('a little-minded man, with ... not one grain of heart ... He loved himself alone'), his haughty and unpopular countess obsessed with rank ('The world with her was divided into two classes – patricians and plebeians; she knew of no shades, no go-betweens') and their spoiled daughter, Lady Anne, who courted flattery by concealing her unpleasant personality beneath a false vivacity. The plot centred on a love story in which the aptly named *nouveau riche* heroine Barbara Birmingham entered society, overcame prejudices about her vulgar origins and married a lord. In its choice of title, plot, characters and style, this highly commercial novel was carefully crafted to engage the middle-class reader by confirming familiar stereotypes of elite life.

Social class, fashionable vices and marriage were the major themes of silver fork novels, many of which were written to a predictable formula, summarised in the *Monthly Review* as 'A love story, of course – which with the usual number of episodes, all tending to the same finale of marriage, must in such compositions make up the outline.' A typical plot appeared in *Traits and Trials*, a two-volume novel published in 1821, where the heroine 'the lovely and virtuous Isabella' found happiness by marrying Lord Clanneron after he recovered his wealth and title from the clutches of a presumptive heir.[41] Marriage and its problems were the focus of Mrs Gore's many novels, such as *Women As They Are, or The Manners of the Day* in which the naïve heroine Helen married Lord Willersdale, only to be led astray by his sister, the licentious Lady Danvers. Her *Mothers and Daughters* revealed the machinations of the marriage market, while *The Hamiltons* explored an unhappy arranged marriage during the political upheaval of the Reform debates.[42]

The most frequently occurring plot described the youthful protagonist's quest for a new identity, featuring either a young man's sexual and political exploits in high society or a young girl's entrance into fashionable life where she was faced with the dangerous temptations of an indulgent existence. They adapted themes from earlier romantic literature to reflect modern debates about power and social change, and created for middle-class readers their ideal of the professional gentleman.[43] The mysterious world of the *Bon Ton* was shown as a secret society with its own rituals, language and code of conduct, which the hero needed to infiltrate in order to be rewarded by love, domestic happiness and public success. Such stories exploring shifting class boundaries clearly resonated with the times. By playing out alternative scenarios of contemporary life, they deliberately set out to present negative stereotypes of dissolute aristocratic behaviour. And by taking marriage, romantic intrigues, seduction or adulterous liaisons as their defining themes, authors drew on the morally dubious love lives of high society which would guarantee sales. The opening scene of *Pelham* described with witty cynicism the failed elopement of the hero's mother, the worldly Lady Frances, with her lover. The hypocritical moral code governing elite circles was satirised in many such novels, including Charlotte Bury's *The Divorced*, which dealt with the fate of female divorcées, and *The Victims of Society* by Lady Blessington, which explored attitudes to fashionable adultery.[44]

Silver fork novels remained hugely popular with avid readers who were dazzled by tales 'that blind one as though the pages were dried with diamond dust!'[45] Less impressionable critics, however, were usually scathing about their poor quality and superficial subject matter, 'affectation and pretension', and they kept wishing in vain that the craze would end for 'a class of literature with which the public, we humbly yet ardently hope, must be nearly satiated'.[46] One reviewer in the *Ladies' Monthly Museum* of September 1830 wrote disparagingly:

> The arts by which the literary appetite of the public has been excited for the last few years, during which the market has … been deluged with a greater quantity of trash than issued from all the purveyors of literature of the previous half century, are becoming too notorious to succeed much longer.

In a review of the novel *The Exclusives*, a critic in the *Edinburgh Literary Journal* of December 1829 commented wearily that 'there is some bold and vigorous painting of passion in this book … The only misfortune is, that we are tired of the whole class of works to which it belongs. We wish the writers in this department would try to strike out something new.'

Many fashionable novels were badly written lightweight romances, ostensibly revealing the hidden truths about the frivolous lives of the great while revelling in all the extravagant detail. But beneath the surface trivia describing fashionable etiquette, some of the better quality novels were sharp satires exploring the relationship between individuals and society. True stories of scandal about actual lords and ladies could be reworked into fictions based on known facts. In one sense they were 'the amber which serves to preserve the ephemeral modes and caprices of the passing day', in the words of a fictional lord from Mrs Gore's *The Manners of the Day*. On the other hand, as another character in that novel observed, 'The worst fault of such productions … is the distortion of their portraiture – the writers … necessarily disfigure the objects of their art'.

This blend of reportage and distortion was used to rework a scandalous true-life story of extra-marital intrigue into the central theme for *The Exclusives*. The three-volume novel by Lady Charlotte Bury was published anonymously in 1830 and proved so popular it rapidly went through several reprints. An advertisement in the *London Literary Gazette* on 2 January 1830 hinted at the 'alleged eminent station of its writer' and promised 'the truest … and the most comprehensive picture of that life, which has yet been presented to the world'. It was described as 'one of the severest satires ever penned upon a certain portion of the fashionable world. The moral certainty is an important one, and, we trust, will not be lost sight of.'[47] The reviewer referred to the existence of 'a list of high and distinguished names, purporting to be a Key to the characters' but added that 'the portraits are sufficiently palpable in resemblance, to serve as their own index'. Another critic, writing in the *John Bull* magazine, praised its 'sallies of wit and humour, enriched by a society whose exclusive pretensions, and whose follies and delinquencies are lashed with a high and masterly hand'.

The Exclusives was intended as a biting satire of high society, and the opening passage of volume one declared its aim of painting:

> ... a picture of the manners, modes, and morals of the times ... to chronicle them for the day would not be without its use. The sensible part of mankind would laugh at the follies ... which the page of such ephemeral history unfolded; while the actors in the scene might possibly view in the mirror held up to them their own lives, and their own actions, in a new and truer light.

The real identities of these actors were unlocked by *A Key to the Royal Novel of The Exclusives* published the same year, which printed 'a Correct List of the Noble and Distinguished Personages alluded to' and included twenty fashionables such as the society hostesses Lady Jersey and Princess Esterhazy, according to *The Age* of 2 February 1830. The novel's heroine Miss Georgina Melcomb, who married Lord Glenmore, was in fact based on the notorious society beauty Jane Digby, who married Lord Ellenborough and divorced in April 1830 after a string of love affairs. The novel's publication was cleverly timed to profit from their sensational adultery case.

The exclusives were described like a mythical alien species observed by a detached narrator acting as an interpreter for the reader, recounting their strange habits and making wry comments. This narrator explained in volume two that 'when set down on paper they may seem exaggerated, yet certainly the fact is not in the least so.' The moral purpose of telling the story was 'to paint so destructive an evil as that of the whole false, futile system of the exclusiveness of *ton*'. The novel presented the interwoven tales of characters for whom 'pleasure is the sole object of their lives' and showed 'the effects of an admission within this Circean circle upon two young and amiable individuals of different sexes'.[48]

The central strand of the plot featuring an innocent young bride being corrupted by society echoed the Duchess of Devonshire's novel *The Sylph* written fifty years earlier, which had also critiqued the suspect moral codes of fashionable life. In *The Exclusives* the familiar criticism was made that the aristocracy disguised its corrupt nature with superficial false performances to mislead observers. The narrator said, 'Whatever vice ... may exist in character, providing it exist with what they call good taste ... is varnished over. The husbands and wives ... agree only in this one point, namely, in being a cloak for each other's follies or vices.' Soon after marriage, the heroine was tutored in the ways of society by the scheming Lady Tenderden (a caricature of the real Lady Cowper) who counselled her that the best way to keep a husband was through indifference and the cultivation of many admirers. Left to her own devices by her unsuspecting husband, who neglected 'the duties of private life' for his political career, the guileless Lady Glenmore was pursued by a charming libertine who saw her 'as a fit play-thing for the hour.'

The Glenmores were both portrayed as sympathetic characters who became the innocent victims of fashionable society, where 'the evil works so insidiously, and under such a variety of masks'. Disapproval of the real Lord Ellenborough's neglect of his wife in the pursuit of his political ambitions was reiterated in a description of the fictional Lord Glenmore. However, Glenmore was presented as a good and well-meaning man who was widely misunderstood. The narrator noted that, although public opinion did not credit Glenmore with 'amiability of feeling, or for the strict principles he really possessed … in addition to warmth of heart, natural affection, and good principles, he possessed talents of a very superior kind'.

Widespread criticism of Ellenborough's ambitious, proud and coldly reserved character was countered in the novel by a persuasive explanation of these faults as positive aspects of the aristocratic role:

> If Glenmore was ambitious (and he was so), his ambition was of a noble kind; and while he sought power, his uprightness of character could never suffer him to abuse its exercise. He was called proud by some: but although impressed with a sense of the dignity of the aristocracy to which he belonged, it was not a blind and foolish estimate of rank which made him value it, but a conviction of the importance and responsibility which everyone placed in the higher grades of society possesses, while fulfilling the duties of the sphere in which Providence places him.

An unpopular real-life public figure was recast as a likeable and misunderstood hero with whom the reader could sympathise.

Fiction conveniently revised the facts of the Ellenborough adultery case to create a fantasy happy ending appealing to sentimental female readers, where morality and virtue triumphed. Lady Glenmore escaped the clutches of her heartless seducer, the workaholic Lord Glenmore chose domestic happiness over ambition and resigned from public office, and the loving couple left the *ton* circle for an idyllic new life together abroad. What actually happened in real life was entirely different.

24

ELEPHANT ELLENBOROUGH, 'A DANDY AMONG POLITICIANS'

Almost sixty years after public indignation at the Duke of Grafton's divorce, another high-profile case created even greater outrage as an appalling example of aristocratic privilege. In April 1830 the 1st Earl of Ellenborough, a cabinet minister and son of the former Lord Chief Justice, was granted a private Parliamentary divorce, and the sensational trial was splashed across the whole front page of *The Times*. Public anger centred on the blatant collusion in the case and the fact that the divorce had been granted without the normal prerequisite of a legal separation order. This exemplified exactly the kind of class inequality that reformers were questioning, and Ellenborough's personal unpopularity as a symbol of the old corrupt aristocracy elevated the scandal into a *cause célèbre*.

The Ellenborough divorce provoked such a public reaction that the following month, in June 1830, a bill was introduced in the House of Commons to give the ecclesiastical courts jurisdiction over divorce, instead of Parliament. Although defeated, it was the first step towards divorce for all, which was eventually made possible by the 1857 Divorce Reform Act.[49] Introducing his bill, Dr Joseph Phillimore said a divorce suit heard in Parliament 'was either a mere mockery of Legislation ... or else the House was made the instrument for covering the guilty connivance of two parties'.[50] Questions of elite privilege were aired during the debate and speakers criticised the unfairness of a legal system which precluded most people from divorcing, because of the vast expense of a private bill.

The number of Parliamentary divorces granted had steadily increased from sixty in the period 1715–75 to seventy-four in the twenty-five years up to 1800 and nearly ninety during the thirty years from 1800–30. The cost of a common divorce bill of around £700 put it well out of the reach of the middle and lower ranks. Dr Phillimore said this went against the principle of English law 'that it should be equal for all parties, for high and low, for poor and rich'. Another MP, Mr O'Connell, asked, 'Were the upper classes of society, who could obtain divorces, more virtuous than the lower who could not? No man would say that they were. And was not divorce a temptation to adultery? Did it not give another argument to the seducer?' Lord Ellenborough's legal costs were believed to have totalled the enormous sum of £5,000 (roughly £300,000 now), proving the point that divorce was a privilege of the wealthy, but he was one of the last peers to be granted a divorce by private Parliamentary bill.

When private life collided with political ambition, trouble was guaranteed. As many peers had discovered, getting entangled in an adultery case was bound to damage public reputation by exposing intimate details of domestic life. The catalyst which transformed a low-key dislike of Lord Ellenborough into widespread public hostility, was the divorce action against his wife after she became pregnant by her lover, the Austrian diplomat Prince Schwarzenberg. The press made the most of the scandal, repeating explicit details of the case for years afterwards to attack him politically and personally:

> In public life Lord Ellenborough is perfect in character, quite as estimable and honourable as we have viewed him in the circle of private society … It is the fate of this Elephant Lord to be as much despised by his own party as he is laughed at by his opponents, and there never was a more unpopular man connected with any Administration.[51]

This article in the *Satirist; or, the Censor of the Times*, written two years after the divorce, gave an exposition of his private character as a 'high moral lesson' to readers:

> His Lordship is not more notorious for those amours which prove the *manliness* of his character, than he is for the lowliness of their *objects* [and seeking pleasure] under a skin most dingy and dirty, and under rags that teem with pestilence and vermin … Honour, eternal honour to his gracious condescension! To take to one's bed and bosom even ugliness and filth … is an act worthy of the holy saints.

It reported that about a week after his marriage 'he was seen at a celebrated watering-place, following a poor, dirty, and unattractive girl – of course with the most benevolent intentions', and that his wife 'was incensed at his early neglect of her – neglect resulting from an unwearied intercourse with the lowly, exposed, and suffering of her own sex!' Many people secretly shared the view of Lady Charlotte Bury, one of the queen's ladies-in-waiting, that 'long attachments, even when not sanctioned by morality' deserved compassion but lust and 'the ephemeral fires of passion, intrigue and pleasure, are loathsome'.

The nickname 'Elephant Ellenborough' referred to his insensitive, thick-skinned personality and habit of roughly trampling opponents underfoot. He was also known as 'the Peacock' because of rumoured vanity about his handsome appearance and thick, dark curly hair. These characteristics were regularly mocked in the press. The reviewer of a painting of the House of Lords, packed with peers for the opening of Parliament, wrote disparagingly that Lord Ellenborough, 'whose qualification for Office of State may be summed up in the single line, that he is a dandy among politicians, a politician among dandies', was painted here 'adjusting the collar of his coat and looking down with a glance of comical satisfaction at the neat display of his own well appointed legs, evidently anticipating the impression his well-tailored figure will make'. Another article, describing government ministers during the closing Parliamentary session of 1829, ridiculed 'the destinies of India aptly entrusted to Lord Ellenborough, because like Samson, his glory lies in his locks'.[52]

The adultery scandal provided extra ammunition to undermine his character, and a satirical item in *The Age* on theatrical performances reported that he would act in three plays entitled *Everybody's Husband*, *Seduction* and *Retribution*.[53] A comment piece on the Parliamentary Reform debate named 'this dandy Lord … he of the curly locks and unchaste wife' as an example of 'profligate corruption', who abused his wealth and title to oppose the people by voting against Reform. He allegedly did this to safeguard his own lucrative sinecure of almost £8,000 a year (around £480,000 now) as chief clerk to his father's court the King's Bench, which he had enjoyed since the age of 22.[54] In short, he seemed to encapsulate all the unacceptable traits of aristocratic privilege which reformers were now determined to expose and eradicate. The extensive press coverage of his divorce compounded a bad reputation, blighted his political career and fuelled a further thirty years of public dislike, during which 'every baseless rumour was given ready credence and public acts given the least generous interpretation'.[55] As one of his biographers later commented, he 'was one of those unfortunate men of whom people were ever ready to accept evil report. Few men of first rate ability have suffered heavier penalties in this respect in their public careers.'[56]

Edward Law, Lord Ellenborough, was born in 1790, the eldest son of a judge who was raised to the peerage as a baron when he became Lord Chief Justice. After Eton and Cambridge, he became MP for St Michael's in Cornwall aged only 23 and soon earned a reputation as a skilful orator in the House of Commons. After his father's death in 1818 he became 2nd Baron Ellenborough (later created Earl) and played an active part in the Lords. A happy marriage to Lady Octavia Stewart, daughter of the Marquis of Londonderry, ended suddenly after five years when she became seriously ill with tuberculosis and died. He was devoted to Octavia and gave up his seat as an MP at the 1818 election so they could spend more time together as her health was failing. But that same winter his father was dying and he was forced to spend many weeks away in London visiting him. The couple wrote every day and Ellenborough grew desperately anxious about his wife's chronic cough, begging her, 'Dearest love, do take care of your own health and do not break me down quite by the double misery of having the two beings most dear to me in the World ill at the same time at a great distance from each other.'[57] In another letter he declared, 'I never knew happiness till I married you and I have hardly save for a moment ceased to enjoy happiness since our marriage except when you have been ill.'[58] As her illness got worse he despaired, writing, 'You do not know how necessary your Health is to my Happiness. What would I do without you?'[59] After her death early the following year, a relative visiting the grief-stricken Ellenborough reported that, 'poor Edward's distress is heart rending'.

Octavia had been the love of his life, but he gradually recovered from the tragedy and five years later in September 1824 he married Jane, the beautiful blonde 17-year-old daughter of Admiral Sir Henry Digby, who had spent much of her childhood at the Palladian mansion Holkham Hall in Norfolk, owned by her wealthy grandfather. Captivated by her huge blue eyes and long golden hair that reached to her waist, Ellenborough poured out his feelings in verse. One poem written during their courtship, poignantly expressed his suffering since Octavia's death:

The thought that I am loved again
And loved by one I can adore,
That I have passed through years of pain
And found the bliss I knew before.

Another romantic love poem written a few months after their wedding declared his passion for Jane, the first and last verses reading:

My bride! For thou art still a bride to me
And loved with all the passion of a soul
Which gave itself at once, nor would be free

And every thought of others is effaced
In dreams of bliss which heaven's behests allow
So wedded truth alone, and love's unbroken vow

The marriage seemed to be happy at first, but things soon began to go wrong as he became more immersed in his political career and Jane was drawn into the *louche* fashionable set, where she met other men only too willing to give her the attention she lacked at home.[60]

Two years after the wedding she began an intense love affair with her cousin Colonel George Anson that started tongues wagging as they went openly about London together. And when her husband was away, she gave George a key to the side-door of their house in Roehampton so he could stay the night. Alarmed at her reckless behaviour, Jane's former governess Margaret Steele warned Lord Ellenborough that his naïve young wife was being led astray by disreputable society friends, but he only laughed and said he 'had unlimited confidence in Lady Ellenborough, and took no notice of it'. When George ended the affair, which was becoming too risky and jeopardised his military career, Jane had a brief romance with Frederick Madden, an academic who was cataloguing manuscripts in the library at Holkham Hall during one of her visits. In his diary, Madden described his first impression of Jane as 'one of the most lovely women I ever saw, quite fair, blue eyes that would move a saint, and lips that would tempt one to forswear heaven to touch them'.[61] Soon after she returned home, Jane realised that she was pregnant, and in February 1828 her son Arthur was born; however, the baby's father was actually George Anson, though she apparently never told her husband.

Delighted to have a son at last, and recently appointed as a minister in the Duke of Wellington's cabinet, Ellenborough's life seemed to be complete. But just three months after the birth, Jane met Prince Felix Schwarzenberg at a ball in the Austrian embassy and they began a torrid affair. Handsome, charming and highly intelligent, the 27-year-old diplomat was immediately struck by Jane's beauty, as men always were, and she did not try to resist the temptation for long. Soon she was visiting his lodgings at No. 73 Harley Street in London several afternoons a week, on the pretext that she was seeing her family who had a house in the same road. A neighbour who lived opposite often noticed Lady Ellenborough arriving, dressed in a riding habit and veil, and driving a green phaeton with two black ponies. On several occasions he looked in through a window across the street, where the blinds were only half-way down, to see Prince Schwarzenberg standing in a first-floor room with Lady Ellenborough, lacing her stays.

The clandestine encounters carried on for the next year in London and at the Norfolk Hotel in Brighton, but by now the affair was common gossip. Ellenborough was busy with his political career and also having his own sexual adventures with two different mistresses, but he was apparently unaware of the seriousness of his wife's entanglement. When he did eventually realise the full extent of her indiscreet liaison, he sent her away to the Roehampton house. It was now too late to avoid a scandal, as Jane realised she was pregnant by her lover and confessed to Miss Steele, 'My situation will soon become visible! God knows what will become of me! The child is not Lord Ellenborough's.' Soon afterwards she left England for Basle, where she hoped Prince Schwarzenberg would join her, and Ellenborough began proceedings for a divorce. The case was bound to be contentious, but no one expected the barrage of hostility it unleashed.

Ellenborough had always been frank about his political ambitions and was well aware that his unpopularity might be exacerbated when he joined the cabinet in 1828, first as lord privy seal, then president of the India Board: 'Undoubtedly the Foreign Office is the object of my ambition ... but I may over-estimate my own powers, and I excite less envy and jealousy by taking at first the incognito office of President of the Board of Control.'[62] He had become resigned to unfavourable press comment, and referring to criticism in *The Times* of recent government appointments, he wrote in his diary, 'As yet it says nothing of me. I expect abuse as a dandy lord. It will be said the affairs of India are given up to those dandy lords, and a priggish lawyer.'[63] Although undoubtedly a conscientious and talented politician with liberal views, Ellenborough's outspoken and arrogant personality had alienated many people since his youth. He could be blunt, sarcastic and impatient, and at his divorce hearings in Parliament, his enemies took their revenge.

The Ellenborough Divorce Bill had a difficult passage through both the House of Lords and House of Commons, due to the unusually meticulous scrutiny of all the evidence, lengthy cross-examining of the witnesses, and strong opposition from many members. There was much criticism of the way he had neglected his young wife, leaving her unprotected and vulnerable to the attentions of her seducer. Lady Ellenborough had been allowed to go about town unattended by her husband several times each week for a year, 'openly, without disguise or attempt at concealment, to the house of Prince Schwarzenberg, where she undressed, went to bed, stayed there two or three hours, and then returned home'. As the Earl of Radnor said, 'there were thousands who would be ready to take advantage of such negligence on the part of a husband', his treatment was not only 'cruel' to 'a young and beautiful woman', but showed 'gross negligence'.[64] Opposing the divorce bill, the Earl of Malmesbury said the House had never before allowed the claims of a husband 'who, through vice or negligence, had delivered over his wife, unprotected, to the dangers of temptation and seduction'.[65] Supporters like the Earl of Rosslyn pointed out that Ellenborough was engaged in public duties and could not be expected to abandon them to constantly watch over his young wife. Lord Wharncliffe agreed, saying that 'there was scarcely a man who had any connexion with public life … but must necessarily be absent at times from his wife, and he must intrust his honour to her own discretion and her just sense of propriety'.

This was a point taken up in the *John Bull* magazine, which said:

> … although Lord Ellenborough never was a favourite of ours, he seems to us to have done no more with regard to Lady Ellenborough than every other nobleman, or gentleman, does and must do by his wife. It is impossible for an official man, whose mornings are employed in public business, and whose evenings are employed in Parliament, to pay those constant atttentions to his 'better half' that smaller people are accustomed to exhibit … If an English wife cannot be trusted by herself, we think the sooner noblemen hire duennas and block up their windows, or perhaps build harems in their back gardens, the better.[66]

In the Commons, many MPs believed the divorce should be refused as a salutary lesson to the higher classes, 'that they were not to be allowed to go on in their career of profligacy and folly, reckless … of consequences', expecting to procure a divorce even when they breached the obligations of marriage and had not 'watched over their wives with care'.[67] The *Observer* commented that 'Lord Ellenborough's Divorce Bill affords another illustration of the remark that all virtue and all affectation of decency will ere long be confined to the middle classes.'

An article in *Bell's Life* said the case had made a mockery of justice and applauded the House of Commons for resisting the bill 'because it is a lesson to men of fashion that they must not hope to be released by the public from the performance of those obligations, in the relations of private life, which by their mild and salutary restraint upon the passions, at once soften and dignify the marriage intercourse'.[68] It pointed out that if male conduct was also assessed in divorce cases, it might bring about an improvement in fashionable life so 'that the public can ultimately be spared much of these exhibitions, which are at once scandalous and lothful'.

The Ellenborough divorce, which came just at a time when reform debates were intensifying, meant that it provided ideal ammunition in the war of words against the aristocracy. Its potential was quickly exploited by the influential campaigning editor of *The Times,* Thomas Barnes, who had long realised the way to boost circulation figures was to court an expanding middle-class readership. He had taken a financial stake in the paper in 1819 and was its editor for the next twenty-two years, making him 'the most powerful man in the country', according to the Duke of Wellington. Under his editorship the newspaper supported popular liberal causes such as reform, and its growing influence on public opinion was recognised in its nickname of *The Thunderer*.[69] Barnes took the unprecedented measure of clearing almost the entire front page on Friday 2 April 1830 to make way for a full verbatim account, across five broadsheet columns, of the Parliamentary hearing on the Ellenborough divorce, including all the witnesses' evidence. On the previous day the case had been reported in one front-page column. Occasionally a section of the front page was used for coverage of major news stories, such as a Lords debate on the contentious Corn Law, but in most editions at this time much of page one was filled with adverts. In contrast to the Ellenborough coverage, Queen Caroline's adultery trial had been given only a single front-page column in July 1820. *The Times* editorial also commented on the 'extraordinary case', calling for the identity of the lady of rank to be revealed who the governess had warned during her testimony was a bad influence on Lady Ellenborough: 'Let the name of this dangerous member of "acceptable society" ... be generally known, that other persons may have the means of avoiding the rock which Lord Ellenborough chose to run against.'

Other newspapers took a lower-key approach to the Ellenborough case, the *Morning Chronicle* and *Morning Post* both allocating it a place on page two and the *Standard* two columns on page one. For Barnes the case was clearly selected as both a political vehicle to support his crusading reformist editorial policy and a commercial vehicle to increase sales among the scandal-loving moral majority. Newspapers in the early nineteenth century were becoming increasingly powerful as agents of change, both reflecting and shaping public opinion, and playing an active part in national affairs by influencing political decision-making. As a form of 'fugitive literature', papers could have an immediate impact on the events they were writing about because they were quick to print and so widely read.[70] Lord Ellenborough acknowledged the power of the press, but his self-confident personality made him disregard the importance of public image, at a time when a display of propriety was expected from a ruling class under attack. Secure in his hereditary right to rule, he assumed the traditional role of haughty and uncompromising statesman, which did not go down well with his contemporaries. As his successor on the India Board Lord Stanley noted, he had 'more about him of the Roman of classical times than ... seems to suit ... our peaceable and commercial community'.[71] Despite undeniable talents and years of public service, his naturally commanding physical presence, stiff and over-bearing manner, abrasive character and insensitive behaviour all made him appear iconic of the despised old aristocracy.[72]

Unfortunately, these highly visible flaws tended to disguise the more sensitive and engaging parts of his nature hidden behind the unappealing public façade. A rare glimpse of the caring family man came in a surprisingly compassionate press comment after the death of 2-year-old Arthur, in February 1830, when *The Times* reported, 'This child was the darling of his father ... The grief of his Lordship will be severe, as the anxious solicitude and devoted attention to his child was so marked, that it became the theme of conversation with every visitor and resident at Worthing.'[73] Jane had left the baby in his care a year earlier, when she followed Prince Schwarzenberg to Europe, and he wrote to break the news to her, enclosing a lock of the little boy's fair hair. Alone and depressed after this bereavement and the breakdown of his second marriage, he retreated to his country home and wrote a moving poem to his beloved lost son:

Poor child! Thy mother never smiled on thee
Nor stayed to soothe thee in thy suffering day!
But thou wert all on earth to me
The solace of my solitary way.[74]

He even considered giving up politics, confiding to his diary, 'I really *could not* remain in London, without any society whatever and having nothing to do in the House. It oppressed my spirits … I feel that my domestic misfortunes have almost extinguished my desire of distinction – indeed *quite.*'[75]

Ellenborough did not marry again, but he went on to father three illegitimate children with a long-term mistress, writing in a letter to his mother that he was very fond of his 'two beautiful boys'. Jane lived with Prince Schwarzenberg in Paris, bearing him two children, until he left her a year after the divorce from Ellenborough. She remained abroad, becoming notorious for her many lovers, including several European royals and aristocrats, an Albanian brigand, two Arabs and finally a Bedouin chief twenty years her junior, with whom she lived in Syria for the rest of her life.

For much of his career Ellenborough kept detailed accounts of his political life in a set of large notebooks, with the words *Publick Memoranda* handwritten on the cover. These contained long daily entries commenting on meetings, letters written and conversations, together with his thoughts on public duties, all written in a bold and illegible scrawl. After the painful year of 1830, he sought consolation in the activities of a busy public life and his skilful mastery of oratory, noting in the diary:

> It is wonderful how I have lost my ambition. To make a fine speech would now give me no pleasure, yet … I must do my duty and regain my proper station by speaking and generally by taking a very active part in politics. It is my nature – and it is only the dreadful distress of mind I have endured that has for the time changed it.[76]

Five months later he wrote, 'I am determined to read Cicero and good English speeches and to think oratorically upon many subjects that will be discussed … As I have abandoned all social engagements, I must be a Public Man or nothing.'[77] Significantly, he defined himself now as a public man, to be judged solely on the competent performance of political duty, according to ancient Roman ideals of leadership which elevated public actions above private family life.[78]

By December that year he was beginning to regain his equilibrium and had found a new sense of purpose by embracing his public role. After a successful performance in the Lords he noted:

I was right to speak. I said just what I intended and I really will now take a part constantly in Debates. It is my forte – I can do it with some credit to myself and advantage to the Country – It will occupy ... my leisure and perhaps give me more of Pleasure in the world than I had expected to enjoy again.[79]

While comments like this revealed the more engaging side of his personality, the tone of many other diary entries showed the forthright, contemptuous manner that alienated others.[80] He dismissed a new book with the terse words, 'The account of Canning's Govnt. by Stapleton is too stupid to be read.'[81] And details about political events were often punctuated with sweeping acerbic comments, such as 'they seem mad', 'a most foolish speech from Lord Wynford, full of fallacies & absurdities' and 'Committee on Poor Laws. The room was insufferably hot & they were twaddling over a Bill requiring returns of money expended, &c. so I left them.'[82]

Ellenborough's political ambitions were fulfilled when he became Governor-General of India in 1841, where he played a decisive role in the war with Afghanistan. As usual he applied himself to the job punctiliously, sometimes spending sixteen hours a day at his desk. But his robust views on how India should be governed and the typically scathing tone of his reports caused resentment among the East India Company directors, who recalled him in April 1844. Not for the first time, his abrasive personality had proved to be his downfall. He was clearly 'honest, painstakingly devoted to duty ... very able, even brilliant. Yet these admirable qualities ... somehow fail to evoke sympathy even where they command respect.'[83] Extracts of his diaries, edited by his nephew Lord Colchester, were published after his death and seemed to confirm him as an arrogant patrician of the old school. In the preface, Colchester wrote that Ellenborough's first ambition was for a military career, but this was forbidden by his father:

On entering public life, his wish, he used to say, was to become a military statesman ... he set himself diligently to the cultivation of oratory as an art, and ... devoted his leisure to the assiduous study of what he thought the best models of ancient and modern eloquence.[84]

Ellenborough's crucial mistake was to disregard the importance of an appealing public image, and take as his model the more autocratic Roman ideal of classical leadership he admired. In doing so, he ignored changing social expectations of public men, which meant that personality was now more important than the actual performance of duty. Ellenborough's diary showed him to be a decisive leader with strongly held convictions. However, while it accurately portrayed him as a conscientious exponent of the aristocratic government he believed to be in the nation's best interests, it was the portrait of an outdated role that no longer fitted the mood of the times.

The social transformation witnessed in the early decades of the nineteenth century fundamentally changed ideas of what aristocracy actually meant. Although for now the nobility still remained at the pinnacle of the social hierarchy, after the 1832 Reform Act wealthy self-made members of the middle classes could realistically aspire to join the ruling class themselves. The Act did not radically alter social power structures, but it did change the entire conception of society. It ushered in fairly moderate political changes to the electoral system, but its major significance was symbolic, signalling a turning point in national consciousness when the whole meaning of aristocracy could be re-imagined. It was the beginning of the end for the old order.

LIST OF ILLUSTRATIONS

1. 'Lady Abergavenny & Mr Liddel amusing themselves', Volume 1, *Trials for Adultery: or, The History of Divorces*, printed for S. Bladon, London, 1779–80. (© The British Library Board. Shelfmark 518.c.8–14)

2. Pompeo Batoni, *Augustus Henry Fitzroy, 3rd Duke of Grafton*, oil on canvas, 1762. (© National Portrait Gallery, London)

3. *Nancy Parsons in Turkish Dress*, c.1771, oil on copper by George Willison. (© Yale Center for British Art, Paul Mellon Collection, USA/Bridgeman Images)

4. *Thomas Lyttelton, 2nd Baron Lyttelton*, attributed to Richard Brompton, oil on canvas, c.1775. (© National Portrait Gallery, London)

5. 'The Female Pilot. A Prime Minister' in *Town and Country Magazine*, March 1769, pp. 113–14. (© The British Library Board. Shelfmark PP 5442.b)

6. 'Miss Roberts sitting naked in Ld Grosvenor's lap at the Hotel in Leicester Fields', Volume 4, *Trials for Adultery: or, The History of Divorces*, printed for S. Bladon, London, 1779–80. (© The British Library Board. Shelfmark 518.c.8–14)

7. *Henrietta Grosvenor (née Vernon), Countess Grosvenor*, mezzotint published by Carrington Bowles, February 1774. (© National Portrait Gallery, London)

8. 'Derby & Joan or the platonic lovers, a farce' (Elizabeth, Countess of Derby; Edward Smith Stanley, 12th Earl of Derby), hand-coloured etching by Robert Dighton, 1795. (© National Portrait Gallery, London)

9. *George Spencer-Churchill, 5th Duke of Marlborough when Marquis of Blandford* by William Whiston Barney; after Richard Cosway, mezzotint, 1803–1808. (© National Portrait Gallery, London)

10. *John Parker and his sister Theresa* by Sir Joshua Reynolds, oil on canvas, 1779. (© National Trust Images/Rob Matheson)

11. The west front of Saltram House, Devon. (© National Trust Images/Rupert Truman)

12. *Portrait of the Hon. Isabella Ingram, later Marchioness of Hertford*, oil on canvas by John Hoppner. (© Leeds Museums and Art Galleries (Temple Newsam House) UK/Bridgeman Images)

13. *Edward Law, 1st Earl of Ellenborough* by Frederick Richard Say, oil on canvas, c.1845. (© National Portrait Gallery, London)

14. *Jane Elizabeth, Countess of Ellenborough*, engraving, c.1828. (© National Portrait Gallery, London)

15. 'Innocent Employment for Foreign Princes', by William Heath, *The Looking Glass* Vol. 1, No. 4, April 1830. (© The Trustees of the British Museum)

Notes

Introduction

1. *Trials for Adultery*, Vol. 1, pp. 5–28.
2. Calculating equivalent present-day values is highly complex, so for simplicity I have used the traditional method of estimation by multiplying Georgian figures by sixty.
3. Cruickshanks, Handley and Hayton (eds), *The History of Parliament, The House of Commons 1690–1715*, Vol 4, p. 715.
4. Delany, M., *Autobiography and Correspondence of Mary Granville, Mrs Delany*, Llanover, Lady (ed.), Vol. 1.

Part One

Chapter 1

1. Graham, W., *On Adultery. A Sermon Preached at Rye, Sussex by Rev Lord Preston*, pp. 7–8.
2. Lamont, D., *Sermons on the Most Prevalent Vices*, p. 55, 59.
3. *Parliamentary History*, 35, 1800, pp. 311, 321–22.
4. Blackstone, Sir W., *Commentaries on the Laws of England*, Vol. 3, pp. 139–40 and Vol. 4, pp. 64–65.
5. Stone, L., *Road to Divorce*, pp. 192–93 and pp. 296–98.
6. Franklin, B., *Reflections on Courtship and Marriage*, p. 57.
7. Locke, J., *Two Treatises of Government*, pp. 262–65.
8. *London Magazine*, September 1772.
9. Friend to Social Order, *Thoughts on Marriage, and Criminal Conversation*, p. vi.
10. *Ladies' Monthly Museum*, 1 July 1821.
11. For information on marriage see Stone, L., *The Family, Sex and Marriage in England, 1500–1800* and Lewis, J.S., *In the Family Way. Childbearing in the British Aristocracy, 1760–1860*. Many historians now dispute Lawrence Stone's theory that a decisive shift from unfeeling arranged marriages to romantic love-matches took place in the eighteenth century.
12. Anon. *A Dictionary of Love. Or the Language of Gallantry Explained*, p. 88.

13. Frost, T., *The Wicked Lord Lyttelton*, p. 83.
14. *Autobiography and Correspondence of Mary Granville, Mrs Delany* (ed. Lady Llanover), 25 December 1729, p. 233.
15. Armstrong, J., *The Forced Marriage, a Tragedy*, p. 8.
16. Franklin, B., *Reflections on Courtship and Marriage: in Two Letters to a Friend …*, pp. 14–15.
17. Fenton, R., 'To a Lady. On her Sentiments of Marriage', in *Poems, by Mr Fenton*, p. 102.
18. Warwickshire County Record Office, Feilding of Newnham Paddox, Letterbooks of 6th Earl of Denbigh, CR2017/244/463, Fld Marshal Sir George Howard to Earl, 30 March 1796.
19. WCRO, Feilding, Letterbooks, CR2017/244/478, Marchioness of Bute to Earl, 28 May 1796.
20. Warwickshire County Record Office, Heber-Percy of Guys Cliffe, CR1707/3, Marriage settlement of Samuel Greatheed, February 1747.
21. Select Committee on Finance 1797, in *Reports from Committees of the House of Commons*, Vol. 13, p. 178.
22. Frost, *The Wicked Lord Lyttelton*, pp. 25–35.
23. Hagley Hall, Lyttelton Correspondence, Vol. 6, Thomas Lyttelton to Sir Richard Lyttelton, undated Toulon 1764.
24. Lyttelton Correspondence, Vol. 6, T. Lyttelton to Sir R. Lyttelton, 19 November 1763.
25. Lyttelton Correspondence, Vol. 6, George Lyttelton to William Lyttelton, 1 January 1765.
26. Lyttelton, T., *Letters of the late Lord Lyttelton*, pp. 74–75.
27. McCahill, M., 'The Bedchamber Lord: Basil, Sixth Earl of Denbigh', in R.W. Davis (ed.), *Lords of Parliament. Studies, 1714–1914*, p. 45.
28. WCRO, Feilding, CR2017/F39, Marriage settlement of 6th Earl, 1757.
29. WCRO, Feilding, Letterbooks, CR2017/C243/66, Earl to Mrs Jane Hart, 3 October 1767.
30. WCRO, Feilding, Unbound correspondence, CR2017/C269/5, Countess of Denbigh to Earl, undated.
31. WCRO, Feilding, CR2017/F41/1–2, Marriage settlement of 6th Earl, 1783.
32. WCRO, Feilding, Letterbooks, CR2017/C244/305, Earl to Viscount Wentworth, 27 July 1783.
33. WCRO, Feilding, Letterbooks, CR2017/C244/334, Earl to Lord Viscount Mount Stuart, 3 December 1785.
34. Gregory, J., *A Father's Legacy to his Daughters*, pp. 91–92.
35. Anon. *Letters from a Peeress of England to her Eldest Son*, p. 141.
36. Anon. *Letters on Love, Marriage, and Adultery*, p. 85.
37. Lovemore, A., *A Letter from a Father to a Son on his Marriage*, pp. 55–56.
38. *London Magazine*, April 1770.
39. *London Magazine*, April 1770.
40. Cobbett, W., *Advice to Young Men … in the Middle and Higher Ranks of Life*, pp. 108–10.
41. *La Belle Assemblee; or, Bell's Court and Fashionable Magazine*, 1 August 1815, *Ladies' Monthly Museum*, 1 October 1828.
42. Gregory, *A Father's Legacy to his Daughters*, pp. 131–32, 145–46.
43. Pennington, Lady S., *An Unfortunate Mother's Advice to her Absent Daughters*, pp. 62–69.
44. Lovemore, A., *A Letter from a Father to a Son on his Marriage*, p. 30.
45. Carey, H., *Cupid and Hymen; a Voyage to the Isles of Love and Matrimony*, pp. 78–79.
46. *Love Letters, which Passed Between his R.H. the D. of C-d, and Mrs Horton. Spectacles for Young Ladies; Exhibiting the Various Arts Made Use of for Seducing Young Women.* Mrs West, *A Tale of the Times.* Ned Ward, *The Comforts of Matrimony; or, Love's Last Shift*, pp. 169–72.

47. Young Lady, A, *The Sylph*, p. 1.
48. *The Whole of the Trial of the Hon. Richard Bingham, for Adultery*, pp. 29–30.
49. Lovemore, A., *A Letter from a Father to a Son on his Marriage*, p. 66.
50. Carey, H., *Cupid and Hymen; a Voyage to the Isles of Love and Matrimony* pp. 109–10.
51. Lovemore, A., *A Letter from a Father to a Son on his Marriage*, pp. 41–46.
52. *The Mercenary Marriage; or, the History of Miss Shenstone*, Vol. 1, p. 4 and Vol. 2, pp. 30–33.
53. Anon. *Letters from a Peeress*, pp. 2, 128–29, 142, 135.

Chapter 2

54. Porter, R., *English Society in the Eighteenth Century*, p. 57.
55. Thompson, *English Landed Society*, p. 63.
56. Details in this chapter on the aristocracy can be found in Thompson, F.M.L., *English Landed Society in the Nineteenth Century*; Cannon, J., *Aristocratic Century*; Habakkuk, J., *Marriage, Debt, and the Estates System, English Landownership 1650–1950*; Langford, P., *Public Life and the Propertied Englishman 1689–1798*; Mingay, G.E., *English Landed Society in the Eighteenth Century*; and Beckett, J.V., *The Aristocracy in England 1660–1914*.
57. Beckett, *The Aristocracy in England*, p. 22.
58. Mandeville, B., *The Fable of the Bees*, Vol. 1, 1723, p. 45.
59. Boswell, J., *Dr Johnson's Table-talk*, pp. 144–46.
60. Mingay, G.E., *English Landed Society in the Eighteenth Century*, p. 13.
61. Stone, L., *An Open Elite? England 1540–1880*, pp. 283, 23–24.
62. Cannadine, D., *Aspects of Aristocracy. Grandeur and Decline in Modern Britain*, pp. 9–31.
63. Knox, T., *Grimsthorpe Castle*.
64. Burke, B., *Genealogical and Heraldic History of the Peerage and Baronetage of the United Kingdom*.
65. Spring, D., *European Landed Elites in the Nineteenth Century*, pp. 2–6.
66. Suffolk Record Office (Bury St Edmunds), FitzRoy Papers, HA513/4/51–80, 1764–5.
67. Wilson, R. and Mackley, A., *Creating Paradise. The Building of the English Country House 1660–1880*.
68. Tyack, G., *Warwickshire Country Houses*, pp. 148–9 and 57–62.
69. Girouard, M., *Life in the English Country House*, p. 3.
70. Namier, L., *England in the Age of the American Revolution*, p. 16.

Chapter 3

71. Paley, R., and Seaward, P., *Honour, Interest and Power*, p. xix.
72. *Trials for Adultery: or, the History of Divorces*, Vol. 1.
73. Aspinall, A., *Three Early Nineteenth Century Diaries*, pp. 81–83, 20 April 1831.
74. Suffolk Record Office (Bury St Edmunds), FitzRoy Papers, SRO(B)/HA513/4/122, Diary Duchess of Grafton, 26 February 1789.
75. SRO(B), FitzRoy Papers, HA513/4/122, Diary Duchess of Grafton, January to December 1789.
76. Aspinall, A., *Three Diaries*, 22 August 1831.
77. Langford, P., *Public Life and the Propertied Englishman 1689–1798*, pp. 561–79.
78. Beckett, J.V., *The Aristocracy in England 1660–1914*, p. 374.
79. Brewer, J., *The Pleasures of the Imagination. English Culture in the Eighteenth Century*, p. xv.
80. SRO(B), FitzRoy Papers, HA513/4/122, Diary Duchess of Grafton, March 1789.
81. Young Lady, A, *The Sylph*, pp. 75–76.

Chapter 4

82. Details of the adultery in *Trials for Adultery*, Vol. 1. For the full story see Hicks, C.,

Improper Pursuits. The Scandalous Life of Lady Di Beauclerk.

83. Jesse, J.H., *George Selwyn and his Contemporaries*, Vol. 2, p. 78, Bolingbroke to Selwyn, undated 1766.

84. *Selwyn*, Vol. 2, pp. 79–80, Henry St John to Selwyn, 21 November 1766.

85. Fyvie, J., *Wits, Beaux and Beauties of the Georgian Era*, pp. 162–65.

86. Cited Hicks, *Improper Pursuits*, pp. 184 and 188.

87. *The Picture Gallery* cited in Hicks, *Improper Pursuits*, pp. 261–62.

Part Two

Chapter 5

1. Boswell, J., *Dr Johnson's Table-talk*, p. 144.

2. Graham, W., *On Adultery. A Sermon Preached at Rye, Sussex by Rev Lord Preston*, p. 7.

3. Stone, L., *Road to Divorce*, pp. 337 and 325.

4. *The Whole of the Trial of the Hon. Richard Bingham, for Adultery with Lady Elizabeth Howard*, p. 45.

5. Rogers, S., *The Elegant Family Bible*, p. 179.

6. *The Protestant's Family Bible*, p. 39.

7. *An Illustration of the New Testament*, pp. 44 and 114.

8. Warwickshire County Record Office, Feilding of Newnham Paddox, CR2017/C269/3, Countess of Denbigh to son, 17 June 1777.

9. Walker, W., *Comments on the Ten Commandments*, p. 33. David Lamont, *Sermons on the Most Prevalent Vices*, p. 55.

10. Fallowfield, J., *Miscellaneous Essays*, pp. 213–14.

11. Graham, *On Adultery. A Sermon Preached at Rye, Sussex by Rev Lord Preston*, pp. 1–6.

12. Legal aspects summarised in Stone, L., *Road to Divorce*, pp. 335–44.

13. *Parliamentary History*, Vol. 17, p. 186.

Chapter 6

14. Family history in Bernard Falk, *The Royal Fitz Roys. Dukes of Grafton Through Four Centuries*.

15. *The Letters of Junius*, p. 79.

16. Barlow, F., *The Complete English Peerage*, p. 86.

17. *Parliamentary History*, Vol. 16, p. 638.

18. *A Vindication of the D- of G-; in Answer to a Letter Signed Junius*.

19. *Junius*, pp. 8, 81–82.

20. *Junius*, pp. 85–86.

21. *Trials for Adultery*, Vol. 3, p. 120.

22. Suffolk Record Office (Bury St Edmunds), FitzRoyPapers, SRO(B)/HA513/4/72, Duchess to Duke, 20 December 1764.

23. *Horace Walpole's Correspondence*, Vol. 21, 14 May 1761 and 16 June 1768.

24. SRO(B), FitzRoy, HA513/4/70, Duke to Duchess, 15 December 1764.

25. SRO(B), FitzRoy, 15 December 1764.

26. SRO(B), FitzRoy, HA513/4/71, Duchess to Duke, 18 December 1764.

27. SRO(B), FitzRoy, HA513/4/67, Duchess to Duke, 7 December 1764.

28. SRO(B), FitzRoy, HA513/4/81, Duke to Lord Ravensworth, 1 July 1768.

29. WCRO, Feilding, CR2017/C243/196, Grafton to Denbigh, 10 March 1769.

30. British Library, Whiteford Papers, Add.36596, ff.205–6, 1769.

31. *Trials for Adultery*, Vol. 3.
32. Almon, *Biographical*, p. 26.
33. SRO(B), FitzRoy, HA513/4/118, Duke to Lord Euston, 24 February 1804.
34. Falk, *FitzRoys*, pp. 214–15.
35. Anon. *Hints, &c. Submitted to the Serious Attention of the Clergy, Nobility and Gentry*, p. 7.
36. Horsley, S., *An Apology for the Liturgy and Clergy of the Church of England: in Answer to a Pamphlet, Entitled Hints, &c ...*, p. 2.
37. Miles, W., *A Letter to the Duke of Grafton*, pp. 2A and 11.
38. William Anson (ed.), *Autobiography and Political Correspondence*, p. 155.
39. SRO(B), FitzRoy, HA513/423/735, Dr John Symonds to Duke, 12 August 1804.

Chapter 7
40. Annesley, G., *Trial for Adultery*, pp. 131–32.
41. Combe, W., *A Letter to her Grace the Duchess of Devonshire*, p. 12.
42. More, H., *Thoughts on the Importance of the Manners of the Great*, p. 2.
43. Hilton, B., *Mad, Bad, and Dangerous People?* pp. 33–37.
44. *Letters on Love, Marriage, and Adultery*, p. 85. Philip Stanhope Dormer, *Letters of the Earl of Chesterfield*, Vol. 2, p. 78, 12 October 1748.
45. Shakespeare, W., *As You Like It*, Act 2.
46. Murphy, A., *The Life of David Garrick*, p. 201.
47. Russell, G., 'Theatre', in McCalman, I. (ed.), *An Oxford Companion to the Romantic Age*, p. 223.
48. Smith, A., *The Theory of Moral Sentiments*, pp. 90–91.
49. Williams, C., *Pope, Homer, and Manliness. Some Aspects of Eighteenth Century Classical Learning*, pp. 41–42.
50. *Lord Chesterfield's Letters*, Roberts, D. (ed), pp. 64–67.
51. Hill, J., *Observations on the Greek and Roman Classics. In a Series of Letters to a Young Nobleman*, p. iii.
52. Hill, J., *Observations*, pp. 10 and 3.
53. Sharpe, G., *The Origin and Structure of the Greek Tongue. In a Series of Letters Addressed to a Young Nobleman*, pp. 1–6.
54. *Elegant Extracts*, pp. 163–4, 206.
55. Halliwell, S., *Aristotle's Poetics*, p. 137.
56. Russell, D., *Ancient Literary Criticism: the Principal Texts in New Translations*, p. 290.
57. Goad, C., *Horace*, p. 14.
58. Lyte, H.C.M., *A History of Eton College, 1440–1898*, pp. 316–28.
59. Hodgson, T., *An Essay on the Origin and Progress of Stereotype Printing*, pp. 117–18. *Repertory of Arts, Manufactures and Agriculture*, p. 79.
60. *Oxford English Dictionary*.
61. *Parliamentary History*, Vol. 34, p. 1559.
62. Barlow, F., *The Complete English Peerage*, p. i.
63. Delamayne, T., *The Patricians: or, a Candid Examination into the Merits of the Principal Speakers of the House of Lords*, pp. 16 and 17.
64. *Monthly Review*, 51, 1774, p. 451.
65. *Lord Chesterfield's Letters*, ed. Roberts, D., p. x.
66. *The Works of Vicesimus Knox*, Vol. 5, pp. 116–17.
67. Hunter, T., *Reflections*, pp. 159, 228–29 and 241.
68. *Monthly Review*, 51, 1774, p. 442.
69. *Gentleman's Magazine*, November 1774, p. 565.
70. Blunt, R., *Thomas Lord Lyttelton, The Portrait of a Rake*, p. 82.

Chapter 8

71. Davis, R.M., *The Good Lord Lyttelton* and Wyndham, M., *Chronicles of the Eighteenth Century*, Vol. 2, pp. 266–82.
72. Wyndham, M., *Chronicles of the Eighteenth Century. Founded on the Correspondence of Sir Thomas Lyttelton and his Family*, Vol. 1, p. 238.
73. Johnson, S., *The Lives of the English Poets*, Vol. 3, pp. 345, 350–51.
74. Lyttelton, G., *To the Memory of a Lady Lately Deceased*, p. 4.
75. Wyndham, M., *Chronicles of the Eighteenth Century. Founded on the Correspondence of Sir Thomas Lyttelton and his Family*, Vol. 1, pp. 227–28.
76. Delamayne, T., *The Patricians: or, a Candid Examination into the Merits of the Principal Speakers of the House of Lords*, p. 16.
77. Lyttelton, G., *Poems by George Lord Lyttelton*, p. viii.
78. Hagley Hall, Lyttelton Correspondence, Vol. 5/41–44, George Lyttelton to William Lyttelton, 20 July 1759.
79. Lyttelton Correspondence, 20 July 1759.
80. *Monthly Review*, 52, 1775, p. 430.
81. *Monthly Review*, pp. 431, 436.
82. *Walpole Correspondence*, Vol. 9, pp. 214–15, 7 July 1775.
83. *Walpole Correspondence*, Vol. 32, p. 243, 3 August 1775.
84. Davis, 'The Correspondents', pp. 215–16, cites letters between two of Lyttelton's cousins.
85. Penny, A., *A Pastoral Elegy on the Death of George Lord Lyttelton*.
86. Lyttelton Correspondence, Vol. 6/325, Lord Chatham to Thomas Lyttelton, 30 August 1773.

Chapter 9

87. Lyttelton Correspondence, Vol. 6/224–5, George Lyttelton to Charles Lyttelton, 11 March 1765. Details of his life from Frost, T., *The Wicked Lord Lyttelton* and Blunt, R., *Thomas Lord Lyttelton, The Portrait of a Rake*.
88. Frost, *The Wicked Lord Lyttelton*, p. 170.
89. Lyttelton Corresp, Vol. 6/190, Thomas to Richard Lyttelton, 11 May 1764.
90. Lyttelton Corresp, Vol. 6/224–5, G. Lyttelton to C. Lyttelton, 11 March 1765.
91. Blunt, R., *Thomas Lord Lyttelton, The Portrait of a Rake*, p. 237. The manuscript letter is now missing.
92. Frost, T., *The Wicked Lord Lyttelton*, pp. 81–86.
93. Lyttelton Correspondence, Vol. 6/305, Thomas to his father, 18 June 1772.
94. Courtenay, J., *The Rape of Pomona*, pp. 1–15.
95. Lyttelton, T., *Letters of the late Lord Lyttelton*, p. 95.
96. Lyttelton, T., *Letters of the late Lord Lyttelton*, pp. 104–7.
97. Anon. *The Diaboliad*, pp. 18–19.
98. Lyttelton, T., *Letters of the late Lord Lyttelton*, pp. 178–79.
99. Lyttelton Correspondence, 11/3.
100. Piozzi Thrale, H., *Thraliana: The Diary of Mrs Hester Lynch Thrale 1776–1809*, December 1779, p. 413.
101. *London Magazine*, Vol. 49, 1779, pp. 534–36.
102. Lyttelton, T., *Poems, by the late Thomas Lord Lyttelton*, p. 6.
103. Wraxall, N., *Historical Memoirs*, Vol. 1, pp. 313–14.

104. Frost points to evidence that Byron had read Lyttelton's poetry, noting the marked similarity of Byron's line 'Born in a garret, in a kitchen bred', Frost, *The Wicked Lord Lyttelton*, p. 236.

105. Byron, G.G., *The Works of Lord Byron*, Moore, T. (ed.), Byron to Robert Dallas, 20 January 1808, pp. 191–92.

106. T. Moore (ed.), *Works of Byron*, Byron to Dallas, 21 January 1808, pp. 193–95.

Part Three

Chapter 10

1. *London Magazine*, Vol. 49, 1779.

2. Stone, L., *Road to Divorce*, pp. 183–210. His calculation should be treated as a rough guide as it was based on the average length of time peers held a title, and estimated the number of title-holders 1770–1830 as 'about 2,050'.

3. W. Blackstone, *Commentaries on the Laws of England* Vol. 3, pp. 139–40.

4. Stone, L., *Road to Divorce*, pp. 295–97.

5. *Trials for Adultery*, Vol. 1, p. iv.

6. Barker and Chalus, *Gender*, pp. 19–28.

7. Piozzi Thrale, H., *Thraliana: The Diary of Mrs Hester Lynch Thrale 1776–1809*, Vol. 1, 17 April 1779.

Chapter 11

8. *Trials for Adultery*, Vol. 1, pp. iii–iv.

9. *The Cuckold's Chronicle*, p. iv.

10. *The Genuine Copies of Letters which Passed Between His Royal Highness the Duke of Cumberland and Lady Grosvenor*.

11. *London Magazine*, Vol. 47, 1777. Tillyard, *Royal Affair*, pp. 178–83.

12. *Trials for Adultery*, Vol. 4, p. 6.

13. *Parliamentary History*, Vol. 35, 23 May 1800, pp. 282–83.

14. *The Whole Proceedings … an Action Brought by The Rt Hon Richard Lord Grosvenor Against His Royal Highness Henry Frederick Duke of Cumberland for Criminal Conversation with Lady Grosvenor*, pp. 11–12.

15. *Trials for Adultery*, Vol. 4, p. 183.

16. Anon. *Harriet: or, the Innocent Adultress*, p. 3.

Chapter 12

17. *Letters from a Peeress of England to her Eldest Son*, pp. 68–69.

18. Pratt, S., *The Pupil of Pleasure*, p. 9.

19. Frost, T., *The Wicked Lord Lyttelton*, p. 207.

20. Blunt, R., *Thomas Lord Lyttelton, The Portrait of a Rake*, p. 226.

21. Hagley Hall, Lyttelton Correspondence, Vol. 6/311–12. Chatham to George Lyttelton, 22 July 1772.

22. Stone, L., *Road to Divorce*, p. 258.

Chapter 13

23. *The Parliamentary History of England*, Vol. 20, pp. 593–99.

24. Stone, L., *Road to Divorce*, pp. 335–44.

25. *London Magazine*, 15 April 1779.

26. Delamayne, T., *The Patricians: or, a Candid Examination into the Merits of the Principal Speakers of the House of Lords*, p. 4.
27. *Trials for Adultery*, Vol. 2.

Chapter 14

28. Almon, J., *Biographical, Literary, and Political Anecdotes*, p. 2.
29. *The Prostitutes of Quality; or Adultery à-la-Mode*, p. iii.
30. For an overview of the press, see Barker, H., *Newspapers, Politics and English Society*.
31. Harris, M., *London Newspapers in the Age of Walpole*, pp. 190–94.
32. Barker, *Newspapers, Politics and English Society*, p.17.
33. Porter, R., *English Society in the Eighteenth Century* p. 234.
34. *Public Advertiser*, 7 April 1769.
35. WCRO, Feilding of Newnham Paddox, CR2017/C243/311, Rev T Fountaine to Denbigh, 31 October 1771.
36. Lyttelton, T., *Letters of the late Lord Lyttelton*, pp. 155–57.
37. Lennard, J.D., *Factual Fictions*, pp. 92–100.
38. Brewer, J., *Sentimental Murder*, p. 160.
39. *London Magazine*, Vol. 49, 1779. *Gentleman's Magazine* quote in Armstrong, J., *Miscellanies*, p. 179.
40. Armstrong, J., *Miscellanies*, pp. 237 and 170.
41. *Evangelical Magazine*, 1793, Vol.1.
42. St Clair, W., *The Reading Nation in the Romantic Period*, p. 1.
43. See Lloyd, S., 'Amour in the Shrubbery' in *Eighteenth-Century Studies*.

Part Four

Chapter 15

1. Philaretes, P., *Adultery Analysed*, pp. 20–27.
2. *Society for Giving Effect to His Majesty's Proclamation against Vice and Immorality*, p. 21.
3. See Innes, J., 'Politics and Morals. The Reformation of Manners Movement in Later Eighteenth-Century England', in Hellmuth, E. (ed.), *The Transformation of Political Culture*, pp. 72–86.
4. For an overview see Bristow, E., *Vice and Vigilance. Purity Movements in Britain Since 1700*.
5. See Bristow, *Vice*, pp. 32–55 and Roberts, M.J.D., 'The Society for the Suppression of Vice and its Early Critics, 1802–1812', *The Historical Journal*.
6. *Brief Statement of the Origin and Nature of the Society*, pp. 16–23.
7. Glasse, S., *A Narrative of Proceedings, Tending Towards a National Reformation*, p. 46.
8. Innes, 'Politics and Morals', pp. 79–86. See also Roberts, *Making English Morals*, pp. 17–58.
9. Langford, P., *Public Life and the Propertied Englishman 1689–1798*, p. 579.
10. Wilberforce, W., *A Practical View*, pp. 388, 416, 418.
11. More, H., *Strictures on the Modern System of Female Education*, p. 4.
12. More, H., *Thoughts on the Importance of the Manners of the Great*, p. 114. *An Estimate of the Religion of the Fashionable World*, p. 205.
13. *Adultery Analysed*, pp. 99–100.
14. *The Evils of Adultery and Prostitution*, pp. 50–51.
15. Anonymous, *Adultery Analysed*, p. 21.

16. See Harvey, K., 'The Century of Sex? Gender, Bodies, and Sexuality in the Long Eighteenth Century', *Historical Journal*, 45, 4 (2002), pp. 899–916 and Hitchcock, T., *English Sexualities*.
17. *Adultery Analysed*, p. 116.
18. WCRO, Feilding of Newnham Paddox, CR2017/244/396, Earl to Archbishop of York, 15 November 1790.
19. *Adultery Analysed*, pp. 45–6, 195–6.
20. Chatsworth House, Chatsworth MSS, CS5/448. Correspondence of 5th Duke, Georgiana Duchess of Devonshire to Countess Spencer, 24–25 October 1782.
21. See Goodrich, A., *Debating England's Aristocracy in the 1790s*.
22. Plymouth & West Devon RO, Parker of Saltram, Correspondence of Hon. Catherine Robinson, 1259/2/154, Theresa Parker to Mrs Robinson, 10 November 1792.
23. PWDRO, Parker of Saltram, Corresp. C. Robinson, 1259/2/155, Theresa Parker to Mrs Robinson, 8 December 1792.
24. WCRO, Feilding of Newnham Paddox, CR2017/244/480, Marchioness of Bute to Earl, 21 June 1796.
25. PWDRO, Parker of Saltram, Corresp. C. Robinson, 1259/2/591, Theresa Villiers to Mrs Robinson, 29 July 1801.
26. PWDRO, Parker of Saltram, Corresp. C. Robinson, 1259/2/677, Theresa Villiers to Mrs Robinson, 8 August 1803.
27. Friend to Social Order, *Thoughts on Marriage, and Criminal Conversation*, p. 39.
28. Wollstonecraft, M., *A Vindication of the Rights of Men*, pp. 22–23.
29. Friend to Social Order, *Thoughts on Marriage, and Criminal Conversation*, pp. 45–46.
30. Stone, L., *Road to Divorce*, p. 261.
31. *Report of the Cause between Charles Sturt, Plaintiff, and the Marquis of Blandford*, p. 90.
32. *Adultery Trial of Lady Valentia*, pp. 126–27.
33. Piozzi Thrale, H., *Thraliana: The Diary of Mrs Hester Lynch Thrale 1776–1809*, Vol. 2, p. 906, 2 January 1795.
34. Leycester, G., *Some Observations on the Inconvenience of the Ten Commandments*, p. 49.
35. *The Whole of the Trial of the Hon. Richard Bingham*, p. 6.

Chapter 16

36. *Bon Ton*, March 1793, p. 18.
37. *Bon Ton*, March 1795, p. 31.
38. *Bon Ton*, January 1792, August 1791, June 1791, January 1796.
39. *Bon Ton*, October 1795, p. 322 and August 1791, p. 203.
40. Lady Craven (eds Broadley, A.M. and Melville, L.) *The Beautiful Lady Craven: the Original Memoirs*.
41. PWDRO, Parker of Saltram, Corresp. Frederick Robinson, 1259/1/115, Morley to Mr Robinson, 1 December 1789.
42. PWDRO, Parker of Saltram, Corresp. F. Robinson, 1259/1/114, Morley to Mr Robinson, 25 November 1789.
43. Cox, M., *Derby. The Life & Times of the 12th Earl of Derby*.
44. *The Testimony of Truth to Exalted Merit*. For life see *The Secret History of the Green Rooms*, Vol. 1.
45. Petronius Arbiter, *Memoirs of the Present Countess of Derby, late Miss Farren*, p. 21.

Chapter 17

46. Hartcup, A., *Love and Marriage*, pp. 48–49.
47. *A Biographical Dictionary of Actors, Actresses*, and Katie Hickman, *Courtesans*, pp. 29–81.

48. Steele, E., *The Memoirs of Mrs Sophia Baddeley*, Vol. 3, pp. 3–4.
49. Steele, E., *Memoirs*, Vol. 1, pp. 120–21.
50. Bicknell, Alexander, *An Apology for the Life of George Anne Bellamy*, Vol. 3, p. 118.
51. *General Evening Post*, 31 March 1785. *Morning Chronicle*, 16 June 1785.
52. Reviews in *Apology for the Life*, Vol. 6.
53. *London Magazine*, July 1782, October 1780, December 1781, October 1782.
54. *London Magazine*, June 1782, p. 259.
55. *Lady's Monthly Museum*, 1 August 1804 and 1 March 1806.
56. The affair is detailed in Levy, M.J., *The Mistresses of King George IV*.
57. Gatrell, V., *City of Laughter*, pp. 325–8, 69–70.
58. WCRO, Feilding, CR2017/C244, Lady Bute to Denbigh, 31 January 1794.

Chapter 18

59. Stone, L., *Road to Divorce*, pp. 335–39, and Andrew, D.T., '"Adultery a-la-Mode": Privilege, the Law and Attitudes to Adultery 1770–1809', pp. 17–21.
60. *Anti-Jacobin Review*, June 1800.
61. *Parliamentary History*, Vol. 34, pp. 1556–57.
62. *Senator; or, Clarendon's Parliamentary Chronicle*, p. 1388.
63. WCRO, Feilding of Newnham Paddox, Letterbooks of 6th Earl of Denbigh, CR2017/244/597, Viscount Wentworth to Earl, 14 June 1800.
64. *Report of the Cause between Charles Sturt, Plaintiff, and the Marquis of Blandford, Defendant, for Criminal Conversation*, pp. 58–59. For Blandford's life see Soames, M., *The Profligate Duke*.
65. *Parliamentary Chronicle*, p. 1389.
66. Gisborne, T., *An Enquiry into the Duties of Men*.

Chapter 19

67. For a fuller account of his life see Norgate, G. Le G., Matthew, H., 'Parker, John, first Earl of Morley (1772–1840)', *Oxford Dictionary of National Biography*. Also Lummis, T. and Marsh, J., *The Woman's Domain*.
68. Anon. *The Evils of Adultery and Prostitution*, p. 71.
69. PWDRO, Parker of Saltram, Correspondence of C. Robinson, 1259/2/202, Theresa to Mrs Robinson, 22 December 1793.
70. 1259/2/147, Theresa to Mrs Robinson, 3 October 1792.
71. 1259/2/148, Morley to Mrs Robinson, 16 October 1792
72. 1259/2/150, Theresa to Mrs Robinson, 28 October 1792.
73. 1259/2/143, Theresa to Mrs Robinson, 19 August 1792.
74. 1259/2/177, Morley to Mrs Robinson, 23 March 1793.
75. 1259/2/179, Morley to Mrs Robinson, 12 July 1793.
76. 1259/2/239, Theresa to Mrs Robinson, 4 January 1795.
77. 1259/2/700, Theresa to Mrs Robinson, 9 July 1804.
78. 1259/2/200, Morley to Mrs Robinson, 23 November1793.
79. 1259/2/205, Morley to Mrs Robinson, 4 January 1794.
80. 1259/2/430, Theresa to Mrs Robinson, 15 January 1799.
81. 1259/2/493, Theresa to Mrs Robinson, 1 January 1800.
82. 1259/2/396, Theresa to Mrs Robinson, 22 August 1798.
83. 1259/2/661, Theresa to Mrs Robinson, 28 October 1802.
84. 1259/2/700, Theresa to Mrs Robinson, 9 July 1804.
85. 1259/2/714, Theresa to Mrs Robinson, 5 November 1804.
86. *The Jerningham Letters*, Vol. 1, p. 308.

87. *Report of the Proceedings under a Writ of Enquiry of Damages, in an Action in the Court of King's Bench … Lord Boringdon was Plaintiff, and the Rt Hon Sir Arthur Paget, K.B. Defendant*, p. 76.

Part Five

Chapter 20

1. *The People or the Peerage?*, p. 10.
2. 'Hints to the Aristocracy. A Retrospect of Forty Years', pp. 68–80.
3. *Rambler's Magazine*, January 1822.
4. *Satirist*, 3 March 1839.
5. Blanchard, J., *The Trial of Lord Charles Bentinck*, p. 31.
6. Gatrell, V., *City of Laughter*, pp. 19–20, 424–25. See also Wilson, Ben, *Decency and Disorder*, pp. 442–45.
7. *Morning Chronicle*, 1 October 1827.
8. *Parliamentary Debates*, House of Lords, 3 October 1831.
9. *Moral Reformer*, 1 November 1832.
10. *Satirist*, 9 October 1831. *The Age*, 27 May 1832.
11. Wade, J., *The Black Book*, pp. 389–90.

Chapter 21

12. *Blackwood's Edinburgh Magazine*, January 1834, p. 75.
13. *The Age*, 21 March 1830.
14. *New Bon Ton*, October 1818.
15. *New Bon Ton*, May, December and June 1818.
16. *New Bon Ton*, December 1818, May 1818, January 1819.
17. *New Bon Ton*, July 1818.
18. Gatrell, V., *City of Laughter*, pp. 508–15. For the full story see Levy, M.J., *The Mistresses of King George IV*.
19. Clark, A., *Scandal: The Sexual Politics of the British Constitution*, pp. 177–207.
20. Sinecure, S., *Fair Play; or, Who are the Adulterers, Slanderers and Demoralizers?*, p. 30.
21. MacRainbow, J., *A Volley at the Peers*, pp. 7, 11.

Chapter 22

22. 'Hints to the Aristocracy' *Blackwood's Edinburgh Magazine*.
23. Paley, R., and Seaward, P., *Honour, Interest & Power*, pp. xvii–xix.
24. Smith, E.A., 'Charles, Second Earl Grey and the House of Lords', in Davis, R.W. (ed.), *Lords of Parliament*.
25. Goodrich, A., *Debating England's Aristocracy*. For more on Reform see Hilton, *Mad Bad*, pp. 421–36 and Beckett, *Aristocracy*, pp. 451–56. Also Pearce, E., *Reform!*
26. WCRO, Seymour of Ragley, CR114A/388, Sir George Francis Seymour, *On the Character of Public Men*.
27. Smith, E.A., *The House of Lords*, pp. 131–36.
28. WCRO, Seymour of Ragley, CR114A/374/9, Diary 11 February 1832.
29. *Parliamentary Debates*, House of Lords, Vol. 7, 5 October 1831.
30. *Parliamentary Debates*, HL, 7 October 1831.
31. Hall, C., 'The Rule of Difference: Gender, Class and Empire in the Making of the 1832 Reform Act', p.110.
32. *Bell's Life*, 15 April 1832.

33. WCRO, Seymour of Ragley, CR114A/644, Diary Francis H. Seymour, 1 January 1835.
34. *Rambler's Magazine*, January 1822.

Chapter 23
35. Burke, J., *A General and Heraldic Dictionary of the Peerage*, p. xiii.
36. *Rambler's Magazine*, January 1822.
37. For a detailed overview see Adburgham, A., *Silver Fork Society*.
38. Kelly, G., *English Fiction of the Romantic Period 1789–1830*, p. 227.
39. *John Bull*, 15 February 1830.
40. *The Age*, 28 February 1830.
41. *Belle Assemblee*, 1 January 1821.
42. Adburgham, A., *Silver Fork Society*, pp. 172–74.
43. Kelly, G., *English Fiction of the Romantic Period 1789–1830* , p. 223.
44. Adburgham, *Silver Fork*, pp. 124–25, 290–91.
45. Gore, C., *The Manners of the Day*.
46. *Belle Assemblee*, September 1830 and September 1829.
47. *Belle Assemblee*, February 1830.
48. *Edinburgh Literary Journal*, December 1829.

Chapter 24
49. For divorce law reform see Stone, L., *Road to Divorce*, pp. 368–82.
50. *Parliamentary Debates,* HC, 3 June 1830, Vol. 24, pp. 1260–93.
51. *Satirist*, 18 March 1832.
52. *Bell's Life*, 3 February 1828 and *The Age*, 21 June 1829.
53. *The Age*, 22 May 1831.
54. *Bell's Life*, 15 April 1832.
55. Imlah, A., *Lord Ellenborough; a Biography of Edward Law, Earl of Ellenborough*, p. 32.
56. Imlah, A., *Lord Ellenborough; a Biography of Edward Law, Earl of Ellenborough*, p. 25.
57. National Archives, Ellenborough Papers, PRO 30/12/7/1, Edward Law to Octavia, 24 October 1818.
58. NA, Ellenborough Papers, PRO 30/12/7/2, Edward Law to Octavia, 10 December 1818.
59. NA, Ellenborough Papers, PRO 30/12/2/2/85–88, Edward Law to Octavia, 18 December 1818.
60. See Lovell, M.S., *A Scandalous Life. The Biography of Jane Digby*.
61. Lovell, M.S., *Scandalous Life*, p. 30.
62. Law, E., *A Political Diary 1828–1830*, 5 September 1828, pp. 207–08.
63. Law, E., *Political Diary*, 12 September 1828, p. 218.
64. *Parliamentary Debates*, HL, 17 March 1830, Vol. 23, pp. 431–55.
65. *Parliamentary Debates*, HL, 17 March 1830.
66. *John Bull*, 5 April 1830.
67. *Parliamentary Debates*, HC, 6 April 1830, Vol. 23, pp. 1339–402.
68. *Bell's Life*, 11 April 1830.
69. *The History of The Times. 'The Thunderer' in the Making*.
70. Phrase used by E.S. Dallas, a correspondent to Blackwood's *Edinburgh Magazine* in 1859, cited Jones, A., *Powers of the Press*, pp. 3–4.
71. *The Diaries of E.H. Stanley, 15th Earl of Derby*, p. 54, cited in Steele, D., 'Law, Edward, first Earl of Ellenborough' *Oxford Dictionary of National Biography*.
72. Imlah, A., *Lord Ellenborough; a Biography of Edward Law, Earl of Ellenborough*, preface.
73. *The Times*, 2 February 1830.
74. Imlah, A., *Lord Ellenborough; a Biography of Edward Law, Earl of Ellenborough*, p. 54.

75. National Archives, Colchester Papers, PRO 30/9/30, Edward Law diary, 21 August 1831.

76. NA, Colchester Papers, PRO 30/9/30, Edward Law diary, 29 May 1831.

77. NA, Colchester Papers, PRO 30/9/30, Edward Law diary, 17 October 1831.

78. Clark, A., *Scandal: The Sexual Politics of the British Constitution*, pp. 10–12, 217–18.

79. NA, Colchester Papers, PRO 30/9/30, Edward Law diary, 15 December 1831.

80. Extracts in *Three Early Nineteenth Century Diaries*, ed. A. Aspinall.

81. Refers to the unreadable *Political Life of G. Canning*. Diary entry 29 December 1831, *Three Nineteenth Century Diaries*, p. 38.

82. *Three Nineteenth Century Diaries*, pp. 31–33, 52.

83. Imlah, A., *Lord Ellenborough; a Biography of Edward Law, Earl of Ellenborough*, preface.

84. Law, *Political Diary*, pp. vi.

BIBLIOGRAPHY

Primary Manuscript Sources

The National Archives, London
Ellenborough Papers, PRO 30/12/7/1–2. Letters between Edward Law and Lady Octavia
PRO 30/12/2/2. Correspondence and papers of Edward Law
Colchester Papers, PRO 30/9/30. Diaries of Edward Law

Chatsworth House, Derbyshire (private collection)
Chatsworth Papers, CS5/448. Correspondence of 5th Duke of Devonshire

Hagley Hall, Hagley, Worcestershire (private collection)
Lyttelton Papers, Six volumes

Plymouth & West Devon Record Office
Parker of Saltram, 1259/2/1–774. Correspondence of Catherine Robinson
1259/1/1-250. Correspondence of Frederick Robinson

Suffolk Record Office, Bury St Edmunds branch
FitzRoy Papers, SRO(B)/HA513/4/51–95. Correspondence relating to separation and
    divorce of 3rd Duke of Grafton
HA513/4/118. Grafton correspondence
HA513/4/122. 1789 Diary of Elizabeth, Duchess of Grafton
HA513/423/735. Grafton correspondence

Warwickshire County Record Office
Feilding of Newnham Paddox (reproduced with kind permission of the Earl of Denbigh)

CR2017/C243 and 244. Letterbooks of 6th Earl of Denbigh
CR2017/C269/1–5. Unbound correspondence
CR2017/F39. 1757 Marriage settlement of 6th Earl
CR2017/F41/1–2. 1783 Marriage settlement of 6th Earl
Heber-Percy of Guys Cliffe, CR1707/3. 1747 Marriage settlement of Samuel Greatheed
Seymour of Ragley, CR114A/388. Essay by Sir G. Seymour
CR114A/374/9. Diary of Sir G. Seymour 1832
CR114A/644. Diary of Francis Seymour 1835

Newspapers and Periodicals

Blackwood's Edinburgh Magazine
Bon Ton Magazine, or, Microscope of Fashion and Folly
Convivial Magazine
Crim. Con. Gazette
Edinburgh Literary Journal
Evangelical Magazine
Examiner
General Evening Post
Gentleman's Magazine
John Bull
La Belle Assemblee; or, Bell's Court and Fashionable Magazine
Ladies' Monthly Museum
London Literary Gazette
London Magazine
Monthly Review
Moral Reformer
Morning Chronicle
Morning Herald
Morning Post
New Bon Ton Magazine, or Telescope of the Times
Public Advertiser
Rambler's Magazine
Ranger's Magazine
Satirist
Senator; or, Clarendon's Parliamentary Chronicle
Standard
The Age
The Times
Town and Country Magazine

Printed Primary Sources

A Biographical Dictionary of Actors, Actresses … in London 1660–1800, Philip H. Highfill, Kalman
   A. Burnim, Edward A. Langhans (eds), (Carbondale, Southern Illinois Univ Press, 1993)
A First Letter to the Duke of Grafton (London, 1770)
A Letter to the Earl of Wilton, on the Commutation of Existing Taxes … (Liverpool, 1830)
A Modest Apology for the Prevailing Practice of Adultery (London, 1773)
Adultery Anatomized (London, 1761)

Almon, J., *Biographical, Literary, and Political Anecdotes* (London, 1797)

An Epistle from N-y P-s to His Grace the Duke of G-n (London, 1769)

An Illustration of the New Testament (fourth edn, Vol. 1, London, printed for R. Goadby, 1770)

Annesley, George, Earl of Mountnorris, *Trial for Adultery. The Whole Proceedings of the Trial of John Bellenger Gawler Esq. for Criminal Conversation with Lady Valentia* (London, 1799)

A.P., *A Pastoral Elegy on the Death of George Lord Lyttelton* (London, 1773)

Anon. *A Dictionary of Love. Or the Language of Gallantry Explained* (London, 1795)

Anon. *A Vindication of the D- of G-; in Answer to a Letter Signed Junius* (London, 1769)

Anon. *Harriet: or, the Innocent Adultress* (London, 1779)

Anon. *Hints, &c. Submitted to the Serious Attention of the Clergy, Nobility and Gentry ...* (London, printed for B. White & Son, and J. Debrett, 1789)

Anon. *The Diaboliad; a Poem* (London, 1777)

Anon. *The House of Peeresses: or, Female Oratory* (London, 1779)

Arbiter, P., *Memoirs of the Present Countess of Derby, late Miss Farren* (5th edn, London, 1797)

Armstrong, J., *The Forced Marriage, a Tragedy* (London, 1770)

Armstrong, J., *Miscellanies* (London, 1770)

Anson, William (ed.), *Autobiography and Political Correspondence of Augustus Henry, third Duke of Grafton* (London, John Murray, 1898)

Aspinall, A. (ed.), *Three Early Nineteenth Century Diaries* (London, Williams and Norgate, 1952)

Bailey, N., *An Universal Etymological English Dictionary; ...* (London, 1778)

Barlow, F., *The Complete English Peerage* (2nd edn, London, 1775)

Bellamy, George Anne, *An Apology for the Life of George Anne Bellamy. Late of Covent-Garden Theatre. Written by Herself* (London, 1785)

Blackstone, W., *Commentaries on the Laws of England* (4 vols. Dublin, 1771)

Blackwall, A., *An Introduction to the Classics: Containing a Short Discourse on their Excellencies; and Directions how to Study them to Advantage* (London, 1746)

Blanchard, J., *The Trial of Lord Charles Bentinck ... for Criminal Conversation with Lady Abdy* (London, 1815)

Boswell, J., *Dr Johnson's Table-talk: Containing Aphorisms on Literature, Life, and Manners ...* (London, printed for C. Dilly, 1798)

Burke, B. (ed.), *Genealogical and Heraldic History of the Peerage and Baronetage of the United Kingdom* (London, 1886)

Burke, J., *A General and Heraldic Dictionary of the Peerage and Baronetage of the British Empire* (2 vols, London, 1833)

Bury, C., *The Exclusives* (London, 1830)

Byron, G.G., *The Works of Lord Byron: With his Letters and Journals*, T. Moore (ed.) (London, 1835)

Carey, H., *Cupid and Hymen; a Voyage to the Isles of Love and Matrimony* (4th edn, London, 1772)

Cobbett, W., *Advice to Young Men ... in the Middle and Higher Ranks of Life* (London, 1829)

Collins, A., *The Peerage of England; Containing a Genealogical and Historical Account ...* (London, 1756)

Combe, W., *A Letter to her Grace the Duchess of Devonshire* (London, 1777)

Courtenay, J., *The Rape of Pomona. An Elegaic Epistle, from the Waiter at Hockrel, to the Honourable Mr. L-tt-n* (2nd edn, London, 1773)

Delamayne, T., *The Patricians: or, a Candid Examination into the Merits of the Principal Speakers of the House of Lords* (London, 1773)

Dormer, P.S., *Letters Written by the late Right Honourable Philip Dormer Stanhope, Earl of Chesterfield, to his Son, Philip Stanhope* (2nd edn, London, 1774)

Elegant Extracts: ... for the Improvement of Scholars ... (London, 1784)

Fallowfield, John, *Miscellaneous Essays, Divine and Moral. Designed to Discourage Vice and Promote Virtue* (3rd edn, Carlisle, 1790)

Felton, H., *A Dissertation on Reading the Classics, and Forming a Just Style* (London, 1753)

Fenton, R., 'To a Lady. On her Sentiments of Marriage' in *Poems, by Mr Fenton* (2 vols, London, 1790)

Franc-Coes, O., *Peerage, Primogeniture, and Aristocracy of England: or, A Plan to Dispose of These Subjects* … (London, 1835)

Franklin, B., *Reflections on Courtship and Marriage: in Two Letters to a Friend* … (London, 1784)

Friend to Social Order, *Thoughts on Marriage and Criminal Conversation* … (London, 1799)

Frost, T., *The Wicked Lord Lyttelton* (reprint, Stroud, Nonsuch Publishing, 2005, of original edn, London, 1876)

Gisborne, T., *An Enquiry into the Duties of Men in the Higher and Middle Classes of Society* … (London, 1794)

Glasse, S., *A Narrative of Proceedings, Tending Towards a National Reformation, Previous to, and Consequent upon, His Majesty's Royal Proclamation* … (London, 1787)

Graham, W., *On Adultery. A Sermon Preached at Rye, Sussex by Rev Lord Preston* (London, 1772)

Gregory, J., *A Father's Legacy to his Daughters* (4th edn, London, 1774)

Hill, J., *Observations on the Greek and Roman Classics. In a Series of Letters to a Young Nobleman* (London, 1753)

Hodgson, T., *An Essay on the Origin and Progress of Stereotype Printing* (Newcastle, 1820)

Horace Walpole's Correspondence, Lewis, W.S. (ed.) (Oxford, Oxford University Press, 1983)

Horsley, S., *An Apology for the Liturgy and Clergy of the Church of England: in Answer to a Pamphlet, Entitled Hints, &c* … (London, 1790)

Hunter, T., *Reflections Critical and Moral on the Letters of the late Earl of Chesterfield* (London, 1776)

Johnson, S., *The Lives of the English Poets: and a Criticism of their Works* (3 vols, Dublin, 1780–81)

Journal of the House of Lords, Vol. 32 (London, 1769)

Laclos, Choderlos de, *Les Liaisons Dangereuses*, trans. P. Stone (reprint, London, Penguin, 1986)

Lamont, Rev. D., *Sermons on the Most Prevalent Vices* (London, 1780)

Law, E., *A Political Diary 1828–1830*, ed. Lord Colchester (London, Richard Bentley & Son, 1881)

Letters from a Peeress of England to her Eldest Son (London, 1784)

Letters on Love, Marriage, and Adultery; Addressed to the Right Honourable the Earl of Exeter (London, 1789)

Lewis, W. *A Peep at the Peers* (London, 1820)

Leycester, G., *Some Observations on the Inconvenience of the Ten Commandments* (Oxford, 1795)

Locke, J., *Two Treatises of Government* (6th edn, London, 1764)

Lord Chesterfield's Letters, Roberts, D. (ed.) (Oxford, Oxford University Press, 1998)

Love Letters, Which Passed Between his R.H. the D. of C-d, and Mrs Horton (London, 1771)

Lovemore, A., *A Letter from a Father to a Son on his Marriage* (London, 1778)

Lyttelton, G., *To the Memory of a Lady Lately Deceased. A Monody* (London, 1747)

Lyttelton, G., *Poems by George Lord Lyttelton* (Ludlow, 1800)

Lyttelton, T., *Letters of the late Lord Lyttelton* (London, 1780)

Lyttelton, T., *Poems, by the late Thomas Lord Lyttelton* (London, 1780)

MacRainbow, J., *A Volley at the Peers, Both Spiritual and Temporal* (London, 1820)

Mandeville, B., *The Fable of the Bees*, Vol. 1 (1723), Hundert, E.J. (ed.) (Indianapolis and Cambridge, Hackett, 1997)

Memoirs of the Amours, Intrigues, and Adventures of Charles Augustus Fitz-Roy … (London, 1769)

Miles, W., *A Letter to the Duke of Grafton* (London, 1794)

More, H., *Thoughts on the Importance of the Manners of the Great to General Society* (London, 1788)

More, H., *An Estimate of the Religion of the Fashionable World* (2nd edn, London, 1791)

More, H., *Strictures on the Modern System of Female Education* (London, 1799)

Mrs West, *A Tale of the Times* (3 vols., London, 1799)

Murphy, A., *The Life of David Garrick* (London, 1801)

N. N., *Directions for a Proper Choice of Authors to Form a Library, Which May Both Improve and Entertain the Mind, and be of Real Use in the Conduct of Life* (London, 1766)

Parliamentary Debates, House of Commons and House of Lords (London, 1830)

Pennington, Lady S., *An Unfortunate Mother's Advice to her Absent Daughters* (7th edn, London, 1784)

Philaretes, P., *Adultery Analysed: An Inquiry into the Causes of the Prevalence of that Vice in these Kingdoms* (London, 1810)

Piozzi Thrale, H., *Thraliana: The Diary of Mrs Hester Lynch Thrale 1776–1809*, Balderston, K.C. (ed.) (2 vols, Oxford, Clarendon Press, 1951)

Pratt, S., *The Pupil of Pleasure* (London, 1776)

Report of the Proceedings under a Writ of Enquiry of Damages, in an Action in the Court of King's Bench ... Lord Boringdon was Plaintiff, and the Rt Hon Sir Arthur Paget, K.B. Defendant (London, 1808)

Rogers, S., *The Elegant Family Bible* ... (London, 1765–67)

Select Committee on Finance 1797, in Reports from Committees of the House of Commons (16 vols, London, 1803–6)

Sharpe, G., *The Origin and Structure of the Greek Tongue. In a Series of Letters Addressed to a Young Nobleman* (London, 1777)

Sinecure, S., *Fair Play; or, Who are the Adulterers, Slanderers and Demoralizers?* (London, 1820)

Smith, A., *The Theory of Moral Sentiments* ... (London, 1774)

Society for Giving Effect to His Majesty's Proclamation against Vice and Immorality (London, 1789)

Spectacles for Young Ladies; Exhibiting the Various Arts Made Use of for Seducing Young Women ... (Cork, 1767)

Steele, E., *The Memoirs of Mrs Sophia Baddeley, late of Drury-Lane Theatre* (London, 1787)

Sturt, Charles, *Report of the Cause between Charles Sturt, Plaintiff, and the Marquis of Blandford ... for Criminal Conversation* (London, 1801)

The Beautiful Lady Craven: the Original Memoirs, Broadley, A.M. and Melville, L. (eds) (London, John Lane, 1914)

The Cuckold's Chronicle; being Select Trials for Adultery (London, 1793)

The Evils of Adultery and Prostitution; with an Inquiry into the Causes of their Alarming Increase, and Some Means Recommended for Checking their Progress (London, 1792)

The Genuine Copies of Letters which Passed Between His Royal Highness the Duke of Cumberland and Lady Grosvenor ... (London, 1770)

The Letters of Junius. Complete in One Volume (London, 1786)

The Letters of Junius, Cannon, J. (ed.) (Oxford, Oxford University Press, 1978)

The Mercenary Marriage; or, the History of Miss Shenstone (London, 1773)

The Parliamentary History of England: from the Earliest Period to the Year 1803 (reprint, New York and London, 1966)

The People or the Peerage? (London, 1835)

The Polite Road to an Estate, or, Fornication One Great Source of Wealth and Pleasure (London, 1759)

The Prostitutes of Quality; or Adultery a-la-Mode (London, 1757)

The Protestant's Family Bible ... (London, 1780–81)

The Repertory of Arts, Manufactures and Agriculture (London, 1803)

The Secret History of the Green Rooms (London, 1790)

The Testimony of Truth to Exalted Merit: or, A Biographical Sketch of the Right Honourable the Countess of Derby; in Refutation of a False and Scandalous Libel (London, 1797)

The Whole of the Trial of the Hon. Richard Bingham, for Adultery with Lady Elizabeth Howard, Wife of B.E. Howard, ... Feb. 24, 1794 (London, 1794)

The Whole Proceedings … an Action Brought by The Rt Hon Richard Lord Grosvenor Against His Royal Highness Henry Frederick Duke of Cumberland for Criminal Conversation with Lady Grosvenor (London, 1770)

The Whole Proceedings on the Trial of John Bellenger Gawler, Esquire, for Criminal Conversation with Lady Valentia (London, 1799)

Thoughts on Marriage, and Criminal Conversation (London, 1799)

Trials for Adultery: or, the History of Divorces. Being Select Trials at Doctors Commons (7 vols, London, printed for S. Bladon, 1779–80)

Wade, J., *The Black Book; or, Corruption Unmasked!! Being an Account of Places, Pensions, and Sinecures …* (London, 1820)

Walker, W., *Comments on the Ten Commandments* (Chichester, 1781)

Ward, N., *The Comforts of Matrimony; or, Love's Last Shift* (London, 1780)

Wilberforce, W., *A Practical View of the Prevailing Religious System of Professed Christians, in the Higher and Middle Classes in this Country* (London, 1797)

Wollstonecraft, M., *A Vindication of the Rights of Men* (Oxford, Oxford University Press, 1999, reprint of 1790 original)

Wraxall, N., *Historical Memoirs of My Own Time* (London, 1815)

Young Lady, A, *The Sylph* (reprint, York, Henry Parker, 2001, of original edn, London, 1779)

Published Secondary Sources

Adburgham, A., *Silver Fork Society. Fashionable Life and Literature from 1814–1840* (London, Constable, 1983)

Andrew, D.T., "'Adultery a-la-Mode': Privilege, the Law and Attitudes to Adultery 1770–1809', *History*, 82, 265 (1997)

Bailey, J., *Unquiet Lives. Marriage and Marriage Breakdown in England, 1660–1800* (Cambridge, Cambridge University Press, 2003)

Baird, R., *Mistress of the House. Great Ladies and Grand Houses 1670–1830* (London, Orion Books, 2004)

Barker, H., *Newspapers, Politics and English Society 1695–1855* (Harlow, Longman, 2000)

Beckett, J.V., *The Aristocracy in England 1660–1914* (2nd edn, Oxford, Blackwell, 1989)

Binhammer, K., 'The Sex Panic of the 1790s', *Journal of the History of Sexuality*, 6, 3 (1996)

Blunt, R., *Thomas Lord Lyttelton, The Portrait of a Rake* (London, Hutchinson, 1936)

Brewer, J., *The Pleasures of the Imagination. English Culture in the Eighteenth Century* (New York, Farrar, Straus and Giroux, 1997)

Bristow, E., *Vice and Vigilance. Purity Movements in Britain since 1700* (Dublin, Rowman and Littlefield, 1977)

Cannadine, D., *Aspects of Aristocracy. Grandeur and Decline in Modern Britain* (New Haven and London, Yale University Press, 1994)

Cannon, J., *Aristocratic Century. The Peerage of Eighteenth-Century England* (Cambridge, Cambridge University Press, 1987)

Christie, C., *The British Country House in the Eighteenth Century* (Manchester, Manchester University Press, 2000)

Clark, A., *Scandal: The Sexual Politics of the British Constitution* (Princeton and Oxford, Princeton University Press, 2006)

Cox, M., *Derby: The Life & Times of the 12th Earl of Derby* (London, J.A. Allen, 1974)

Dabhoiwala, F., 'Sex and Societies for Moral Reform, 1688–1800', *Journal of British Studies*, 46 (2007)

Davidoff, L., and Hall, C., *Family Fortunes. Men and Women of the English Middle Class 1780–1850* (rev. edn, London and New York, Routledge, 2002)

Davidoff, L., *The Best Circles: Society, Etiquette and the Season* (London, Croom Helm, 1973)

Davis, L.J., *Factual Fictions. The Origins of the English Novel* (New York, Columbia University Press, 1983)

Davis, R., *A Political History of the House of Lords 1811–1846: From the Regency to Corn Law Repeal* (Stanford, Stanford University Press, 2008)

Davis, R.M., *The Good Lord Lyttelton. A Study in Eighteenth Century Politics and Culture* (Bethlehem, Penn, Times Publishing, 1939)

European Landed Elites in the Nineteenth Century, Spring, D. (ed.) (Baltimore and London, John Hopkins University Press, 1977)

Falk, B., *The Royal Fitz Roys. Dukes of Grafton Through Four Centuries* (London, Hutchinson, 1950)

Foreman, A., *Georgiana. Duchess of Devonshire* (London, HarperCollins, 1998)

Gatrell, V., *City of Laughter. Sex and Satire in Eighteenth-Century London* (London, Atlantic Books, 2006)

George Selwyn and his Contemporaries, Jesse, J.H. (ed.) (London, Richard Bentley, 1882)

Gillis, J.R., *For Better, For Worse. British Marriages, 1600 to the Present* (Oxford, Oxford University Press, 1988)

Girouard, M., *Life in the English Country House. A Social and Architectural History* (New Haven and London, Yale University Press, 1978)

Goodrich, A., *Debating England's Aristocracy in the 1790s: Pamphlets, Polemics and Political Ideas* (London, Boydell & Brewer, 2011)

Habakkuk, J., *Marriage, Debt, and the Estates System. English Landownership 1650–1950* (Oxford, Clarendon Press, 1994)

Hall, C., 'The Rule of Difference: Gender, Class and Empire in the Making of the 1832 Reform Act', in I. Blom, K. Hagemann and C. Hall (eds), *Gendered Nations: Nationalisms and Gender Order in the Long Nineteenth Century* (Oxford, Bloomsbury Academic, 2000).

Harris, M., *London Newspapers in the Age of Walpole. A Study of the Origins of the Modern English Press* (Cranbury and London, Associated University Presses, 1987)

Harvey, K., 'The Century of Sex? Gender, Bodies, and Sexuality in the Long Eighteenth Century', *The Historical Journal*, 45, 4 (2002)

Hickman, K., *Courtesans* (London, HarperCollins, 2004)

Hicks, C., *Improper Pursuits. The Scandalous Life of Lady Di Beauclerk* (London, Pan Macmillan, 2001)

Hilton, B., *A Mad, Bad, and Dangerous People? England 1783–1846* (Oxford, Clarendon Press, 2006)

Hitchcock, T., *English Sexualities, 1700–1800* (Basingstoke, Palgrave Macmillan, 1997)

Honour, Interest & Power. An Illustrated History of the House of Lords, 1660–1715, Paley, R. and Seaward, P. (eds) (Woodbridge, Boydell & Brewer, 2010)

Imlah, A., *Lord Ellenborough; a Biography of Edward Law, Earl of Ellenborough, Governor-general of India* (Cambridge, MA, and London, Harvard University Press, 1939)

Innes, J., 'Politics and Morals. The Reformation of Manners Movement in Later Eighteenth-Century England', in E. Hellmuth (ed.), *The Transformation of Political Culture. England and Germany in the Late Eighteenth Century* (Oxford, Oxford University Press, 1990)

Jones, A., *Powers of the Press. Newspapers, Power and the Public in Nineteenth-Century England* (Aldershot, Scolar, 1996)

Katritzky, L., 'Junius: An Orthodox Rebel', in R. Hewitt and P. Rogers (eds), *Orthodoxy and Heresy in Eighteenth-Century Society* (Lewisburg, PA and London, Associated University Presses, 2002)

Kelly, G., *English Fiction of the Romantic Period 1789–1830* (London and New York, Longman, 1989)

Langford, P., *A Polite and Commercial People. England 1727–1783* (Oxford, Oxford University Press, 1989)

Langford, P., *Public Life and the Propertied Englishman 1689–1798* (Oxford, Clarendon Press, 1991)

Levy, M.J., *The Mistresses of King George IV* (London, Peter Owen, 1996)

Lewis, J.S., *In the Family Way. Childbearing in the British Aristocracy, 1760–1860* (New Brunswick, Rutgers University Press, 1986)

Lovell, M.S., *A Scandalous Life. The Biography of Jane Digby* (London, HarperCollins, 1995)

Lummis, T. and Marsh, J., *The Woman's Domain. Women and the English Country House* (London, Penguin, 1990)

Matthew, H.C. and Harrison, B. (eds), *Oxford Dictionary of National Biography* (Oxford, Oxford University Press, 2004)

Lyte, H.C.M., *A History of Eton College, 1440–1898* (London, Macmillan, 1899)

McCahill, M., 'The Bedchamber Lord: Basil, Sixth Earl of Denbigh', in Davis, R.W. (ed.), *Lords of Parliament. Studies, 1714–1914* (Stanford, Stanford University Press, 1995)

Mingay, G.E., *English Landed Society in the Eighteenth Century* (London, Routledge, 1963)

Namier, L., *England in the Age of the American Revolution* (New York, Macmillan, 1966)

News, Newspapers, and Society in Early Modern Britain, Raymond, J. (ed.) (London, F. Cass, 1999)

Pearce, E., *Reform! The Fight for the 1832 Reform Act* (London, Pimlico, 2004)

Peers, Politics and Power. The House of Lords 1603–1911, Jones, C. and D. (eds) (London, Hambledon Press, 1986)

Porter, R., *English Society in the Eighteenth Century* (London, Penguin, 1991)

Raven, J., 'The Book Trades', in Rivers, I. (ed.), *Books and Their Readers in Eighteenth-Century England: New Essays* (Leicester, Leicester University Press, 2001), pp. 1–31

Rea, R., *The English Press in Politics* (Lincoln, Nebraska, University of Nebraska Press, 1963)

Roberts, M.J.D., *Making English Morals. Voluntary Association and Moral Reform in England, 1787–1886* (Cambridge, Cambridge University Press, 2004)

Roberts, M.J.D., 'The Society for the Suppression of Vice and its Early Critics, 1802–1812', *The Historical Journal*, 26, 1, (1983), pp.159–76

Smith, E.A., *The House of Lords in British Politics and Society 1815–1911* (London, Longman, 1992)

Smith, E.A., 'Charles, Second Earl Grey and the House of Lords', in Davis, R.W. (ed.), *Lords of Parliament. Studies, 1714–1914* (Stanford, Stanford University Press, 1995)

Soames, M., *The Profligate Duke* (London, Collins, 1987)

Stapleton, H., *Heirs Without Title. A History of the first Earl of Morley and his Natural Children* (York, published by the author, 1974)

Stone, L., *The Family, Sex and Marriage in England, 1500–1800* (London, Penguin, 1977)

Stone, L., *Road to Divorce* (Oxford, Oxford University Press, 1990)

Stone, L., *Broken Lives: Separation and Divorce in England, 1660–1857* (Oxford, Oxford University Press, 1993)

The History of The Times. 'The Thunderer' in the making 1785–1841 (London, The Times, 1935)

Thompson, F.M.L., *English Landed Society in the Nineteenth Century* (London, Routledge and Kegan Paul, 1963)

Tillyard, S., *A Royal Affair. George III and His Troublesome Siblings* (London, Chatto & Windus, 2006)

Turner, D.M., *Fashioning Adultery. Gender, Sex and Civility in England, 1660–1740* (Cambridge, Cambridge University Press, 2002)

Tyack, G., *Warwickshire Country Houses* (Chichester, Phillimore, 1994)

Wilson, B., *Decency and Disorder. The Age of Cant 1789–1837* (London, Faber, 2007)

Wilson, R., and Alan Mackley, *Creating Paradise. The Building of the English Country House 1660–1880* (London, Hambledon, 2000)

Wyndham, M., *Chronicles of the Eighteenth Century. Founded on the Correspondence of Sir Thomas Lyttelton and his Family* (London, Hodder and Stoughton, 1924)

INDEX

Abdy, Lady Anne 196
Abergavenny, Lady 9–14, 23, 104, 109
Abergavenny, Lord 9–11, 12–13
adultery, definition 19–20, 59
Alfieri, Count Vittorio 110–11
Ancaster, Duke of 164, 166
aristocracy, definition 35–7
arranged marriages 21, 23, 26, 27–8, 31, 33,
   79, 188, 189–90, 216
Auckland, Lord 85, 173, 174, 179

Beauclerk, Topham 51, 52–5, 124
Bedford, Duke of 73, 160, 164–5
Belasyse, Lady Elizabeth 31
Bellamy, George Anne 167–8
Bentinck, Lord Charles 196
Bertie, Lady Mary 25
Bingham, Richard 31, 154–6
Bird, William 127–8
Bisset, George 120
Blake, Lady Annabella 120
Blandford, Marquis of 153, 175–9
Bolingbroke, Lady (Diana Spencer) 50–6,
   109, 124
Bolingbroke, Viscount 43, 50–6, 165
Bon Ton Magazine 157–60, 200–1
Boringdon, Lord (1st Earl of Morley)
   181–90
Boscawen, George 120
Bunbury, Lady Sarah 123
Burke, Edmund 34, 151
Burke's Peerage 38, 212
Bury, Lady Charlotte 214, 216, 217–18, 222

Bute, Marchioness of 24–5, 152, 172
Byron, John 133
Byron, Lord 102–4

Carlisle, Earl of 171, 174, 179
Carmarthen, Marchioness of 116, 123, 133
Caroline, Queen 171–2, 204, 214, 227
Chesterfield, Lord 79, 80, 82, 86–7, 101, 124
Clarence, Duke of 159, 175
Complete English Peerage, The 75, 85
Cotton, Mary 26
courtesans 55, 61, 63, 67, 100, 113, 116, 117,
   118–19, 161, 164–72
   see also prostitution
Coventry, Lady 51
Craven, Baron 160, 168
Craven, Lady Elizabeth 132, 160
criminal conversation ('crim. con.') 14, 19,
   20, 61, 78, 92, 106–7, 109, 151, 152–4,
   158, 173, 174
criminal conversation ('crim. con.'), cases
   12, 13, 50, 54–5, 71, 74, 111, 112–13,
   116–17, 120–1, 133, 136, 141–2, 154–5,
   175–6, 188, 193, 194, 196
Cumberland, Duke of 30, 82–3, 112,
   116–18

Denbigh, 6th Earl of (Basil) 24, 26–7, 41,
   71, 89, 132, 138, 151, 172, 174
Denbigh, Countess of 26–7, 59–60
Derby, Countess of (Elizabeth Farren) 161–3
Derby, Countess of (Elizabeth Hamilton)
   30, 161–2

Derby, Earl of 30, 140, 161–2, 165
Devonshire, Duke of 30, 45, 48, 171
Devonshire, Georgiana, Duchess of 30, 45, 48, 78, 125, 127, 151, 161, 218
Digby, Jane (Lady Ellenborough) 218, 223–9
Disraeli, Benjamin 214
divorce 14, 18, 32–3, 50, 59, 85–6, 173–4
divorce and Parliament 55, 58, 61–2, 71, 106–7, 129–30, 153, 174–5, 220–1
Dorset, 3rd Duke of (John Sackville) 30, 72, 73, 161, 165
dowries (marriage portions) 21, 24–6, 39, 50

Egremont, 3rd Earl of 164, 186
Eldon, Lord 174, 175, 179
Ellenborough, Earl of (Edward Law) 43, 44–5, 218, 219, 220–31
Ellenborough, Lady (Jane Digby) 218, 223–9
Erskine, Thomas 19, 31, 109–10, 155, 156, 176

Fane, Lady Augusta (Lady Boringdon) 187–9
Farren, Elizabeth 161–3
Fielding, Henry 13, 89
Fisher, Kitty 84
FitzRoy, Lord Augustus 74
Foley, Lady Ann 141–2
Fox, Charles 82, 129–30, 165
France 39, 144, 147, 150–2, 156, 173–4
Franklin, Benjamin 23–4

Gentleman's Magazine 56, 72, 87, 140
gentry 24, 25, 36–7, 38, 39, 45, 47, 76, 82, 106
George III, King 58, 144
George IV, King 170–1, 186, 201, 202–3, 204
Gisborne, Thomas 78, 147, 180
Gore, Catherine 214, 216, 217
Grafton, Duchess of (Anne) 40, 61, 64, 67–72, 73–4, 76, 93, 109, 116, 132
Grafton, Duchess of (Elizabeth) 43–4, 48, 71, 73, 75
Grafton, Duke of (Augustus Henry FitzRoy) 43–4, 61, 63–77, 138, 140, 146
Grey, Earl, Charles 48, 197, 203, 206, 207

Grosvenor, Lady (Henrietta Vernon) 82–3, 112–13, 116–18, 119, 132
Grosvenor, Lord, Richard 113, 118–19

Halford, Lady Sarah 27
Hamilton, Duke of 159
Hamilton, Lady Elizabeth (Countess of Derby) 30, 161–2
Harrington, Lord and Lady 83–4
hereditary power undermined 14, 78, 108–9, 129, 144, 192, 210
Hertford, Marchioness of 201, 202–4
Howard, Lady Elizabeth (Duchess of Norfolk) 31, 59, 110, 113, 116, 124, 154–6
Hunter, Dr William 53–4, 70–1

Jersey, Earl of (George Villiers) 68, 170–2, 187
John Bull magazine 214, 217–18, 226
Johnson, Samuel 36, 58, 90, 101, 137
Junius 65–6, 76

Kenyon, Lord 59, 78, 146, 152–3, 155, 174, 175, 183–4, 189

Ligonier, Lady Penelope 110–12
London Magazine 20, 28, 101, 106, 112, 130, 140, 163, 169
London Season 37, 41, 42, 123
love and marriage 18–33, 156
Lyddel, Richard 9–11
Lyttelton, 1st Baron (George) 25, 41, 86, 87, 88–94, 96, 97, 98, 125–6
Lyttelton, 2nd Baron (Thomas) 22–3, 25–6, 88–9, 92, 94, 95–104, 125, 138–9

March, Earl of 52, 54
marriage, institution of 18–33, 58–9
marriage portions (dowries) 21, 24–6, 39, 50
Melbourne, Viscount 166, 167
memoirs 29, 74, 77, 139, 165–9, 212
middle class 24, 41, 108, 186–97, 205, 206–7, 208, 212–13, 215, 226, 227, 231
Mildmay, Sir Henry 193–6
Monck, Lady Elizabeth 185–7, 190
Montagu, Elizabeth 89, 97
Monthly Review 86, 92–3, 215–16
morality 14–15, 18–19, 35, 46–7, 58–9, 60, 78–81, 86–7

More, Hannah 78–9, 147
Morley, 1st Earl of (Lord Boringdon) 181–90
Morning Chronicle 54, 121, 131, 168, 178, 189, 195, 197, 227
Morning Post 98, 121, 127, 138, 142, 154, 177, 178, 188, 195, 227
Mountnorris, Earl of 153, 159

Norfolk, Duchess of (Elizabeth Howard) 31, 59, 110, 113, 116, 124, 154–6
Norfolk, Duke of (Bernard Howard) 31, 154–6
novels and public opinion 89–90, 140–1, 147, 148–50, 163, 212–19

Parliament and adultery 14, 18–19, 61, 109, 114, 118, 129–32
Parliament and divorce 55, 58, 61–2, 71, 106–7, 129–30, 153, 174–5, 220–1
Parsons, Nancy 67, 68, 69, 72–3, 161, 165
Patricians, The 75, 85, 91, 132, 157
Peach, Apphia 92, 93–4
Pennington, Lady Sarah 29
Percy, Baroness, Anne 113, 123, 124, 125, 126–8
Peterborough, Earl of 141–2
press as agent of social change 14, 82–6, 117, 135–42, 144, 157–60, 193, 199–204, 205–11, 227–8
  see also memoirs; novels; trial reports
propriety, growth of 192–3, 196–7
prostitution 145–6, 165, 175
  see also courtesans
Public Advertiser 65, 66, 72, 138, 142

Radnor, Earl of 46, 146, 194, 226
Rambler's Magazine 120, 137, 142, 193, 200
Reform Bill debates 196, 197, 206, 207, 208, 209–10, 216, 222
Robinson, Mary 100, 168
Rochester, Bishop of 173–4, 179
Rosebery, Lady 193–6

Sackville, John (3rd Duke of Dorset) 30, 72, 73, 161, 165
Schwarzenberg, Prince 221, 224–5, 226, 228, 229
Selwyn, George (MP) 52, 54
servants as witnesses 9–11, 50–1, 52–4, 67–8, 74, 110–11, 115–16, 117, 120, 122, 124, 128, 133–4
Seymour, Sir George Francis 207
Smith, Adam 79–80
Smith, Charles Loraine 121
Sylph, The 30, 48, 125, 218

Tenducci, Ferdinando 119–20
theatre 79, 158, 159, 160–1
Thrale, Hester 101, 109, 153
Thurlow, Lord Edward 130–1
Times, The 84, 136–7, 171, 188–9, 194, 196, 220, 225, 227, 228
Town and Country Magazine 55, 63, 73, 82–3, 99–100, 117, 126, 160, 166
trial reports 114–22, 123, 128, 156, 176–7, 188–9, 193, 196, 227
Trials for Adultery: or, the History of Divorces 13, 56, 114–15, 117, 119, 121, 128, 132–3, 138
Tyrconnel, Lord and Lady 109, 121–2

Upper Ossory, Earl of (John Fitzpatrick) 70, 71

Villiers, Frances (Countess of Jersey) 132, 170–2, 186–7, 202, 218
Villiers, Theresa 151, 152, 181–7

Walpole, Horace 41, 68, 82, 90, 93
Wellington, Duke of 168, 207
Wilberforce, William 19, 145, 147
William IV, King 79, 207
Wilson, Harriette 168
Wollstonecraft, Mary 108, 148, 152
women, expected behaviour 109, 147–9, 170, 182–3, 197
Worsley, Lady Seymour Dorothy 120